THE STORY OF YORKTOWN

Told by the Men Who Were There

Jack Darrell Crowder

Clearfield Company

For
My wife, Peggy, for her help with this book
and supporting my trips to Yorktown.

&

My best friend Blair for joining me on one of the trips
to Yorktown and other battlefields.

Copyright © 2023
Jack Darrell Crowder
All rights reserved. This book may not be reproduced, transmitted, or stored in whole or in part by any means, including graphic, electronic, or mechanical, without the expressed consent of the Publisher or the Author for brief quotations in critical articles and reviews.

Published for Clearfield Company by
Genealogical Publishing Company
Baltimore, Maryland

ISBN 9780806359618

Cover illustration: Storming of Redoubt #10, by H. Charles McBarron, Jr., U.S. Army Chief of Military Historians Office. This work is in the public domain in the United States.

Books by Jack Darrell Crowder from Clearfield Company:

Women Patriots in the American Revolution: Stories of Bravery, Daring, and Compassion

The First 24 Hours of the American Revolution: An Hour by Hour Account of the Battles of Lexington, Concord, and the British Retreat on Battle Road

Strange, Amazing, and Funny Events that Happened during the Revolutionary War

Victory or Death: Military Decisions That Changed the Course of the American Revolution

Contents

Preface **5**

Introduction **7**

Chapter 1 Yorktown **11**

Chapter 2 The Siege Begins **17**

Chapter 3 British Leave a Gift and a Hero Falls **31**

Chapter 4 Preparations and the First Skirmish **39**

Chapter 5 Quiet before the Storm **57**

Chapter 6 Artillery of Yorktown **73**

Chapter 7 The Allies Roar Back **79**

Chapter 8 Closer to the British Lines **95**

Chapter 9 The Noose Tightens **107**

Chapter 10 A Desperate Attempt to Escape **127**

Chapter 11 Capitulation **137**

Chapter 12 Agreeing to Terms of Surrender **147**

Chapter 13 Surrender Ceremony **155**

Chapter 14 Personal Accounts of the Surrender **173**

Chapter 15 Prisoners Begin to Leave **183**

Chapter 16 Final Days **193**

Conclusion **203**

End Notes **209**

Bibliography **227**

Index **235**

Preface

There are two battles that occurred during the American Revolution that had a major influenced on the outcome of the war and impacted the leading countries in Europe. The defeat of the British at Saratoga was the first. It proved to be the turning point of the war and convinced the French that the rebels could win, which led to French aid in the effort. It also forced England into a global conflict.

The second battle would be the Siege of Yorktown. This gave the Americans their final major victory that eventually led to peace. It did not end the war, for it continued on a much smaller scale for two more years. Also, Yorktown finally convinced the British parliament that the conflict in America was simply not worth continuing. Independence for America also encouraged other colonies to challenge the old order in Europe.

There have been countless books written about the Siege of Yorktown. This account of the siege is primarily told by the people that participated in this great event. The stories of the participants have been taken from letters, journals, diaries, memoirs, newspapers, and pension applications. **The spelling and grammar has been left the way it was written. Some stories may not agree with the accepted time frames of the event, or the accounts may vary.** The persons recording their recollections may have a bias, or their memory may be distorted by the passage of time. There is, however, no mistaking the frustrations, fears, and anger that is expressed with each person's story. They also make no attempt to hide the respect and admiration that the men felt for their comrades and leaders.

The weather conditions, given for most of the days, describes the weather in the Yorktown area. The weather data came from diaries and letters. The story begins on September 28, 1781 when the last of the allied troops reach Yorktown and it ends on October 26, 1781 when they left.

Introduction

"It is equally certain that our Troops are approaching fast to nakedness & that we have nothing to clothe them with."

----Letter from George Washington to John Laurens

As the year 1781 began, General George Washington warned anyone that would listen, that his army was tired and the supporters of the war had grown discontent. In a letter to John Laurens from George Washington that was dated January 15, 1781, he wrote, "The people are discontented, but it is with the feeble and oppressive mode of conducting the war, not with the war itself."[1]

John Adams feared that France, faced with growing debts and the lack of progress in the war, might stop her support within the year. It appeared that if there was not a major American victory in 1781, the fate of the country would be decided at a conference table consisting of the great European powers.

The fighting had put the Americans deeply in debt, and because most of their soldiers had not been paid, there were desertions and occasionally mutinies. In 1781, pay for the soldiers of the Continental Army was suspended. It was decided that the army would be paid in debt certificates or land grants until the peace treaty was signed.

Continental money was almost worthless, and the money issued by the separate states was even of less value. The currency finally collapsed in May of 1781. People marched in Philadelphia with Continental dollars in their hats as paper plumes to protest its collapse. A very unhappy dog ran alongside the marchers, while tarred and pasted with the worthless dollars. General Philip Van Cortlandt wrote in his memoirs, "At Hanover Court House I was given the choice of paying, for a bowl of apple toddy, five hundred dollars in continental money or one dollar in silver."[2]

On April 9, 1781, George Washington wrote a letter to John Laurens, who was in France assisting with the work of Benjamin Franklin. The letter paints a bleak picture for the hope of independence,

> As an honest & candid man—as a man whose all depends on the final and happy termination of the present contest, I assert this—While I give it decisively as my opinion, that without a foreign loan our present force (which is but the remnant of an Army) cannot be kept together this Campaign; much less will it be increased, & in readiness for another. And, if France delays a timely, & powerful aid in this critical posture of our affairs it will avail us nothing should she attempt it hereafter; for we are at this hour, suspended in the Balle—not from choice, but from hard and absolute necessity—for you may rely on it as a fact, that we cannot transport the provisions from the States in which they are assessed to the Army, because we cannot pay the Teamsters—Who will no longer work for Certificates—It is equally certain that our Troops are approaching fast to nakedness & that we have nothing to clothe them with—That our Hospitals are without Medicines, & our Sick without Nutriment except such as well men eat—That all our public works are at a stand, & the

Artificers disbanding. but why need I run into the detail, when it may be declared in a word, that we are at the end of our tether, & that now or never deliverance must come.[3]

After six years, the war in the colonies was growing unpopular back home in England. The British controlled only a handful of coastal cities in American and around the world they were in a war with Spain and France.

Many individuals in England were not in favor of the war, because they were no longer getting taxation out of America, so their own taxes began to go up. At first, personal items were taxed, such as ink, paper, and even rabbit hair for women's hats. Later, their property taxes were raised. Also, some merchants began to oppose the war because there was no trade with America.

Prominent men such as Horace Walpole, 4th Earl of Oxford, a former member of parliament and a man of many letters, began to become critical of the war. In a letter to the Countess of Ailesbury, July 10, 1779, he wrote, "We could not conquer America when it stood alone; then France supported it, and we did not mend the matter. To make it still easier, we have driven Spain into the alliance. Is this wisdom?"[4]

In May 1781 the focus of the war in the south was in Virginia. There were nearly 7,000 British troops in Virginia, and some of the leadership on both sides believed that the war could be decided there. General Washington, however, was focused on capturing New York City, and British commander Sir Henry Clinton was determined to prevent it.

Clinton wanted Cornwallis to select a spot in Virginia, where he could easily embark some of his troops to return to New York and reinforce Clinton. He directed Cornwallis to take a strong position on the Chesapeake. He first ordered him to Portsmouth and then later to Yorktown to build fortifications for a deep water port.

On July 6, 1781 the French and American armies met at White Plains, which was about thirty miles north of New York City. The Americans needed help from the French, and without it their revolution most likely would be lost.

Washington and the French commander General Rochambeau discussed where to launch their joint attack. Washington wanted New York, because with the combined forces the British would be outnumbered three to one. Rochambeau did not agree. He said, that since the French fleet was going to sail from the West Indies under Admiral De Grasse, and because the Admiral wanted to return to the Indies by mid-October, an attack on the Chesapeake area was a better option.

French commander General Rochambeau---National Archives

Later when Washington realized that a campaign against New York City was no longer possible, he turned his attention toward Cornwallis in Virginia. Lafayette was directed to make a disposition of his army, as it would prevent Lord Cornwallis from saving himself by a sudden march to Charleston. Once Washington abandoned his plan to take New York, he began to prepare his army for the march south to Virginia.

By the middle of August the British army was at either Yorktown or nearby Gloucester, and Cornwallis began working to defend Yorktown. On August 24th, Hessian soldier Stephen Popp was concerned that the British were not in a good situation when he wrote in his journal, "Trenches dug and lines thrown up in Yorktown, but there are reports that we are in a very bad situation."[5]

In August the British fleet under Sir Thomas Graves was sent from New York to meet the French fleet at Chesapeake Bay. When the French arrived at Chesapeake Bay the British underestimated the size of it and in the afternoon of September 5th, the two fleets prepared to fight. Because of a failure of British tactics and confusion in commands, the British fleet broke off the fight after heavy losses. Since they were outnumbered by the French, they later chose to withdraw to New York. Cornwallis was now surrounded with little chance for escape.

Heat, illness, and a shortage of food was taking a toll on his men. Daily desertions had become common place. His officers informed him that they believed they could hold out for only a few more weeks, unless they received aid from General Clinton in New York.

General Clinton knew that Cornwallis was in a very dangerous situation. He raised the hopes of Cornwallis, when he told him that he was making preparations to send him a relief force. Cornwallis welcomed this news, but he was concerned that the aid would come too late.

The allied army that would face Cornwallis at Yorktown was made up of three parts; American Continental, American Militia, and French auxiliaries. Most of the 3,000 militia were from Virginia and North Carolina. The allied total number of troops was over 18,000. Cornwallis had around 8,000 British and German troops.

It was clear that one side needed to score a knock-out blow and seize the victory. Both Cornwallis and Washington saw that this knock-out would come at Yorktown, Virginia in 1781.

Chapter 1

Yorktown

"We are busily employed in fortifying this post, which will be a work of great time and labor, and after all, I fear, not be very strong." ----letter from General Cornwallis to General Leslie

Description of the village:

Yorktown was a small village on the south side of the river, which bore its name. In December 1774, the people of Yorktown staged a miniature "Tea Party" in Yorktown Harbor, and later Thomas Nelson Jr., a resident, was a signer of the Declaration of Independence. When the British arrived, there was a garrison of 300 militiamen, but they marched sixteen miles away to Williamsburg.

Yorktown was located on a long peninsula eight miles wide between the York and the James Rivers. The harbor was deep and two miles wide. The James River wound more than twenty miles inland, and was navigable only by small ships.

When the British arrived, the village consisted of around 300 houses, which were mostly brick and many in ruins and abandoned. The York River made a bend or curve, in the center of the town in which it was is situated. The town consisted of a row of houses built on a high bank, with wharves and warehouses below on a level with the water. On the right side of town there is a considerable ravine.

Yorktown was built above the cliffs which in some locations were almost straight up and as tall as a three story house. There was a narrow strip of beach from the base of the cliff to the water's edge. The beach was from 50 to 75 yards wide. Photo Courtesy of the Colonial Historical National Park, NPS.

On the opposite shore is Gloucester Point, a piece of land projected deep into the river. Gloucester Point was fertile country, where forage for the cavalry was abundantly gathered and would be the most likely point of junction for the promised relief from Sir Henry Clinton. Both these posts were occupied by Lord Cornwallis. The communication between Yorktown and Gloucester Point was commanded by the batteries and by some ships of war, which lay in the harbor.

The memoirs of British General Samuel Graham provided a description of the town and surrounding area,

> On the right side of the town there is a considerable ravine, and on the angle of the opposite bank was constructed a pretty strong redoubt with an abates [a defensive obstacle with felled trees that have been sharpened and face the enemy] formed by as a defence on the right flank. The town was then surrounded by a ditch and thick parapet [wall] having a horn work in its center, in both of which were batteries, the embrasures lined with fascines. The parapet ran to the river on the left flank, having two advanced redoubts with abates constructed on that flank, one on the brink of the bank over the river, the other advanced, and in a line with the town's parapet and base of the hornwork. The parapet was formed of trees cut in the woods and placed inside; outside it was formed of fascines [long bundles of sticks of wood bound together] and the earth from the ditch, which was sandy and gravelly, was thrown into the space between; it had a fraise made of fence rails kept in line and projecting by the earth thrown into the opening of the parapet, giving it an appearance of strength which it little merited.[1]

Slaves in Yorktown:

During the siege of Yorktown, over 3,000 slaves helped Cornwallis in hopes of gaining their freedom if he was victorious. They were mainly used as manual labor, and were used to build the fortifications. When food became scarce during the siege, rations to blacks were either cut or eliminated completely.

Both sides saw slaves as pawns on the chessboard of war. As the British soldiers moved through the south, they would divide up plunder from plantations they raided, which also included the slaves. The Rebels and Tories did the same as they marched through the south. The captured slaves were either sold for profit or used as personal servants. Sometimes in the American Army slaves were used as payment for serving, or an enticement to enlist.

Thomas Jefferson, when Governor of Virginia, signed a bill that gave every white male who enlisted for the duration of the war, "300 acres of land plus a healthy sound Negro between 20 and 30 years of age or 60 pounds of gold or silver.[2]

Why Yorktown:

The location made a good naval station which would need to be defended, but otherwise it was a bad selection. Cornwallis had the choice to fortify either Old Point Comfort as ordered by Sir Henry Clinton, or Yorktown, which was where Cornwallis chose to defend. Why did he choose Yorktown, when it had no high ground, and if Gloucester Point was taken his only escape would be by water?

At Yorktown the York River narrowed and was deep enough for the British men-of-war ships, and there were marshes on both of the town's flanks. This would make the attack on the town by land more difficult. Gloucester was located just a mile across the river from Yorktown and could house a gun battery and fort. Also, if American land forces threatened Yorktown, the British could escape across the river into Gloucester.

Standing on the beach at Yorktown, looking across the York River toward Gloucester Point. --Photo by author

Cornwallis believed he had the best soldiers in the world, because he had Tarleton's Legion, a large group of Hessians, and the Royal Navy to protect him. When he considered these advantages, he could not believe that he could be trapped at a base of his own choosing.

Defenses of Yorktown:

While setting up defenses at Yorktown, Cornwallis never anticipated the possibility of a siege. The defenses of Yorktown were not particularly strong. The town backed up against the York River, and it stood on the bank of the river, thirty or forty feet above the water. A strong line of inner entrenchments ran around the town and 300 to 400 yards out from the town. This inner line contained redoubts and batteries, and they were strengthened by long narrow trenches called fosses.

Of the ten redoubts in this inner line, two covered the right and faced the river road to Williamsburg, three stood back of the town, and three on the left, looked down the river. The two remaining redoubts, known as Nos. 9 and 10, stood disconnected in advance of, and as an additional strength to the left. A projecting redoubt, called the horn-work, guarded the road to Hampton. The fourteen batteries constructed along the line had sixty guns that had been mounted. None of these guns were larger than eighteen pounders. These guns were stripped from the frigate *Charon* which was anchored in the river.

There were additional lines of batteries along the river bank. The town was situated between the mouths of creeks, whose beds were deep ravines, and these natural advantages were also skillfully made available. There were numerous abatis, which were defensive obstacles with felled trees that had been sharpened and faced the enemy. The main body of the army of Cornwallis was encamped on the open grounds inside the inner line of Yorktown.

The outer line of defense encircled the inner line and was about 1,200 yards out from the town. On the northwest side of the line was a strong star or Fusiliers' redoubt. West of town was the Pigeon Quarter, a low hill, where three redoubts were built. Trees were felled, fences were thrown up, and batteries were constructed at the points which were deemed most vulnerable. The outer defenses, including Pigeon Hill, were abandoned by Cornwallis on the 28th of September. This gave the Allied army a good position for their own artillery.

Across the river, about a mile wide, was the village of Gloucester. It had been fortified before Yorktown, and its defenses consisted of a line of entrenchments with four redoubts and three batteries. The line ran from east to west across the peninsula. The defenses here had a total of nineteen guns and were established to prevent an advance by the enemy from the north. The point was out of range of the French fleet, and several British ships were stationed there. The stream below was obstructed by several sunken ships.

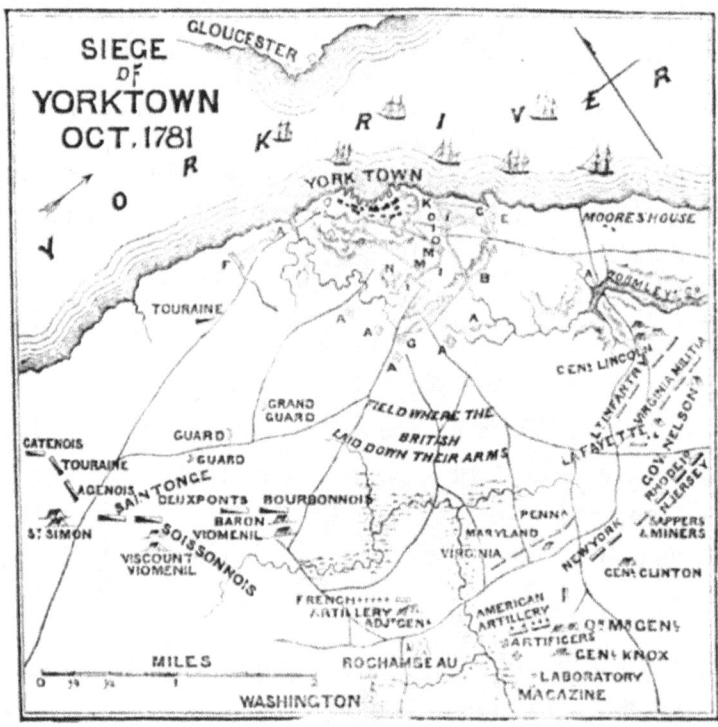

Battle Plan of Yorktown from *A Pictorial History of the United States* by S.G. Goodrich, 1875.

Redoubts:

The slaves did most of the hard work building redoubts. These were earthen forts with dirt walls high enough that a man could stand up inside and not be seen by the enemy. Fascines were made of sticks and branches stripped of foliage and bound together for flooring, if the ground was marshy. They were also used to strengthen the sides of the dirt walls of the redoubt.

On the outside of the redoubt a deep trench was dug around the dirt wall or berm. Around six feet up from the bottom of the trench the defenders installed an abatis. This obstacle consisted of logs driven into the dirt walls and they had one end pointed outward. The outward end of the log was sharpened. These sharpened logs formed a close ring around the redoubt. As you approached the trench of the redoubt, you would encounter stacked branches acting as a fence around the redoubt.

To attack the redoubt you had to get through the fence of branches, go down the moat, climb several feet up it, somehow get past the sharpened abates, and finally climb the remaining several feet of the dirt wall. You would be under constant fire from above.

British redoubt at Yorktown, in the background is the York River---Library of Congress

Chapter 2

The Siege Begins

"We had several little engagements with the enemy before they were himed in at said town a Council of War was held by our officers and some were in favour of storming the enemies fort then under General Wallace [Cornwallis] but General Washington was opposed to that counsel and recommended a siege as I was told." ---Pension application of Edward Elley

---

Friday September 28, 1781

(A very warm day)

The entire allied force was now at Yorktown, and the British were preparing for an attack. Some skirmishes did take place, but for the most part there was no major fighting. The allies sent a small force to Gloucester to seal up a possible escape route for Cornwallis. Washington met with his officers to discuss if they should attack, or lay siege to the British positions. Both sides spent the week preparing for a battle.

British forces:

Bartholomew James, ready for battle, later wrote in his journal, "At noon the enemy appeared in front of our works in force about twenty-six thousand, extending from right to the left of our lines; and a number of them advancing to reconnoiter a ravine in from of my battery, I opened fire on them until they were dispersed."[1]

The British force numbered 9,000 British, Loyalist, and Hessian troops. The French fleet now blocked the entire Chesapeake Bay, including the York and James Rivers.

In his memoirs, twenty-five year old Scottish Lieutenant Samuel Graham of the 76th Highlanders wrote of his first encounter with the Americans at Yorktown,

> On the 28th September, information was given by a picquet [a small military post] in front of a working party that the enemy were advancing in force by the Williamsburgh Road. The army immediately took post in the outward position. The French and Americans came on in the most cautious and regular order. Some shots were fired from our field-pieces. The French also felt the redoubt on our right flank, defended by the 23rd and a party of marines. But did not persist. The two armies remained some time in this position observing each other. In ours, there was but one wish, that they would advance. While standing with a brother captain (Mont Blanc), we overheard a soliloquy of an old Highlander gentleman, a lieutenant, who, drawing his sword, said to himself, 'Come on, Maister Washington, I'm unco glad to see you; I've been offered money for my commission, but I could na think of gangin' hame without sight of you. Come on.'"[2]

The whole camp was in alarm for a strong attack of the American forces. Tents were hastily removed and all the baggage taken into the town. Some thirty of the English and Hessians were killed or wounded. At night, all the troops in the camp were quietly moved into the new lines thrown up around the town.[3]

Johann Conrad Döhla wrote about the advancing enemy troops, "There was an alarm at noon in our camp because the enemy approached from all sides and fired on our outer pickets. We struck our tents and took all our equipment back into the city. At night, I went on command at the defenses."[4]

American/French forces:

Claude Blanchard, Commissary of the French Auxiliary Army, was in Williamsburg helping with the French troops in a hospital. He wrote in his journal, "I had 300 sick persons and a single employee; of these 300 sick, 10 officers were harder to please than all the rest."[5]

At daylight on September 28, Washington led the whole combined army out of Williamsburg to march twelve miles to surround Yorktown. After marching about seven miles, the road parted and the American army took the right and the French the left side. The Marquis de Saint-Simon was at the head of the French troops. He had left his sickbed, ill with malaria, but he was determined to lead his men to Yorktown.

As the British lines came into view at about three o'clock, a group of British Dragoons traded fire with the allies, and then they raced back to the safety of the British fortifications. When they reached Yorktown the French camped on a plain with a large marsh in their front. The Americans went a little farther towards the river and camped about a mile from the British fortifications.

The troops all moved in light marching order, ready for action at a moment's notice, and were doubtless eager for the opportunity to fulfill the instructions of General Washington issued the day before,

> If the enemy should be tempted to meet the army on its march, the General particularly enjoins the troops to place their principal reliance on the bayonet, that they may prove the vanity of the boast which the British make of their peculiar prowess in deciding battles with that weapon. He trusts a generous emulation will actuate the allied armies; that the troops in general, that have so often used it with success, will distinguish themselves on every occasion that offers. The justice of the cause in which we are engaged, and the honor of the two Nations, must inspire every breast with sentiments that are the presage of victory.[6]

Washington wanted his arrival at Yorktown to be a surprise before Cornwallis could break out and escape. So, he ordered his men to use bayonets if they were attacked by small groups of British soldiers, so that gunfire would not alarm the British garrisons at Yorktown. The Americans encountered no major British resistance as they marched.

19th Century painting of Private Joseph Martin and his wife Lucy, unknown author.

Twenty year old Private Joseph Plumb Martin was in the continental Army during much of the war. He mentioned the general's instruction in his diary,

> Here, or about this time, we had orders from the Commander-in-chief, that in case the enemy should come out to meet us, we should exchange but one round with them and then decide the conflict with the bayonet, as they valued themselves at the instrument. The French forces could play their part at it, and the Americans were never backward at trying its virtue. The British, however, did not think fit at that time to give us an opportunity to soil our bayonets in their carcases; but why they did not we could never conjecture, we as much expected it, as we expected to find them there.[7]

Colonel Richard Butler wrote in his journal about marching to Yorktown and encountering the British,

> The Army marched according to orders, and took post three quarters of a mile from the town of York, and in open view of the enemy, on our approach Lord Cornwallis at the head of his Dragoons turned out to reconnoiter us, some riflemen and two pieces of artillery moved towards them, and a few shots made them scatter and move off into their works. The General [Washington] reconnoitred them and ordered the heavy artillery which landed at Harrod's landing below Burril's ferry to be moved up as fast as possible. The French army have the left fronting the British right, the Americans the right facing the British left. The British General seems determined to stand a siege having prepared in the best manner possible.[8]

Washington sent Duc De Lauzun's cavalry and infantry to Gloucester to reinforce the 1,200 men under the command of George Weedon. Cornwallis had sent all his cavalry and a large amount of infantry to Gloucester, and Washington feared that Cornwallis might try to retreat that way. Lauzun wrote of General Weedon in his memoirs,

> Weedon, rather good commander, but hating war which he had always refused to wage, and being specially in mortal fear of gun shots. Having become a brigadier-general by chance, the respectable officer was my senior in command; General Washington regretted this more than I, for he intended to give me the command. He told me that he would write to General Weedon that he could continue to hold honours of his rank, but that he would forbid him to meddle with anything. I explained to him that we did not understand this manner of serving, that if General Weedon were under my orders, I should certainly make him obey his every order, that I had no objection to serve under him, if he wished it, and that he might count on me to get along very well with him.[9]

Washington wrote in his diary,

> Having debarked all the Troops and their Baggage, Marched and Encamped them in Front of the City and having with some difficulty obtained horses & Waggons sufficient to move our field Artillery, Intrenching Tools & such other articles as were indispensably necessary, we commenced our March for the Investiture of the Enemy at York.[10]

Charles Strong was eighteen years old when he served at Yorktown in the Virginia militia. He stated in his pension application [31994],

> Some where about the last of August or first of September of the same year he was drafted again for three months and marched to Williamsburg where he laid about one month & from there he marched to Little York—most of his time in this tour was taken up in performing guard duty—he also assisted in unloading our vessels loaded with artillery, mortars, bombs, &c, at Trebell's Landing on James River, was busily at York Town during the whole siege & for a few days after the siege he guarded the country stores.

On the 27th Washington had sent Lauzun's cavalry and infantry to Gloucester to reinforce the 1,200 men under the command of General George Weedon. Lauzun felt he was more qualified to take command, instead he was placed under the command of Weedon, of whom he had little respect. He believed that Weedon, a former tavern keeper, was promoted too quickly and did not like war.

Apparently, General Weedon was aware of this by what he wrote in his letter to Washington, " …for my own part shall with the greatest cheerfulness take the orders of any senior Officer your Excellency may please to send here, and I am sure the Duke de Lauzun will also pay the most perfect respect to your wish."[11]

Twenty-two year old John Burch was drafted into the Maryland militia for the second time and wrote in his pension application [W5238],

> I was drafted in the summer before Cornwallis was taken & marched down to Fredricksburgh [Fredericksburg] on the Rappahonnock [sic, Rappahannock] River under Capt. Peter Evans, first Lieutenant Robert Overhaul, he thinks & 2nd Lieutenant Pur. Harrison & were commanded shore by Genl. Weedon & Major Armistead. While at Fredricksburgh, orders were received from Genl. Washington to clear out a road around the tide water of Ockoquon river in order that Genl. Washington, the troops & baggage from the north

might march along that road down to Little York where Cornwallis was besieged. While I was engaged with the rest in cutting out the road, Genl. Washington & some other officers passed on to the Little York, & the baggage & troops came on after the road was finished. After they (the North Army) had gone on some days met & my company were marched down the Little York by Captain Evans & were stationed with the militia on the opposite side of York River from Little York, for the purpose, as was said, of preventing Cornwallis from escaping. I continued there until the surrender of Cornwallis.

In his memoirs, Count Rochambeau described the French army leaving Williamsburg for Yorktown,

We left Williamsburg on the 28th at daybreak, and proceeded direct to York. I commenced investing, with the French troops, from the upper part of the river down as far as the marshes near the residence of Colonel Nelson, taking advantage of the woods, the curtains, and the marshy creeks, to confine the enemy within pistol-shot of their outworks. The three French brigades encamped very near, but under cover of the enemy's fire by the nature of the ground. Vinomenil commanded the grenadiers and chasseurs of the van-guard, and our investing operations were effected without the loss of a single man. On the same day, General Washington was obliged to double in our rear, and to halt on the brink of the marshes, of which all the bridges had been broken up; he employed the rest of the day and the ensuing night in repairing them.[12]

Twenty-nine year old St. George Tucker was a Lieutenant Colonel in the Virginia Militia under General Nathanael Greene. After the war he served as a judge of the General Court of Virginia. He wrote in his journal,

Fryday September 28th, 1781. This Morning at five OClock the whole Army marchd from Williamsburg, Mulenburg's Brigade of Infantry Lewis's Corps of Riflemen & the Light Dragoons forming the advanced Guard—The continental & French Troops march'd by the ordinary Road of Burwells Mill; after passing the half way house the former filed off to the Right & falling into the White Marsh road were joined By Nelson's Division of Militia who had march'd down the Warwick Road from Williamsburg passing over Harwoods Mill—The french Troops continuing their March on the ordinary Road took post on the left & part of the rear of York Town—The continentals having march'd to Secretary Nelson's quarter on the Mulberry Island road, discovered Tarlitons Legion [Banastre Tarleton] posted at their Ordinary Quarters about a mile below York at the forks of the Hampton & Warwick roads (at one Hudson Allens I think). At the Appearance of our Troops Tarliton paraded his horse & came down within three hundred yards of a Meadow which lay between him & our reconnoitring party—4 field pieces were brot. down to the Brow of the Hill to drive him off, & cover some Pioneers who were sent to repair Munfords Bridge where the Army were to cross—the second shot produced the desired Effect—The Bridge being mended Genl. Mulenburg passed over & occupied the Ground on the opposite side of the Meadow. A few more Shot were fired but I believe without Execution.[13]

Lieutenant William Feltman of the 1st Pennsylvania Regiment wrote about the march to Yorktown in his journal,

28th, The whole army took up the line of march this morning five o'clock. I conjecture the whole of our army, I mean the French and our Continental troops, to be Fifteen Thousand Veteran Troops. Besides the militia; they are so numerous that I have not been able to ascertain their number. The American army consist of six Brigades.

The American troops encamped in a wood within a mile of the Enemy's left line, and the French troops encamped on their right. Our troops remained under arms all night with their respective companies and platoons. The French troops saluted Col. Tarleton's Horse with a few shot of three pounders which made them retreat immediately. A number of prisoners taken this night who had been straggling through the country.[14]

Major Ebenezer Denny of the 7th Pennsylvania Regiment wrote of the march to Yorktown in his journal,

> The whole army moved in three divisions toward the enemy, who were strongly posted at York, about twelve miles distant. Their pickets and light troops retire. We encamped about three miles off- change ground and take a position within one mile of York; rising ground (covered with tall handsome pines) called Pigeon Hill, separates us from a view of the town. Enemy keep possession of Pigeon Hill. York on a high, sandy plain, on a deep navigable river of same name. Americans on the right; French on the left, extending on both sides of the river; preparations for a siege. One-third of the army on fatigue every day, engaged in various duties, making gabions, fascines, saucissons, &c., and great exertions and labor in getting on the heavy artillery. Strong covering parties (whole regiments) moved from camp as soon as dark, and lay all night upon their arms between us and the enemy. Our regiment, when on this duty, were under cover, and secured from the shot by Pigeon Hill; now and then a heavy shot from the enemy's works reached our camp. Our patrols, and those of the British, met occasionally in the dark, sometimes a few shot were exchanged-would generally retire. Colonel Schamel, adjutant-general to the army, with two or three attendants, on a party of observation, ventured rather close; they were seen and intercepted by a few smart horsemen from the British. Schamel forced his way through, and got back to camp, but received a wound, of which he died next day. His death was lamented, and noticed by the Commander-in-chief in his orders. Possession taken of Pigeon Hill, and temporary work erected. Generals and engineers, in viewing and surveying the ground, are always fired upon and sometimes pursued. Escorts and covering parties stationed at convenient distances under cover of wood, rising ground, &c., afford support. This business reminds me of a play among the boys, called Prison-base.
>
> At length, everything in readiness, a division of the army broke ground on the night of the 6th of October, and opened the first parallel about six hundred yards from the works of the enemy. Every exertion to annoy our men, who were necessarily obliged to be exposed about the works; however, the business went on, and on the 9th our cannon and mortars began to play. The scene viewed from the camp now was grand, particularly after dark-a number of shells from the works of both parties passing high in the air, and descending in a curve, each with a long train of fire, exhibited a brilliant spectacle. Troops in three divisions manned the lines alternately. We were two nights in camp and one in the lines; relieved about ten o'clock. Passed and repassed by a covert way leading to the parallel.[15]

Ebenezer Denny {{PD-US}}

Joseph Plumb Martin was marching toward Yorktown when he met some very friendly Pennsylvania troops who took advantage of him,

> We marched from Williamsburg the last of September. It was a warm day; when we had proceeded about half way to Yorktown we halted and rested two or three hours. Being about to cook some victuals, I saw a fire which some of the Pennsylvania troops had kindled a short distance off; I went to get some fire while some of my messmates made other preparations. I had taken off my coat and unbuttoned my waistecoat, it being very warm; my pocketbook, containing about five dollars, was in my waistcoat pocket. When I came among the strangers they appeared to be uncommonly complaisant, asking many questions, helping me to fire, and chatting very familiarly. I took my fire and returned, but it was not long before I perceived that those kind hearted helpers and helped themselves to my pocketbook and its whole contents. I felt mortally chagrined but there was no plaster for my sore but patience, and my plaster of that, at this time, I am sure was very small and very thinly spread, for it never covered the wound.[16]

The approach of the allies toward Yorktown met no resistance. Had Cornwallis tried to stop them, it would have been a waste of British troops. When the allied troops appeared, the British pickets began to fall back.

The troops of Lieutenant Colonel Robert Abercrombie, who commanded the British left wing, were the first to give the alarm of the approaching allied army. Rochambeau sent forward Baron Viomenil with troops and two cannons toward the British, which sent the British soldiers in retreat.

Colonel Tarleton's Legion covered the British left. After a few cannon shots from the allied army, Tarleton withdrew to the Moore House, below Yorktown. There were no causalities the first day as the American and French troops camped within a mile of the British posts. Washington's order for the evening was, "The whole army, officers and soldiers, will lay on their arms this night."[17]

On the 28th the American and French forces came within sight of the British forces at Gloucester Point. All three leaders of each army had a different perspective of the encounter. General Lauzun's perspective was tainted, because he had very little respect for his commander General Weedon. Lauzun believed that Washington should had given him the command.

Lauzun and Weedon also came from different social circles. Lauzum was a member of French nobility, and Weedon had started life as an innkeeper. Lauzun also felt that Weedon shied away from gunfire, which was far from the truth. Weedon had fought with courage at Brandywine and Germantown, where there was much gunfire.

The American version according to Weedon was sent to Washington on the 29th,

I yesterday [28th] made a forage at Abington Church of some Oats & Barley belonging to Col. Warner Lewis, by that Gentleman's desire. The covering party consisting of 3 Militia Battalions of Infantry; were advanced as low down as Sewells, they were supported by 100 Horse from the Duke de Lauzuns Legion with 30 Militia Dragoons.

While the Waggons were loading the Duke & Self reconnoiter'd the Country below, & were within a Mile of Gloster; the Enemy lay quite still & have not been out since the 24th Inst. We had a view of one side of their Works, saw no one on them, & Deserters say they have not worked any for some days. The last forage they made, our parties had a sight of each other, they fired a few Field pieces at us, but returned with a small Quantity of Corn that they had cut down in a Field near Town, not choosing to venture a single Yard after Mr [Simcoe] reconnoiter'd us with his Glass who swore to his people, "our Rifle Men were as thick as the Stalks in the Corn Field." If your Excellency have not already pointed out a place for the Marines to debark at, I would recommend Mr Frank Willis's on Ware River, he lives not more than a Mile from Mobjac Bay, good navigation & 3 Mile from the left of our encampment & 10 from the Fleet laying in York River.[18]

This is the French version according to Lauzun,

I proposed to him [Weedon] to advance towards Gloucester, and to go the next day [28th] and reconnitre along the English posts; he consented, and we started with fifty hussars. When we were within six or seven miles of the enemy, he told me that he considered it useless and very dangerous to go any further, and that we could learn no more; I pressed him so, that he did not dare refuse to follow. I forced back the enemy's posts, and approached sufficiently to get an exact idea of their position. My general was in despair; he told me he would go no further with me; that he did not wish to get killed.[19]

This is the British version according to Colonel Tarleton,

> At four o'clock the same day [28th] Lieutenant-colonel Tarleton was informed that a body of French and Americans had passed the swamp which divided the ground in front of the royal army, and that they were extending towards the left flank of the legion. The cavalry were immediately mounted, and formed into three squadrons in front of the British center. In this situation they watched for an opportunity of striking at any detachment who might pass the Hampton Road; but the enemy were cautious, and cannonaded the legion dragoons across the morass, who retired at sunset.[20]

Here we have one skirmish, three different accounts, and each with their own agenda.

Washington's army moved by different roads toward Yorktown. About noon all the columns reached their ground, and, after driving in the pickets and some cavalry, encamped for the evening.

Lieutenant William Feltman described the six allied brigades in his journal,

> The whole army took up the line of march this morning five o'clock. I conjecture the whole of our army, I mean the French and our Continental troops, to be Fifteen Thousand Veteran Troops, beside the militia: they are so numerous that I have not been able to ascertain their number. The American army consists of six Brigades, viz: Col. Von's, Lt. Col. Barber's and Lt. Col. Gemot's Battalion of Infantry will form one brigade and to be commanded by Brigadier Gen. Muhlenberg.
>
> Col. Gaskin's Virginia Reg't and the two Battalions of Pennsylvania's, a Brigade to be commanded by Brigad'r Gen. Wayne.
>
> The two Jersey battalions and the Rhode Island Reg't, a Brigade to be commanded by Col. Dayton.
>
> The third and fourth Maryland Regt's, a Brigade to be commanded by Brigad'r Gen'l Clinton.
>
> The American troops encamped in a wood within a mile of the Enemy's left line—and the French troops encamped on their right. Our troops remained under arms all night with their respective companies and platoons.
>
> The French troops saluted Col. Tarleton's Horse with a few shot of three pounders which made them retreat immediately. A number of prisoners taken this night who had been straggling through the country.[21]

The 3rd Pennsylvania Regiment was on the march as recorded in the journal of an unknown soldier,

> This day the Whole French American & Militia at 5 o'clock for the Enemy lines we Encamped about sun set within two miles of their works some Cannon Shot was Exchanged between the French troops & the Enemy His Excellency Genl. Washington rode the enemy within one mile of their works marched this day 12 miles.[22]

Allied defenses at Gloucester Point, earlier manned by 1,500 Virginia militia troops under Weedon, were now commanded by General Marquis de Choisy and 1,400 French troops.

Twenty-one year old Thomas Lowry was drafted into the Virginia militia for a second time in 1781. He wrote in his pension application [W2139],

> I was drafted in a company of Militia commanded again by Captain George Mountjoy. The Company was raised in Stafford County Virginia. It was marched to Falmouth where the company received our arms. It was then marched through Fredericksburg, & through Spotsylvania, Caroline, King and Queen and on to

Williamsburg and from there to Springfield, where it joined the brigade commanded by Colonel Dark. After being at Springfield for some time, we were marched to Pigeon Hill to drive the British back into York, they having erected some pieces of cannon on said hill. We were then commanded by General Stevens The British spiked there cannon and retreated into York, and we occupied the ground they had left. I was drafted for a tour of three months, and before my time had expired, whilst I was at the siege of York.

Charles Moreland was seventeen, when he joined the Virginia militia in March of 1781. He stated in his pension application [S1920],

> We joined the main Army at Williamsburg & was attached to the Brigade of General Nelson & the Regiment of Colonel William Darke, at this place General Washington joining the Army & from this place marched to York, which place the British had possession of. They also had possession of Pidgion Hill [Pigeon Hill]. General Lafayette heading the French troops marched up & attacked the British & was compelled in the first instance to retreat. But having been reinforced he again attacked them & made them retreat, on that evening or the following General Washington commenced building a Fort on Pidgion Hill, also built breastworks.

When the combined American and French armies arrived at Yorktown, there was discussion whether to attack Cornwallis or to lay siege. The Americans had very little experience in siege warfare.

Edward Elley had served several times in the Virginia militia. He joined again at the age of twenty-nine and marched to Yorktown. He stated in his pension application [S8403],

> The third term I was drafted for the service I hired a substitute who filled my place and was in General Lafayette's Army when he passed on by Elleys ford in Culpepper County Va by circuitous rout through Spotsylvania County and into Culpepper in order to strengthen his Army and he joined I think General Morgans Army at the Fork Church in Culpepper County and crossed over the Rapidan River at the Racoon ford into Orange County and so on down towards Williamsburg on the James River and whilst passing Elleys ford some fifty or sixty of Lafayettes officers and soldiers called at my house near said ford and gave them dinner it being that time of day when the army passed. A short time after this army passed another requisition of men was called as a relief which included me and having just hired a substitute and not feeling myself able to hire if I could have obtained another substitute I determined to fill my own place and took my horse and joined Lafayettes Army before it reached Williamsburg. I do not recollect the day or month when this term of myself or my substitute commenced or on the armies halted a short time at Williamsburg to receive reinforcements from the surrounding country and then marched down to York Town in Virginia and we had several little engagements with the enemy before they were himed in at said town a Council of War was held by our officers and some were in favour of storming the enemies fort then under General Wallace [Cornwallis] but General Washington was opposed to that counsel and recommended a siege as I was told. The enemy frequently fired upon us whilst engaged in making preparations for the siege and killed a few of our men.

Washington ceded the intellectual leadership of the siege to Rochambeau. The French knew much more about how to conduct a siege than he did. Rochambeau had led, or at least participated in, fourteen sieges in Europe. Washington's pride was not involved, and he did not have to be persuaded to yield to the French suggestions on how to go about squeezing Cornwallis into surrendering. Most of the French had a high regard for Washington. Going into battle with him was, for many of the French, more that an opportunity to inflict revenge on an old enemy, but it was also an honor.

Soon the combined American and French armies would have the British surrounded on three sides. The French fleet in Chesapeake Bay would complete the circle around the British. The battle Washington had longed for so long was about to begin.

The French forces, like the Americans, were energetic. They were incessant in the work of opening entrenchments, while redoubts were quickly built and parallels were rapidly advanced. Under the cover of night, the men with pickaxes and spades marched noiselessly to the posts of labor, and in the morning, as if by magic, there appeared to the anxious eyes of the British a new evidence of power and skill.

Washington reconnoitered the British defenses and decided that they could be bombarded into submission. The Americans and the French spent the night of the 28th sleeping out in the open, while work parties built bridges over the marshes. Some of the American soldiers hunted down wild hogs to eat. According to Irving's *Washington,* the general slept under a mulberry tree, with the root serving as his pillow.

Saturday September 29, 1781

(A warm day)

British forces:

Lieutenant Bartholomew James was in command of several cannons, when the Americans attacked his line. He described the action in his journal,

> His lordship having in vain offered the enemy battle with his little force of five thousand men on this and the preceding day, and finding them very intent on their determination of attacking him on the left flank with every advantage, he removed into the works on this night, not doubting in the least but the garrison, acting on the defensive, would be enabled to hold out till the much-expected and long-looked-for fleet and army relieved us. A body of French horse and foot attacked the Legion, who retreated under cover of a battery to the left. Some of the enemy advancing in front of the works, I discharged seven eighteen-pounders at them.[23]

Cornwallis displayed a mood of confidence, when he sent this letter to Sir Henry Clinton,

> I have this evening received your letter of the 21st, which has given me the greatest satisfaction [Clinton offers to send him troops]. I shall retire this night within the works, and have no doubt, if relief arrives in any reasonable time, York and Gloucester will be both in possession of his Majesty's troops.[24]

Henry Clinton, Library of Congress   General Charles Cornwallis---National Archives

Cornwallis must had felt very confident about help being sent, because he pulled back his troops from his outer line of works which they occupied. The troops were moved into the town, which left the outer works to be taken by the Americans the next day.

The main body of the British were entrenched in the open grounds about Yorktown, with the intention of checking the progress of the allies, while an inner line of works near the village had been provided for his ultimate defense.

Stephen Popp, a Hessian soldier, wrote in his journal, "One of our men killed and two wounded, many of the English and Hessians too, at night moved into our lines, as the enemy was advancing on them. Eight of our men deserted to them."[25]

Johann Dohla got his exposure to war at Yorktown and wrote in his diary,

> At ten o'clock in the morning Private Zeilmann of Quesnoy's Company was fatally wounded by a small weapon's ball while on picket duty and died a short time later. I helped bury him.
>
> Following this, at twelve o'clock noon, Private Hammerlein was wounded while on duty at the same post. The ball was cut out later from between the two shoulder blades as I watched and held him. Also at this post, a Private Grunbeck, and three other men were severely wounded. Today more than thirty English and Hessians on duty at the outpost were killed or wounded.[26]

American/French forces:

Washington and other general officers rode to Pigeon Quarter at an early hour and surveyed the works, which were in full view. The group, attracting the British's attention, were fired at by cannons which struck the trees above them. Washington remained under fire until he had finished his observations.

Washington again reminded his troops of their duty, "The advanced season and various conditions render it indispensably necessary to conduct the attacks against York with the upmost rapidity. The General therefore expects and requires the officers and soldiers of this army to pursue the duties of their respective departments and stations with the most unabating ardor."[27]

The American troops began marching at seven o'clock in the morning and formed in front of a marsh before the enemy's works about half a mile out. The day before the Americans had spent the entire day and most of the night repairing the bridges over the marsh. Two brigades crossed the marsh and were met with cannon shot. One soldier lost a leg due to a cannon ball. Dr. James Thacher assisted in amputating the man's leg. One American reported, "A twelve and a four pound ball paid us a visit in our camp, but did no damage." The two sides skirmished several times during the day.

Washington wrote in his diary,

> Moved the American Troops more to the right, and Encamped on the East side of Bever dam Creek, with a Morass in front, about Cannon shot from the enemys lines. Spent this day in reconnoitering the enemys position, & determining upon a plan of attack & approach which must be done without the assistance of Shipping above the Town as the Admiral (notwithstanding my earnest sollicitation) declined hazarding any Vessells on that Station.[28]

At the age of eighteen Henry Muirhead joined the Virginia militia in May of 1781. He joined Lafayette's army, and he was discharged August 1st. On the 15th of August he joined the army again as a substitute for his brother Andrew. For the next few weeks he marched with his regiment chasing Cornwallis. He wrote in his pension application [S30609],

> Hearing that Cornwallis had encamped at York Town, we fell back to Williamsburg. Here they heard that General Washington was coming on, and in a short time after, an express came on for them to join him, as I understood at the time: but in a few days General Washington and suite came to Williamsburg; – General Washington & suite went on board a vessel then lying in the River, and went down the River, for the purpose, as he understood at the time of conducting measures of cooperation. Soon after which they took up their line of march from Williamsburg, and in 4 or 5 days (or thereabouts) they joined General Washington and the French Officers, some 10 or 12 miles from York Town, about 2 o'clock in the evening, and the next morning took up our line of march towards York Town, when within a short distance of the River we separated from Washington, he Washington, crossing the River a little above the town, and us under Wayne (who commanded the left wing) & Lafayette (who commanded the right) were stationed at Gloucester Point.

Washington moved the army closer to Yorktown, and British gunners opened fire on the infantry. Throughout the day several British cannons fired on the Americans, but there were few casualties. Lieutenant William Feltman wrote in his journal, "The two Brigades [American] crossed the morass, who were immediately saluted with a few cannon shot. One of their soldiers unfortunately lost his leg by a cannon ball."

St. George Tucker described a small skirmish with the British in his journal,

Sat. 29. This morning about eight o Clock the Enemy fired a few shot from their advanced Redoubts, our Right wing having now passed over Munford's Bridge. About nine or ten the Riflemen & Yagers exchanged a few shot across Moores Mill pond at the Dam of which the British had a redoubt—a few shot were fired at different times in the Day and about Sunset from the Enemy's Redoubts—we had five or six men wounded; one mortally & two others by the same Ball. The Execution was much more than might have been expected from the Distance, the dispersed situation of our Men and the few shot fired.[29]

General Nathanael Greene wrote to a friend on September 29, "We have been beating the bush, and the General [Washington] has come to catch the bird. Never was there a more inviting object to glory. The General is a most fortunate man and may success and laurels attend him."[30]

Eighteen year old Major Groom had served several tours in the Virginia militia, when he was sent to Yorktown. He described his time there in his pension application [S31073],

That not long afterward sometime in 1781 as well as I remember I was again drafted to go to York—that two Companies were drafted from his County, and rendezvoused at Williamsburg, and from there marched to Yorktown and there joined Gen'l Washington, who was besieging Cornwallis at that place. The enemy had built a battery on a small creek a small distance from the town & annoyed, much annoyed our men digging entrenchments-- this creek ran into the river below the town -- battery was aboned in a short time as rifle men approached under cover within gun shot & compelled them to retreat. The American Army was posted on both sides of river, & the French fleet was below the town, so that the town was completely surrounded. Washington's plan was to entrench himself & so advance by degrees to protect his men from the enemy's fire & in about ten days our batteries were raised & we returned the fire -- the first battery was raised below the town & the firing continued without intermission until Cornwallis surrendered under both the posts of Yorktown & Gloucester Point.

During the night the right wing of the army, consisting of Americans, occupied the ground east of Beaver Dam Creek, while the left wing, consisting of French, was stationed on the west side of the stream.

Chapter 3

British Leave a Gift and a Hero Falls

"We were agreeably surprised this morning, to find that the enemy had, during the preceding night, abandoned three or four of their redoubts." --- Doctor James Thacher's journal

---

Cornwallis, in a controversial move, pulled his forces back from their outer defense line. He still held out hope that General Clinton would send a relief force to his rescue. Washington decided to lay siege to Yorktown, and his troops quickly occupied the abandoned redoubts. Unfortunately, the Americans lost a popular officer during a skirmish. September ended as the allied troops began digging trenches to encircle the British, and they started to move up their siege guns.

Sunday September 30, 1781

British forces:

During the night, Cornwallis pulled back his forces from the outer defenses, except for redoubts 9, 10, and the Fusiliers redoubt. The troops from the abandoned redoubts were sent to occupy the earthworks surrounding the town. Cornwallis was expecting 5,000 reinforcements from Clinton by the next week, so he was trying to tighten his lines. Cornwallis knew that he might be relieved by sea, so he decided to consolidate his position at Yorktown. By withdrawing his forces inward, he believed it would increase his chances to hold out until the British navy came to his rescue.

The Americans and the French occupied the abandoned defenses and began to establish their own batteries there. With the British outer defenses in their hands, allied engineers began to lay out positions for the artillery. The men improved the occupied works and deepened their trenches. The British also worked on improving their defenses.

Henry Clinton wanted to reassure Cornwallis that he would come to his aid on land or water with this letter,

> Your Lordship may be assured that I am doing every thing in my power to relieve you by a direct move, and I have reason to hope, from the assurances given me this day by Admiral Graves, that we may pass the bar by the 12th of October, if the winds permit and no unforeseen accident happens: this, however, is subject to disappointment, wherefore, if I hear from you, your wishes will of course direct me, and I shall persist in my idea of a direct move, even to the middle of November, should it be your Lordship's opinion that you can hold out so long; but if, when I hear from you, you tell me that you cannot, and I am without hopes of arriving in time to succor you by a direct move, I will immediately make an attempt upon Philadelphia by land, giving you notice, if possible, of my intention. If this should draw any part of Washington's force from you, it may

possibly give you an opportunity of doing something to save your army; of which, however, you can best judge from being upon the spot.[1]

Colonel Tarleton thought Cornwallis was too quick to give the order to abandon the outer line. He later wrote in his book, "That great time would have been gained by holding and disputing the ground inch by inch, both to finish the works of Yorktown and to retard the operations of the combined army."[2]

Bartholomew James described the second day of battle in his journal,

> The enemy broke ground and began to throw up two redoubts, moving on the same time in three columns towards our centre, and took possession of two of our redoubts we had evacuated on withdrawing into the town. At eleven o'clock the enemy attacked the right and left of the town with an intention of storming the flanking redoubts, and, after a smart action of two hours, they were repulsed with some loss, retreating into the woods with the utmost precipitance and confusion, our batteries having much galled them.[3]

Stephen Popp wrote in his journal about the capture of Colonel Alexander Scammell and the treatment of the dead and wounded,

> A wounded rebel Colonel captured by our light horse. The rebels made three attacks on our right redoubt, but were driven back by our batteries and the fire of our frigates—with heavy loss. The French sent a flag of truce asking leave to bury the dead and carry off the wounded—this was granted, provided they came without arms,---this they agreed to, and the dead were buried, the wounded removed to Williamsburg where they were hospitals, their loss was over 440, we have had a trying month, much labor and little food.[4]

Johann Conrad Döhla also mentioned the capture of Colonel Scammell in his journal,

> This morning the English Light Horse brought a wounded rebel colonel in as a captive. The enemy probed our right wing today and stormed the outermost redoubt. However, he was chased back into the forest, with losses, by the grape shot from our batteries, as well as from one of the frigates standing in the river. The French Grenadiers appeared among those making the attack.[5]

American/French forces:

Washington had been encouraged to travel to Yorktown without his heavy guns. On this morning the heavy cannons were being unloaded just six miles away at Trebell's Landing on the James River. Until these guns could be brought to the front, there could be no movement toward the outer positions of the British. This would be the first time in the war that Washington would have superior firepower, combined with trained artillerymen.

On the morning of the 30th, Rochambeau sent Charles de Lameth and Guillaume-Mathieu Dumas, at the head of a hundred grenadiers and chasseurs of Bourbonnais [assault troops], to occupy the strongest of these redoubts, called Pigeon Hill. When they got there the redoubt was empty. Fifty chasseurs of the regiment of Deux-Ponts occupied the second redoubt, and the Americans took command of the third redoubt.

The French also attacked the Fusiliers redoubt twice, but each attack failed. The French detachment engaged the pickets of the Twenty-third Regiment (Welsh Fusiliers). The Fusiliers redoubt, very close to the York River, was supported with cannon fire from the frigate *Guadeloupe*, which was anchored near the redoubt. This redoubt was the strongest of the British outer works and was never captured. One French soldier was killed, one broke an arm, and another had a leg broken by a cannon ball. This was the only skirmish of the day.

Doctor James Thacher noted in his journal, "We were agreeably surprised this morning, to find that the enemy had, during the preceding night, abandoned three or four of their redoubts, and retired within the town, leaving a considerable extent of commanding ground which might have cost us much labor and many lives to obtain by force."[6]

Count Axerl de Fersen, an aide-de-camp to Rochambeau, wrote about the abandoned redoubts in his diary. He was also critical of the decision of Cornwallis to give them up,

> On the 30th the enemy evacuated their advanced works and retreated within the body of the place. The works consisted of two large redoubts, and a battery of two cannon, which were separated from the town by a deep ravine of twelve hundred yards. We took possession; and this advanced our own work very much, leaving us the ability to put our first parallel on the other side of the ravine. Though that was a blunder made by Cornwallis, it is, perhaps, excusable, because he had express orders from General Clinton to retire within the place, and a promise that he (Clinton) would relieve him.[7]

Rochambeau wrote in his memoirs of the British forces pulling back from Pigeon Hill during the night, "The enemy fearing an attack by surprise in the very extensive position in which they had entrenched themselves, abandoned the entrenched camp at Pigeonhill, and confined themselves within the walls of their fortifications."[8]

The French soldiers found that the redoubts were well placed. However, their walls were thin and made of sand. Rochambeau had some men reinforce the walls. While they were working, the British fired several rounds without scoring a hit.

Afterwards, de Rochambeau and several men, including Colonel de Deux-Ponts, surveyed the area. The Colonel wrote in his journal, "I advanced three hundred paces nearer the town [Yorktown] and saw a ravine, nearly twenty-five feet deep, which surrounds the whole place, and enters York River above and below the town. This ravine seems to me to be an excellent defense, and I do not understand why the enemy left it."[9]

Washington wrote in his diary,

> The Enemy abandoned all their exterior works, & the position they had taken without the Town; & retired within their Interior works of defence in the course of last Night—immediately upon which we possessed them, & made those on our left (with a little alteration) very serviceable to us. We also began two inclosed Works on the right of Pidgeon Hill—between that & the ravine above Mores Mill.[10]

Lieutenant Ebenezer Wild wrote in his journal,

> The enemy have abandon all their outworks except two redoubts, which are about 150 years advanced of their main works; in consequence of which detachment of our troops have moved, and taken possession of them (the abandoned works). A large part of the army are ordered to making fascines and other material for carrying on a siege. At 9 o'clock a.m. the Light Infantry marched to the lines, where we continued as a covering party all day. Colonel Scammel was unfortunately wounded and taken prisoner as he was

reconnoitering near the enemy's lines. The enemy have kept a moderate fore on us all day. Several of our men were killed & wounded during the night.[11]

Colonel Richard Butler recorded in his journal that both sides had a busy day preparing for battle,

> The American and Allied army took possession of the abandoned redoubts in proper military form. The engineer began to lay out work for the artillery and every thing goes on with spirit; 1,200 men for fatigue, forming faseines,&c. The enemy very busy all day at the works around the town. This morning Col. Seammel was unfortunately wounded and taken prisoner when reconnoitereing too close to the enemy.[12]

De Choisy asked for a detachment of French troops to reinforce the troops stationed at Gloucester. De Grasse gave him 800 men, which landed there on October 3rd.

There were times that British forces would send people infected with smallpox toward American lines, which was what may have prompted this general order issued September 30th. Lieutenant William McDowell encountered people infected with smallpox and wrote in his journal, "Left one negro man with the small pox laying on the road side in order to prevent the Virginia Militia from pursuing them [British], which the enemy frequently did, left numbers in that condition starving and helpless."[13]

You would think that American soldiers would not have to be told not to wear red coats around a battlefield. These were the general orders for the day,

> All Deserters and others coming from the Enemies Lines are to be stopped at the outposts and reported to the General Officer of the day who is desired to find such as are capable of giving useful information to Head Quarters, the rest are to be disposed of as the Governor or person appointed by him may direct—in the first examination of them at the Outposts the most scrupulous attention is to be used, to prevent any person infected with the small pox from entring either the French or American Camps—All Officers and others are strictly forbid for obvious reasons to wear red Coats.[14]

Washington sent a letter to General Weedon, who was in command of the troops on the Gloucester side. He was alerting the general to keep a close watch, because Cornwallis might use Gloucester as an escape route,

> I have just received your Favor of Yesterday—Last Night the Enemy evacuated their exteriour Works,& left us in Possession of Pigeon Quarter, & some other Works which they had occupied, contracting their Defences near the Town. This Circumstance has created a Jealousy in some Minds similar to what you mention—that Ld Cornwallis may throw himself with his Troops upon the Gloster Side,& endeavour by a rapid movement to attempt an Escape—I can hardly perswade myself that this will be his Policey—he ought to be watched however on every point—You will therefore pay the utmost Attention to all their Movements which can fall under your Eye—approachg as near as you can with Safety & prudence, so as not to hazard too much—In Case any Intention of an Escape should be discovered, you will give me the most instantaneous Information—send immediate Notice to the Inhabitants to remove from this probable Rout, all the Cattle & Horses that can be of any Use—And at the same Time, give every Impediment to their March that you possibly can—that I may have Time to throw my Army in their Front.
>
> I am this Day informed that some Troops are crossing the River to Glousster—whether this is to replace a Corps of Germans wh. are said to have come from that side Yesterday or for some other purpose I can not say—three Boats with men, I saw cross myself.[15]

Rochambeau wrote in his memoirs about the British attacking New London and the arrival of British troops in New York,

> The whole day of the 30th was employed by us in establishing ourselves in the out-works abandoned by the enemy, and by so doing we were enabled to confine them within a much smaller circle, and thereby secure an imminent advantage over them.
>
> We were informed that Arnold had been sent at the close of the month of August on a plundereing expedition to New London in Connecticut. He burned the town with a part of the merchant ships in the harbor; but this diversion intended in no way to impede our operations. We received intelligence, at the same time, of the arrival at New York of Admiral Digby, with three ships of the line, and a body of troops on board with Prince William-Henry, one of the King of England's sons, who had been sent out by the Court to retake possession of the Government of Virginia. We were informed that this farther assistance of land and naval forces had enabled General Clinton to embark part of his army on board the English fleet, consisting of twenty-six sail, besides several fifty-gun ships and a few fire ships; and we were also informed that active preparations were making at New York to second this new attempt to succor Cornwallis, but which, in the extremity to which the latter was reduced, was too tardy to be efficient.[16]

The French and Americans had their main camp two miles from the British. They broke ground and began digging trenches and the installing of gun batteries around Yorktown.

Lieutenant William Feltman wrote in his journal,

> This morning about 8 o'clock, upon strict examination, we found that the enemy had evacuated all their outworks, which we immediately took possession of. The French and British had a severe engagement this morning. One of the French officers lost his leg, and a number of privates were killed and wounded. Col. Scammell was wounded and taken prisoner this morning.
>
> Lt. Tilden and self took a walk to view their works which they evacuated last night, which was within musket shot of their main works, when we perceived a flag advancing toward us, which we immediately went to meet, and on Examination found that he had a letter for Lieut. Col. Huntington of Col. Scammel's Reg't, informing him of his capitivity, where he would be sent on parole as soon as his wound was dressed.
>
> This day Capt; Davis laid a bet with me of a beaver hat that Lord Cornwallis and his army would be prisoners of war by the next Sunday.[17]

Later in the day, Colonel Philip Van Cortlandt was on picket at one of the captured redoubts, when visited by General George Washington. He wrote of the unexpected visit by Washington and the attack by British artillery in his memoirs,

> That morning the Commander in Chief with almost all the General officers came to my picket and was in my front while I was seated on the platform of the popular redoubt Viewing their Battery about one mile distant, the enemy fired over their heads and cut branches of the Tree which fell about me, but as the Generals did not move the Second Ball struck directly in my front. Struck and went in the ground about 3 rods before the Generals m(had it raised it must have passed thro the Cluster and have killed Several) when they all retreated except the Commander in Chief who remained with his spying glass observing their works and altho he remained sometime alone directly in their View and in my front they did not fire again. The General then came toward me which observing I rose and mett him when after some Remarks and Enquiries he directed me to keep my men as they were at present disposed of out of sight of the Battery until the Evening then to surround the town with my centinels from the Redoubt which was to the right all the way to the York River and that Baron Viominal with the French pickets should do the same to the left.[18]

This would not be the last time that General Washington would expose himself to British cannon fire. At times the men became upset with him for standing in the open where he could be injured or killed.

Death of Colonel Scammell:

The day was clouded only by the fall of the brave and much-loved Colonel Scammell of New Hampshire. When the pickets reported the evacuation of the enemy's outer position, the Colonel went forward about 5:40 in the morning, with a small party, as field officer of the day to reconnoiter the deserted works. Proceeding alone a short distance toward Yorktown, he was suddenly surprised near the Fusiliers' redoubt by some troopers of Tarleton's Legion, under Colonel Cameron. The British probably reached the area called Poplar Tree Fort around six in the morning.

Alexander Scammell from *The Granite Monthly* Vol. XIV No. 9, September 1892, following page 272.

Colonel Alexander Scammell, a Harvard educated lawyer, was wounded while reconnoitering British fortifications that had been abandoned the day before. He became separated from his scouting party, when he was discovered by a squad of Tarleton's light dragoons led by Lieutenant Allan Cameron. Scammell's men escaped but were nearby when the Colonel was surrounded. He was shot in his side either before or after he surrendered. His captives hurried him roughly into Yorktown, where his wound was dressed.

Colonel Scammell was one of the first to discover that the British had abandoned their advance redoubts and forts. General Washington was given this information immediately. Later in the day, a British soldier, under a white flag, approached one of the redoubts. He gave a letter to an American soldier, from Colonel Scammell, requesting that his servant and some clothing be sent to him at Williamsburg where he would go to be paroled. He was paroled due to his severe wound and moved to the Continental Army hospital at Williamsburg, where he died around five in the afternoon on October 6, 1781.

The British placed Scammell in one of their boats and sailed it up the York River, and then they rowed up Queen's Creek to Capitol Landing. The trip of twelve miles took around five to six hours. On guard duty at the landing was Erasmus Chapman, a twenty-two year old member of the Virginia militia, and in his pension application [R1867] he gave his account of the arrival of the Colonel,

> I frequently stood sentry at a place called the Stone Bridge which was made over a creek that emtied into York river not far distant; while on duty one night a Boat sailed or was rowed up the creek to the bridge, I hailed it, and detained the Boat, till a file of men and an Officer from our camp came; the Boat proved to be

a Brittish one, and came with a flag bearing an American Colonel who had been taken prisoner by them and was dangerously wounded I may have forgotten his name but I now think the Col'os. name was either, Scamel, or Campbell, he was immediately sent to the Doctors at Williamsburg on a litter the Brittish boat was suffered to return.

It was first thought that the Colonel would recover. He told several visitors of the events leading up to his capture,

> ...he [Scammell] mistook a few of the enemy's light horse for Moylan's [Col. Stephen]; he thought he knew the officer in front and was therefore not alarmed. Two of them rode up to him, one of which seized his bridle, while the other pointed a pistol at him. Being thus in their power, and enquiring who they were, a third rode up and shot him in the back, at so near a distance as to burn his coat with the powder; another soldier then made a pass at him with his sword, but being weakened with his wound, and his horse starting at the report of the pistol, he happily fell to the ground and avoided the stroke. He was then plundered, taken to York.[19]

Scammell's men were close enough to see what had happed but could do nothing in time to help. Colonel Philip Van Cortlandt had just arrived with his men to relieve Colonel Scammell, and he was told what happen. He wrote in his memoirs,

> I found his men and relieved them; but the Colonel had before my arrival observed that [the British] had retired from the Poplar Tree Redoubt to the road in front, and mistook a British patrol of Horse for our Men was under the necessity of surrendering, when one of their dragoons coming up, fired, and wounded the Colonel after his Surrender but whether the dragoon knew of the Surrender, being behind him I cannot say but from all the information I could obtain it was after his Surrender. The Colonel was first taken to the Town then paroled to Williamsburg where he died in our Hospital and buried with the honors of War.[20]

Quartermaster-General Pickering said of the wounding, "He was barbarously wounded. After two dragoons had him their prisoner, a third came up and shot him through the side ...lamented by all who knew him, and who valued friendship, integrity, and truth. The enemy in York treated him kindly afterwards, particulary the Suregons. He was suffered to go to Williamsburg on Parole."[21]

Lieutenant John Bell Tilden wrote in his journal about the wounding of Colonel Scammel and skirmishes with the British,

> This morning about 8 o'clock, upon strict examination, we found the enemy had evacuated their outworks, which we immediately took possession of. After a severe cannonade, the French took one of their redoubts with a number of prisoners. Col. Scammell was wounded and taken prisoner this morning. A flag from the town this afternoon informing us of his captivity and desiring his servant and baggage be sent to Williamsburg. Mount picket at sunset in front of a redoubt building by our troops, the picket consisted of two Captains, four lieutenants and one hundred men, with non-commissioned officers in proportion. Received orders from the Baron who was general of the day, that the subaltern officers of the guard should patrol by themselves as near the enemy as possible, without exposing themselves too much. Myself and another officer, at different times were fired at by the British sentinels. Discovered nothing of any consequence, heard a confused noise of tearing down buildings, for making fortifications.[22]

Dr. James Thacher wrote in his journal about the wounding and capture of Colonel Scammell,

An occurrence has just been announced which fills our hearts with grief and sorrow. Colonel Alexander Scammell being officer of the day, while reconnoitering the ground which the enemy had abandoned, was surprised by a party of their horse, and after surrendered, they had the baseness to inflict a wound which we fear will prove mortal; they have carried him into Yorktown.[23]

St. George Tucker noted in his journal the capture of a British redoubt, and the wounding of Colonel Scammell,

Sunday 30th. This morning it being discovered that the Enemy had abandoned all their advanced Redoubts on the South & East Ends of the Town a party of French Troops between seven & eight OClock took possession of two Redoubts on penny's Hill or Pigeon Quarter, an eminence which it is said commands the whole Town—About ten a smart firing was heard on the upper End of the Town, accompanied by some Guns from the Ships—Being at this time in one of the Redoubts at penny's Hill I saw some of the British retreating or rather running very hastily across the sandy Beach into the Town; soon after which the firing ceas'd & a very considerable smoke (on the upper side of the town across the Creek) indicated the Destruction of their advanced Redoubt on that Quarter by the French Troops; and this I take to be really the Case; but if it should prove otherwise I shall mention it in the sequel—A party under Major [Joseph R.?] Reid having advanced pretty near to their Works on our right, were obliged by a few well directed shot from them to retire. It is now conjectured by many that it is Lord Cornwallis's Intention to attempt a retreat up York river by West point, there being no Ships yet above the Town to prevent such a Measure. This morning Coll. Scammell of the Lt. Infantry reconnoitring the Enemies Works rather too near was wounded & taken prisoner.[24]

Doctor Eneas Munson was the surgeon of Colonel Scammell's Regiment at the beginning of the siege of Yorktown. He attended to him when he was wounded and taken to Williamsburg. "I probed the wound," said Doctor Munson, "but could not find the ball."[25]

General Henry Lee, in his memoires, expressed very kind words about Colonel Scammel and the impact of his death on the army, "This was the severest blow experienced by the allied army throughout the siege; not an officer in our army surpassed in personal worth and professional ability this experienced soldier."[26]

Chapter 4

Preparations and the First Skirmish

"I discovered very quickly that we are young soldiers in a siege, however, we are determined to benefit ourselves by experience; one virtue we possess, that is perseverance." --- Colonel Richard Butler wrote in his journal, Oct. 2, 1781 at Yorktown

The Americans had no experience with siege warfare, but fortunately the French were very experienced. Washington approved the plans for the siege, upon advice from French General and chief engineer, Du Portail, and General Rochambeau.

When the operations against Yorktown began, General Von Steuben asked Washington for a regular command. Washington was happy to give him the command of the Virginia, Maryland, and Pennsylvania divisions. These division, totaled 2,309 men. Steuben was the only American officer who had ever taken part in a regular siege.

Washington wrote in his journal, "From this time [September 30] until 6th of October nothing occurred of importance."[1] During the first week at Yorktown, the American sector had most of the men engaged in labor. Many were sent into the woods, where they cut down small trees and branches from larger ones. The wood was tied together to make fascines to be used for filling in marshy or soft ground and to strengthen the sides of the trenches. Heavy, thick boards were made to provide platforms for the cannons.

The English sent troops across the York River to fortify Gloucester. Washington, aware that Gloucester could be an escape route for Cornwallis, sent French troops and Virginia militiamen to secure Gloucester. There the allies and British had the opening skirmish of the Siege of Yorktown.

The British began to prepare for a siege by cutting rations by a third. Food was scarce for the horses and the several thousand slaves that were used to construct fortifications. Cases of smallpox began to break out, especially among the slaves. Residents of Yorktown that remained were turned out of their homes, so that they could be used by the British soldiers. Help from General Clinton in New York was promised, but would it arrive in time?

Monday October 1, 1781

(Pleasant weather)

British forces:

Ample food was not available for the British horses and hundreds were slaughtered on the beach of Yorktown. Many were seen floating in the York River. Also, large groups of starving Negroes were released and sent to the American lines. Some of them were infected with smallpox.

Bartholomew James, a British naval officer, wrote in his journal,

> A rebel colonel was taken about noon this day, having been shot through the back by an officer of the Legion. The enemy constantly employed throwing up works, and all our batteries cannonading their working parties, which in great measure impeded their operations, though they were, from their great numbers, carried on with astonishing briskness. At midnight a negro fellow was caught deserting to the enemy, with a letter enclosing a state of the garrison's distress from a merchant in the town, who was immediately taken into custody.[2]

American/French forces:

Quartermaster General Timothy Pickering wrote an optimistic letter to his wife on this day, "The enemy have abandoned some of their outer works, which will probably, in some degree, shorten the siege."[3]

General Timothy Pickering---Library of Congress

Count William de Deux-Ponts, of the French Army, went out to survey the area while his men were working on the trenches. He wrote in his journal,

I made a special reconnaissance on the enemy's left, and I did not find the defenses better than on the side that I had already seen. The land is a little more open, and gives greater facility to the enemy to direct his shots at our works; but that is the only advantage which this side has for the enemy. I went as far as the York River, and I saw all the English vessels, the position of Gloucester, and the French ships which blockade the river.[4]

Early in the morning the Americans broke ground for a redoubt about 300 yards east of the main British redoubt. The plain on which these redoubts were located was called Pigeon Hill.

Captain James Duncan, a Princeton graduate, was preparing for the ministry, when he volunteered to serve in Colonel Hanson's Regiment until the end of the war. He was twenty-six years old when he wrote in his journal at Yorktown,

Ten companies were ordered out early this morning for fatigue, of which I had the honor to command one. Until 11 a.m. we were employed in cutting and stripping branches for gabions [a type of wall used to protect soldiers from enemy fire]. On being furnished with shovels, spades, pickaxes, etc., we were ordered up to the lines, where we continued inactive until about an hour before sunset. In the meantime, the engineers were employed in reconnoitering the enemy's works, and fixing on proper places to break the first ground. Let me here observe that the enemy by evacuating their works had given us an amazing advantage, as the ground they left commanded the whole town, and nothing but the reasons before alleged could have justified them in doing so, as by contrary conduct they must have very much retarded the operations of the siege.

The engineers having fixed on and chained off the ground in two different places to erect their works within point blank shot of the enemy, the parties were called on. Five companies were ordered to an eminence on the right and five to another on the left.

We were now conducted to a small hollow near the ground. Five men were ordered by the engineer to assist in clearing away the rubbish, staking out and drawing the lines of the work. This was in the face of open day, and the men went with some reluctance; a little before this we had a shot from the enemy which increased their fears. At dusk of evening we all marched up, and never did I see men exert themselves half so much or work with more eagerness. Indeed, it was their interest, for they could expect nothing else but an incessant roar of cannon the whole night. We were relieved about daybreak, and scarcely had we left the trenches when the enemy began their fire on both works from three pieces.[5]

Colonel Richard Butler, of the 5th Pennsylvania Regiment, wrote in his journal, "Last night a good deal of firing between the patrols and pickets, two works were traced out and carried with great vigor. The enemy began to cannonade at daybreak, and also a few shells, which did no damage till evening, when two men were killed on the works."[6]

On the Gloucester side, the allies had a legion of cavalry under the Duke de Lauzum and a force of Virginia militia under General Weedon. Eight hundred marines from the ships of Count de Grasse landed to reinforce the allies.

John Hudson had been in camp for about a week, and he wrote about hearing of Colonel Scammel's death,

On reaching my company I heard discharges on cannon fired in quick succession, and the sound of their balls sticking some object. Inquiring what was doing, of my associates, I was told, that they had raised a redoubt the morning of their arrival and that the balls were from the enemy, who were striking a large oak tree in front of the redoubt. On that very day, as I afterwards learnt, Col. A. Scammel, who was out with a reconnoitering party was taken prisoner by Tarleton's light horse and inhumanly murdered after his capture. I was told also, that the night before, the Marquis de la Fayette, with a party of Frenchmen who had been landed from the fleet had stormed two batteries of two twelve pounders to each battery, putting every man to the sword—literally—as the very privates among the French wore that weapon. [7]

Orders were given in regard to the health of the soldiers, "The health of the troops is an object of such infinite importance, that every possible attention ought to be paid to the preservation of it."[8] Quartermasters were ordered to furnish straw, good bread, and one gill of rum per man each day.

Lieutenant Feltman of the Pennsylvania Line recorded in his diary,

> This morning the enemy discharged a number of their horses, which were so poor that they were scarcely able to walk. This afternoon, three o'clock, his Excellency Gen. Washington, Gen. Duportail and several other engineers crossed at the mill dam to take a view of the enemy's works. His Excellency sent one of his aides de camp for Capt. Smith and his guard of fifty men to march in front of his Excellency as a covering party, which we did, and went under cover of a hill, where we posted our guard, when his Excellency Gen. Washington and Gen Duportail with three men of our guard advanced within three hundred yards of the enemy's main works, which is the town of York.
>
> Capt. Smith, and Lt. Parker and self took a walk to the York river, where we had the pleasure of seeing all the enemy's vessels of which they had four of them sunk this side of the river in order to prevent the French shipping from passing this side. We observed at a great distance down the river three of the French ships riding at anchor.
>
> The enemy this whole day keep up a cannonading at our fatigue parties who were throwing up works in front of them at so short a distance as half a mile, but did very little damage.
>
> We waited this whole day very impatiently, but all to no purpose, in expection of being relieved from picquet, but to our great mortification we found that we were to be continued which we very agreeably consented to, and built ourselves a fine bowery of pine bushes to spend the night and keep the dew from us.[9]

Captain John Davis reported in his journal that, "A warm fire continued all this day, about 40 guns to the hour, on an average & 10 by night to the hour 2 men only killed one of them in the works." [10]

General Washington wrote a letter to the commander of the French fleet, Admiral de Grasse, because he was concerned that Cornwallis would be able to retreat by going up the York River and then take his army on to West Point. Washington hoped to convince de Grasse to move some of his ships up the York River to prevent this from happening.

> Upon the whole, I can assure your Excellency [de Grasse], that this seems to be the only point in which we are defective. The enemy have already abandoned all their exterior works, and withdrawn altogether to the body of the place, and given us great advantage for opening the trenches. The engineers have had a near and satisfactory view of the works, without interruption, and satisfactory view of the works, without interruption, and we have most to apprehend Lord Cornwallis's escape.
>
> For these reasons I earnestly entreat, that you will be pleased to authorize and enjoin the commanding officer of the ships in York River, to concert measures with me for the purpose above mentioned. In this case

an additional ship may be necessary to remain at the mouth of the river. If upon mature examination of the passage, it should appear too great a risk for the ships, I would at least solicit your Excellency, that the vessels may advance higher up the river, and take a more menacing position with respect to the enemy.[11]

Admiral de Grasse---National Archives

Count de Grasse declined to send any ships up the York River, because he feared that the large ships would not be secure. The narrow channel of the river would not allow his ships to maneuver, if they were attacked by fire-ships.

A few days later, however, the French reconnoitered the area of the river above Yorktown and found it to be safe. De Grasse agreed to send the ships up the river, if Washington would provide row-boats that could be used to protect the ships against enemy fire-ships. It took many days for replies to the letters that went back and forth between Washington and de Grasse. By the time Washington was ready to execute the plan Cornwallis had purposed to surrender.

Tuesday October 2, 1781

(Pleasant weather)

British forces:

During the night, the British opened fire with their cannons to cover the movement of troops to Gloucester. Tarleton crossed over the York River with his Legion to reinforce the troops at Gloucester, and he soon assumed command of all the forces there. This location was considered by Cornwallis to be his escape route and an area that would provide food for his men and horses.

Johann Conrad Dohla wrote in his diary, "Our side cannonaded the enemy heavily because they were entrenching themselves and throwing up batteries about two English miles from York. Also, they occupied two defensive positions that we had previously vacated and destroyed, with large forces, in order to restore their use."[12]

Captain Johann Ewald of the Field Jager Corps received some promising news to write in his diary, "An American galley blew up in the mouth of the York River. At about the same time a guard boat arrived from New York, which brought us the assurance again that Admiral Graves and General Clinton would do everything in their power to relieve us."[13]

British defensive line at the horn facing west toward the allies, firing cannons as the allied trenches are being dug. Photo Courtesy of the Colonial Historical National Park, NPS.

American/French forces:

There was a delay in transporting the siege pieces, which were located about six miles away at Trebell's Landing on the James River. Washington believed it was so urgent to receive the cannons that he sent his own baggage wagons over and ordered his generals, field, and other officers to send theirs. He said that it was, "of the utmost importance that the Heavy Artillery should be brought up without a moment's loss of time."[14]

Firing from the British continued at the redoubt workers, and one of the Maryland troops deserted to the British. According to Colonel Butler, the enemy fired three hundred and fifty one shots between sunrise and sunset. The Americans made no reply but kept digging away until the redoubts were finished.

Colonel Butler wrote, "The fire of the enemy more severe this morning about 10 o'clock. They brought up two 18 pounders in additional to what they had yesterday. About 10'clock p.m. a heavy firing of the ships in the bay. I discovered very quickly that we are young soldiers in a siege, however, we are determined to benefit ourselves by experience; one virtue we possess, that is perseverance."[15]

Captain James Duncan and his men were finishing their work on the fortifications. He wrote in his journal, "The works were so far finished in the course of the preceding night that the men worked in them this day with very little danger, although the enemy kept up an almost incessant fire from two pieces of artillery. A drummer, rather too curious in his observations, was this day killed with a cannon ball."[16]

Lieutenant Feltman of the Pennsylvania Line wrote, "One Maryland soldier's hand was shot off and one Militia man killed. One of the Maryland soldiers deserted to the enemy this afternoon from his post, my waiter was in pursuit of him, but could not overtake him, and in his pursuing him made him drop his arms and accoutrements, which he brought off with him."[17]

Lieutenant Colonel St. George Tucker was a twenty-nine year old Virginia lawyer in the militia. He was one of the 3,500 Virginia militiamen that made up 40% of the American troops at Yorktown. He wrote in his diary disturbing sights he saw,

> The Firing from the Enemies works was continued during the whole night at the distance of fifteen or twenty Minutes between every Shot—By these means our works were interrupted altho' no Execution was done—Since Sunrise this Morning the firing has been much more frequent the Intermissions seldom exceeding five Minutes and often not more than one or two Minutes—Our Men are so well covered by their Works that I have not heard of any Execution done to day. This Forenoon I rode down to the mouth of Wormeley's Creek but could not descry any of the French Ships in the River—As the Wind has been perfectly favourable yesterday & to day I am apt to conclude it is not intended that they shall cooperate with the Army in the Siege—but whether this is really the Case or not I can not hear—The British Ships are stretch'd across the Channel of the River between York & Gloster point—It is said five of them are fire ships chaind to each other. But of this Circumstance I have not been inform'd from good Authority. This Afternoon from Mr. [Augustine] Moores I cou'd discover two of the French Ships which were conceald by a point of Land from Wormeley's Creek—I discovered by the Assistance of a Glass from seventy to an hundred horses dead on the shore of York or floating about in the River—This seems to indicate a Want of Forage & no Intention of pushing a March. I could also discover that the British had sunk several square rigged Vessels near the Shore and at the distance of one hundred and fifty, or two hundred Yards from it. Whether this was meant as a precaution against the French landing from their Ships of a general Assault I can not determine.[18]

Portrait of St. George Tucker by Charles B.J.F. de Saint-Mémin. {{PD-US}}

Wednesday October 3, 1781

(Pleasant weather)

British forces:

Tarleton is attacked:

A large portion of Tarleton's troops on Gloucester Point left at dawn to go out foraging. By 10'oclock the wagons were loaded with supplies and about three miles from Gloucester with the infantry covering their return.

As the British were returning with their wagons, their rear guard was attacked by Lauzun's Legion and the Virginia militia, both commanded by General Duc de Choisy. Tarleton, being more experienced, formed his men in the woods and then advanced as he led his men. Lauzun, on the other hand, charged across open ground and attacked Tarleton without halting. After a brief skirmish, Tarleton withdrew to his lines.

Lauzun had many of his troops cut down by British volleys, and the rest of his men decided to retreat. Colonel John Francis Mercer covered the French retreat with his Virginia militiamen. Tarleton and Lauzun might have met in personal combat had Tarleton's horse not gone down. The British had thirteen men killed and wounded, the French had three killed and sixteen wounded, and the American casualties were not known.

General de Choisy was very impressed with the brave conduct of the Virginia militiamen, which brought great pride to the Virginian George Washington. Choisy declared the skirmish a victory for the allies. This would be the last British foraging party in Gloucester and the final action in this area.

Accounts of the battle:

Colonel Tarleton gave his account of the skirmish,

> At day-break in the morning, Lieutenant-colonel Dundas, who commanded the post, led out detachments from all the corps in his garrison to forage the country in front. About three miles from Gloucester the wagons and the bat horses were loaded with Indian corn, and at ten o'clock the infantry of the covering party began to return. The rear guard, composed of dragoons, formed an ambuscade for some militia horsemen who made their appearance, and who came near enough to give effect to the stratagem. The wagons and infantry had nearly reached York river before the cavalry began to retreat. When they had proceeded to the wood in front of Gloucester, Lieutenant Cameron, who had been sent with a patrole to the rear, reported, that the enemy were advancing in force. A column of dust, and afterwards some French hussars, became visible.
>
> Part of the legion, of the 27th, and of Simcoe's dragoons, were, ordered to face about in the wood, whilst Lieutenant-colonel Tarleton, with Lieutenant Cameron's party, reconnoitered the enemy. The superiority of their horses enabled this detachment to skirmish successfully with the hussars of Lanuzun. At this point of time. Brigadier-general de Choisy was moving down the road with a corps of cavalry and infantry, to sustain his people in front; and the English rear guard was forming at the edge of a wood upwards of a mile distant, in fight of the skirmish upon the intermediate plain; when a dragoon's horse of the British legion, plunged, on being struck with a spear by one of the hulans, and overthrew Tarleton and his horse. This circumstance happening so much nearer to the body of the French than the British cavalry, excited an apprehension in the latter for the safety of their commanding officer. Impelled by this idea, the whole of the English rear guard set out full speed from its distant situation, and arrived in such disorder, that its charge was unable to make impression upon the Duke of Lauzun's hussars, who at this period were formed upon the plain.
>
> Meanwhile Tarleton escaped the enemy, and obtained another horse, when perceiving the broken state of his cavalry, occasioned by their anxiety for his safety, and which now precluded all vigorous efforts, he ordered a retreat, to afford them opportunity of recovering from their confusion.[19]

Lieutenant Colonel Banastre Tarleton---National Archives

Lieutenant Colonel John Simcoe had recently rejoined his unit in Virginia, and he was in very poor health. Simcoe was a heavy set man, six feet tall and with the appearance of a John Bull.

He could be at times solitary, aloof, and headstrong. He had the peculiar habit of referring to himself in the third person.

Lieutenant Colonel John Simcoe---Archives in Ontario

Simcoe was currently stationed on the Gloucester side with Tarleton. Because of his health, he earlier was forced to give up the command of the troops at Gloucester and turn command over to Colonel Tarleton. When the skirmish started with the allies, Simcoe got up from his sick bed to join in with the fight. He wrote in his journal,

> One of the foragemasters saying Col. Tarleton was defeated, Lt. Col. Simcoe sent him to Earl Cornwallis, ordered the troops to their post, and, being carried from his bed to his horse, went himself to the redoubt occupied by the rangers. Capt. Shank, on his return, reported to Lt. Col. Simcoe, that being on the left when the line was formed he had received no orders; but when the right, composed of the legion, advanced to charge, he did the same, in close order, but necessarily not in equal front: on the legion giving way, the Rangers followed, quitting the field the last, and in such order as prevented a rapid pursuit, and returned to the charge with Lt. Col. Tarleton, when he, having again offered the enemy combat, which they devlined, remained master of the field. Lt. Col. Simcoe, on whom the command of Gloucester devolved, was obliged from want of health, to give up its duties to Lt. Col. Tarleton.[20]

De Lauzun described his account of the skirmish in his memoirs,

> A moment before entering the plain of Gloucester, the dragoons of the state of Virginia came very much frighten to tell us that they had seen English dragoons outside, and that, in fear of some accident, they had come as fast as their legs could carry them, without further investigation. I went forward to try and learn more. I perceived a very pretty woman at the door of a small house, on the main road, I questioned her, she told me that, at the very moment, Colonel Tarleton had left her house; that she did not know if many troops had come out of Gloucester; that Colonel Tarleton was very anxious "to shake hands with the French Duke." I assured her that I came expressly to give him that pleasure. She was very sorry for me thinking, I believe, by experience, that it was impossible to resist Tarleton; the American troops were of the same opinion.
>
> I had not gone a hundred paces, when I heard my advance guard firing pistols. I advanced at full gallop to look for ground on which I could arrange my troops for battle. On arriving I perceived the English cavalry three times more numerous than mine; I charged it without stopping, and we came together. Tarleton picked me out, came to me with pistol raised. We were going to fight between our respective troops when his horse was thrown down by one of his dragoons who was being pursued by one of my lancers. I ran on him to take him prisoner, a company of English dragoons threw itself between us and protected his retreat, his horse was left to me. He charge me a second time, without breaking my ranks; I charged him a third time, upset a portion of his cavalry, and pursued him to the intrenchments of Gloucester. He lost one officer, some fifty men, and I made a rather large number of prisoners.[21]

De Lauzun did not relate in his memoirs what was seen by another officer. This event, written by another officer, speaks of the character of de Lauzun. "As he [Lauzun] returned with his troop, he perceived one of his lancers of his legion, at some distance, defending himself against two of Tarleton's lancers. Without saying a word to any one, he gave his horse his head and went to his soldier's aid."[22]

Charles Bettisworth was a twenty year old militia man from Virginia. He stated in his pension application [S32117],

> He states that there was a company of Militia Grenadiers formed who were commanded by Colo. Mercer of Virginia. He states that during the siege he had in common with that brave army many trials and hardships to endure they were poorly supplied with provisions, were very sickly & almost continually on Picket Guard and constant watching. He states that during the siege the British made a sortie & with about 300 horse and a regiment of infantry approached the American lines Weedens Brigade was put in motion to meet them & marched forward with two small field pieces to oppose them but while marching they were passed by about 40 French Dragoons some mounted Militia and Mercers Corps of Grenadiers who dashed forward in advance of the army encountered them and put them to flight killing their colonel &c & taking 2 of the Queens Rangers prisoner before Weedens brigade got near enough to take part in the engagement.

After the skirmish General Duc de Choisy established his main camp on the battlefield. His advanced post was placed within a mile and a half of Gloucester, and it remained there until the end of the siege. The British remained close to their lines during this time.

On the 25th of September, Sir Henry Clinton had sent a letter to Cornwallis telling him that relief troops would be sent and to apprise him of the situation he faced. Cornwallis received the letter on the 2nd and replied to it the next day,

> I received your letter of the twenty-fifth September, last night. The enemy are encamped about two miles from us. On the night of the 30th of September they broke ground, and made two redoubts about eleven hundred yards from our works, which, with some works that had been constructed to secure our exterior position, occupy a gorge between two creeks which nearly embrace this post.
>
> They have finished these redoubts, and I expect they will go on with their works this night. From the time that the enemy have given us, and the uncommon exertions of the troops, our works are in a better state of defense than we had reason to hope. I can see no means of forming a junction with us but by York River; and I do not think that any diversion would be of any use to us. Our accounts of the strength of the French fleet have in general been, that they were thirty-five or six of sail of the line and one frigate lie at the mouth of this river, and our last accounts were, that the body of the fleet lay between the tail of the Horse-shoe and York-split. And it is likewise said that four line of battle ships lay a few days ago in Hampton Road. I see little chance of my being able to send persons to wait for you at the capes, but I will if possible.[23]

American/French forces:

Enoch Breeden, a twenty-two year old militia man from Virginia, described the French troops that were sent to Gloucester in his pension application [S1747], "They crossed York river at White house ferry, in the month of August as well as this affiant recollects, where they joined General Weedon's army. They were then marched down to Ware Church in Gloucester County where they were joined by the French Horse under Duke Lauzan. Those troopers all wore large mustachios on their upper lip, and very large whiskers."

Colonel Richard Butler wrote in his journal about the skirmish with British Colonel Tarleton. He expressed his dislike for Tarleton in his biased account of the skirmish, "The ruffian Tarleton, with a body of troops, went to Gloster yesterday, with a body of troops, after killing all his poor horses and mounting men on the officers horses, (who Lord Cornwallis ordered to part with them) pushed out to forge, but fell in with the Duke de Lauzun and his legion, who treated them very roughly, and obliged them to retire to their lurking places with the loss of above fifty killed, wounded and taken. Tarleton himself was rode down by his own men, whose hurry caused them to be very impolite to their commander."[24] After the skirmish, General Choisy moved his troops within a mile or so of the British lines. Gloucester was now sealed off as an escape route for Cornwallis.

Claude Blanchard, the Commissary of the French Auxiliary Army, was present at Trumbell Landing to watch the landing of the heavy artillery. As some of the heavy cannons and howitzers arrived at Yorktown, the British stopped firing at the redoubt workers. Later, two French and one American deserted to the British.

Captain James Duncan wrote in his diary about the death of a good soldier and how another lost his life by being foolish,

> Last night four men of our regiment, detached with the first brigade, were unfortunately killed by one ball; one of the men belonged to my own company, a loss I shall ever regret as he was, without exception, one of the finest men in the army. A militia man this day, possessed of more bravery and prudence, stood constantly on the parapet and said, "damn my soul if I would dodge for the buggers [the cannon balls]". He had escaped longer than could have been expected, and, growing fool-hardy, branished his spade at every ball that was fired, till, unfortunately, a ball came and put an end to his capers. This evening our brigade was ordered for an evening party, and in the course of the night a deserter went to the enemy, informing them of our situation, in consequence of which they directed a few shots our way, but did not harm.[25]

General "Mad" Anthony Wayne---National Archives

General Anthony Wayne wrote a very frank and optimistic letter to President Reed of the Pennsylvania Executive Council,

> The enemy abandoned their advanced chain of works the same evening, leaving two enclosed redoubts almost within point-blank shot of their principal fortification; this was not only unmilitary, but an indication of a confused precipitation; these works were immediately possessed by the allied troops, and we are now in such forwardness that we shall soon render his Lordship's quarters rather disagreeable.

> However, the reduction of that army will require time and some expense of blood, for we cannot expect that Lord Cornwallis will tacitly surrender 6,000 combatants, without a severe sortie—his political and

military character are now at stake—he has led the British king and ministry into a deception by assuring them of the subjugation of the Carolinas, and his maneuver into Virginia was a child of his own creation, which he will attempt to nourish at every risk and consequence.[26]

Wayne added at the end of his letter a request for shoes, shirts, and overalls, and some needles and thread to be used to make their coats a little longer.

During the siege, Washington was in continuous activity, and at times he was in the saddle the entire night. He was constantly observing the British lines, and at times he placed himself in danger. The following account occurred when Washington was at the Poplar Redoubt that had been earlier captured from the British,

> At the battle of Yorktown, Mr. Evans was standing beside Washington when a cannon ball in full sweep struck the earth at his very feet and sent s shower of dirt over his hat. Washington glanced at the chaplain to see how he took it, but the latter was as imperturable as himself. Without stirring from the spot, he took off his hat, and seeing it covered with sand, said quietly as he held it up, "See here, general." Washington smiled and replied, "Mr. Evens, you had better take that home and show it to your wife and children."[27]

At the age of seventeen John Suddarth was in the Virginia Militia at Yorktown. He was impressed with the courage of Washington, as he stated in his pension application [R10293],

> Your declarant during the progress of these works witnessed a deed of personal daring & coolness in General Washington which he never saw equaled. During a tremendous cannonade from the British in order to demolish their breastworks a few days prior to the surrender, General Washington visited that part of our fortifications behind which your declarant was posted, and whilst here discovered that the enemy were destroying their property & drowning their horses &c. Not however entirely assured of what they were doing, he took his glass & mounted the highest most prominent & most exposed point of our fortifications, and there stood exposed to the enemy's fire, where shot seemed flying about as thick as hail, & were instantly demolishing portions of the embankment around him for ten or fifteen minutes, until he had completely satisfied himself of the purposes of the enemy. During this time his aides &c were remonstrating with him with all their earnestness against this exposure of his person, and once or twice drew him down. He severely reprimanded them & resumed his position. When satisfied he dispatched a Flag to the Enemy and they desisted from their purpose. Your declarant continued at York Town till the surrender of Cornwallis.

Thursday October 4, 1781

(Pleasant weather)

British forces:

Bartholomew James wrote in his journal, "A flag came in on this morning from the enemy, who as before were employed on their works; and we kept up as heavy fire on them as our want of ammunition would allow."[28]

On Gloucester Point Colonel Tarleton reported that communication between the country and Gloucester had been cut off with the earlier reinforcement of French Marines.

American/French forces:

Colonel St. George Tucker wrote in his diary about the skirmish with Colonel Tarleton. As usual the second hand news contained several falsehoods,

> We are Told that Tarliton made an Excursion yesterday with two hundred Horse into Gloster; it is also said a Firing was heard on that side & that Tarliton was repulsed but we have not yet heard any particulars of the affair—the number of dead horses seen yesterday by some Gentlemen amounted to near four hundred—A few shot fired during the Course of the Day—This Evening it was mentioned in Gen. Orders that the Duke de Lozun's Legion [Armand Louis de Gontaut, duc de Lauzun] with Mercers Corps of Grenadier Militia (about I50) repuls'd Tarliton yesterday & drove him back to the Enemy's Lines—Our loss was three Hussars Kill'd, eleven and an officer wounded—the Enemy lost fifty Men in kill'd and wounded—The Officer commanding the Infantry was kill'd & tarliton himself badly wounded. [A marginal note made said that Tartleton was not wounded]
>
> It is said his own men rode over him in the precipitancy of their Retreat—About three Days ago about nineteen hundred French Troops were landed from the Fleet in Gloster—Our Force there amounts to near four thousand men at present I am told. It is said his own men rode over him in the precipitancy of their Retreat—About three Days ago about nineteen hundred French Troops were landed from the Fleet in Gloster—Our Force there amounts to near four thousand men at present *I am told.* [29]

Lieutenant John Bell Tilden wrote in his journal an extract from Washington's General Orders of the day about the skirmish with Tarleton,

> He requests the Duke de Lauzun to accept his particular thanks for the judicious disposition and the decisive vigor with which he charged the enemy, and to communicate his warmest acknowledgements to the gallant officers and men by whom he was so admirably seconded. He feels particular satisfaction at the inconsiderable loss on our part, that no ill effects are to be apprehended from the honourable wounds which have been received in this affair and that at so small an expense. The enemy amounting to 600 horse and foot, were completely repulsed and conducted to their very lines.[30]

Claude Blanchard wrote in his journal some good news concerning the British navy, "I learnt that the English admiral Digby, who was expected from Europe with a strong squadron, had arrived with only three vessels, two of which were in a bad condition."[31]

After the naval battle on the 5th of September, it was also learned that the English ship *Terrible* of seventy-four guns was so badly damaged that the British blew her up. Also, the *London, Shrewsbury, Robust,* and the *Prudent,* were in bad condition.

Much needed horses and oxen arrived to move the heavy guns from Trebell's Landing to Yorktown. During the evening British cannons, that had been pretty much silent during the day, fired most of the night at allied advance parties causing the death of one American soldier.

Lieutenant Feltman reported, "Very little firing this day. A number of heavy pieces of artillery arrived in camp this day."[32]

Ebenezer Wild wrote in his journal, "At sunrise the Brigade was turned out, and marched into the woods (for the purpose of making sausesons [bags of sand shaped like sausage], gabions, &c where we continued till 5 o'clock at which time we marched to our tents and were dismissed."[33]

Eighteen year old Shadrach Beal was drafted into the militia at the age of sixteen. He reported in his pension application (S6596), "We were stationed in rear of the regulars and so near that I recollects there was a ceadar Tree that the men used to climb up and look in the Enemys Fort until they discovered us and fired several cannon shot at us which we desisted peeping at them."

Joseph Plumb Martin wrote in his diary about one of the greatest inconveniences the American troops faced in camp,

> We were on duty in the trenches twenty-four hours and forty-eight hours in camp. The invalids did the camp duty, and we had nothing else to do, but to attend morning and evening roll calls, and recreate ourselves as we pleased the rest of the time, till we were called upon to take our turns on duty in the trenches again. The greatest inconvenience we felt, was the want of good water, there being none near our camp but nasty frog ponds, where all the horses in the neighborhood were watered, and we were forced to wade through water in the skirts of the ponds, thick with mud and filth, to get a t water in any wise fit for use, and that full of frogs. All the springs about the country, although they looked well, tasted like copperas water, or like water that had been standing in iron or copper vessels.[34]

Friday October 5, 1781

(Rainy, a cold wind off the bay, and very dark at night)

British forces:

Hessian soldier Johann Conrad Dohla described in his diary what it was like to be on picket near the enemy lines,

> At night I went on duty at a detached picket, which was outside our lines. This picket post was a dangerous position. During the two hours on post it was necessary to sit or lie down so that the enemy outposts, which were often hardly five or six hundred yards from us, could not see us against the starlit heaven. When it was quiet, all reliefs and patrols could be heard, and first the French, then the English or the German called out, "Who goes there!" "Friend!" This picket therefore went to its assigned place at twilight and pulled back at daybreak and every night the location of the post was changed to prevent the enemy becoming aware of it. Everything connected therewith was done in silence; neither relief nor patrols were challenged, but only a previously agreed-upon sign was given. Smoking was also forbidden, and no fire could be made. It was called, and rightly so, "the lost post."[35]

Bartholomew James sounded as if he was looking forward to a fight with the rebels when he wrote in his journal, "The French hoisted five stand of colours on their works, and the rebel flag was also displayed before the garrison, whose sanguine expectations of a relief had taught us to look for the hour that was to enable us to march out and beat the enemy, who was making such a rapid approaches towards attack."[36]

American/French forces:

Lieutenant Feltman of the Pennsylvania Line reported that a soldier met with a very unfortunate death, "A Corporal was shot through the rump with a nine-pounder as he was relieving the sentinels. He was immediately brought into the fort and the doctor sent for, who informed us that his life was but short. The doctor then ordered him to be carried to camp, where he lived but a short time."[37]

Colonel Jonathan Trumbull was a friend and advisor to General Washington throughout the Revolutionary War. He wrote in his journal, "Park of Artillery begins to look respectable, & preparations for offensive measures ripen fast."[38]

A Corps of Engineers for the United States was authorized by Congress on March 11, 1779. Engineer soldiers were called sappers and miners. A sapper could either prepare defenses around fortifications, or lead assaults through fortified enemy fortifications. They would sometimes dig a tunnel up to and under the enemy's wall. Sappers that did this and placed explosives under the walls were called miners.

Washington was almost ready to open the first parallel. During the night sappers and miners worked at putting strips of pine on the ground to mark the path of the trenches.

In 1780, Corporal Joseph Plumb Martin of the 8th Connecticut Regiment transferred to one of the companies of sappers and miners. He wrote in his journal about the dangers of his work and a surprise visit from a stranger,

> We now began to make preparations for laying close siege to the enemy. We had holed him and nothing remained but to dig him out. A third part of our Sappers and Miners were ordered out this nigh to assist the Engineers in laying out the works. It was a very dark rainy night. However, we repaired to the place and began by following the Engineers and laying laths of pine woods end to end upon the line marked out by the officers, for the trenches.
>
> We had not proceeded far in the business, before the Engineers ordered us to desist and remain where we were, and be sure not to straggle a foot from the sport while they were absent from us. In a few minutes after their departure, there came a man alone to us, having on a surtout, as we conjectured, (it being exceeding dark,) and inquired for the Engineers. We now began to be a little jealous for our safety, being alone and without arms, and within forty rods of the British trenches. The stranger inquired what troops we were; talked familiarly with us a few minutes, when, being informed which way the officers had gone, he went off in the same direction, after strictly charging us, in our case we should be taken prisoners, not to discover to the enemy what troops we were. We were obliged to him for his kind advice, but we considered ourselves as standing in no great need of it, for we knew as well as he did, that Sappers and Miners were allowed no quarters, at least, are entitled to none, by the laws of warfare, and of course should take care, if taken, and the enemy did not find us out, not to betray our own secret.
>
> In a short time the Engineers returned and the aforementioned stranger with them; they discoursed sometime, when by the officers often calling him "Your Excellency," we discovered it was Gen. Washington. Had we dared; we might have cautioned him for exposing himself so carelessly to danger at such a time, and doubtless he would have taken it in good part if we had. But nothing ill happened to either him or ourselves.[39]

Colonel Richard Butler reported in his journal, "Cannonading all morning. Corporal Organ, a brave and honest soldier, was unfortunately killed by a cannon shot. [the same death reported by Lieutenant Feltman] A great deal of firing through the night."[40]

Two British deserters came into the American camp and claimed that 2,000 British soldiers were in the hospital, and the other troops had barely enough to live on. They also said that the British slept with their weapons every night expecting an attack.

St. George Tucker also wrote that the British were expecting an attack at any time,

> Our patrolling parties & the Enemy's meeting last night between the Lines occasioned a little skirmishing in which we lost one Man—As soon as the Enemy's Patroles retired within their Works a general Discharge of Cannon and Musketry in platoons took place along their whole Lines—Some Deserters who came out yesterday say that the Besieged lie on their Arms every night apprehending a general Assault & Storm. A good deal of our Ordnance being now brought up we may expect that some of it will be mounted in a few days.[41]

Ebenezer Denny wrote in his journal that all the activity with soldiers being fired upon, sometimes pursued, and keeping from being caught by the other side, reminded him of "a play among boys, called Prison base."[42]

Note: [Prison base is an old running game. You play it on a large field with a small area marked off on each end called a prison. You start the game by having someone on each side try to rescue an imprisoned team member and bring him back to their side without being caught. If the runner gets caught or tagged, then he also becomes a prisoner.]

Chapter 5

Quiet Before the Storm

General Washington asked her if she "was not afraid of the cannonballs?" She replied "no, the bullets would not cheat the gallows, that it would not do for the men to fight and starve too." --- Sarah Osborn at the Siege of Yorktown

---

Much of the activity on the allied side revolved around quietly digging trenches, constructing four redoubts, and hauling cannons to their positions. The soldiers doing the digging were exposed to cannon fire from the British, and they were probably not very happy that their own cannons did not return the fire. Fortunately, casualties were light during this time.

It was decided that a series of parallels (trenches), fortifications that ran parallel to the British defenses, were to be built. The first parallel was 600 yards from the British line. Later, a second parallel would be built just 300 yards from the British line. These parallels would allow the allies to bring their heavy cannons close to the British and to hit them with greater accuracy. After a few days the British rarely returned fire from their cannons in order to save ammunition.

Since most of the troops doing the digging were young men, a friendly rivalry between the French and Americans, as to their completions of the fortifications, sprang up. However, one thing that both armies shared was their admiration and respect they had for General Washington. Washington watched carefully every movement that went on. His presence could be seen anywhere day or night.

The cannons were put ashore six miles away at Trebell's Landing on the James River. There was a shortage of horses and oxen to haul them to Yorktown, which caused a delay of several days to start the siege. When it was time to bring in the cannons, it became a slow and tedious process to put them in place. The troops were pleased that soon they would be able to fire back at the British.

Saturday October 6, 1781

(Cloudy with a gentle rain most of the day)

British forces:

On the night of October 6, the British concentrated their fire on a trench opened on the French left and on the redoubts on Pigeon Hill and the Hampton Road. Not only did they fire cannons from their batteries, they also fired from the ships in the bay. At times, the shots were fired at one minute intervals. Apparently, they were unaware of the work continuing on the first parallel during the night.

Cornwallis had made his headquarters at the very visible and elegant mansion of Secretary Nelson, which was just outside of town. From there most of his fortifications were visible.

American/French forces:

Digging the first parallel:

About 4,300 men, both French and Americans, marched in the late afternoon to the front. There they waited, while sheltered by the ravine until nightfall. There were 1,500 men to do the digging and the remainder to stand ready to repel an attack. Part of the materials had been taken to the spot under cover. The soil was sandy and easy to dig in, which helped to speed up the work.

Orders were given that the men who did the digging were to be counted, when they went into the trench and counted when they came out. There was to be no straggling, and during the digging the greatest silence had to be maintained.

Sentries were posted at proper intervals in the lines, protected by sand bags, to alert the approach of anyone coming from the town. They were told to shout when the British fired shells, but not to shout if it was musket shot. If an attack occurred, then the diggers were to quickly leave, and the artillery was directed to fire at the attacking forces. When the attacking enemy retreated, they were not to be pursued.

At night, while it was raining, the troops moved out to dig the first parallel. The soldiers were told to remain silent a distance of one mile out. With the noise of the rain and the cloudy night, the British were not aware of what was going on just in front of them. George Washington ceremoniously struck several blows with a pick axe to start the first trench.

The engineers had decided that the trench was to be 2,000 yards long, and running from the head of Yorktown to the York River. It was to be ten feet wide and four feet deep. It would be wide enough for many men to pass through and also to move cannons through. At four feet deep and mounds of dirt added at the top of the trench, men would be able to walk through the trench without being seen by the British.

It was dug 600 yards from the British lines, which would place the troops beyond the range of grape and small arms fire. Half of the trench was to be commanded by the French and the other half by the Americans. On the northernmost end of the French line, a support trench was dug so that they could bombard the British ships in the river.

As work was going on, the French were ordered to distract the British with a false attack on the Fusilier redoubt away from where the allies were digging. Unfortunately, the British were told of the plan by a French deserter from the Touraine Regiment, who left his post when it became dark. He told the British that his regiment was going to attack the Fusilier redoubt in an all-out attack. It was not uncommon for deserters to tell a really good story in hopes of being treated better by their former enemy.

Guard dogs around the Fusilier redoubt began to bark, which made other dogs in the British camp bark. The British artillery at once began firing at the French line. The French were working on a small trench, and when the bombardment began they were forced to retire. Work continued without incident in the main trench being dug by the Americans. As one group of diggers became tired, they would be replaced by a fresh group. It was a race against the clock, because it had to be completed by the time the sun rose. Once the sun was up, they would be seen by the British.

Daniel Trabuel first enlisted in the Virginia Militia at the age of sixteen in 1776. He was involved in several skirmishes, and in 1781 he delivered dispatches for General Lafayette. According to his pension application (S14727), he was at the siege of Yorktown, not as a soldier, but there "as a settler of my own business." Daniel and his brother Edward were there selling "spirits" to the officers. He described the first parallel in his journal,

> The Ditch was nearly half a mile from the Fort, and the two ends ran into the River. It was nearly 2 1-2 miles long, and about every 25 yards they made a Battery for cannon or a morter to fling bombs. And men could walk around in it and could not be seen by the enemy.
>
> When our men were working at these Batteries the Enemy fired on them heavily. They kept a man on the watch, and when they saw a match going to the cannon our men would fall down in the Ditch, and you could hear the Ball go by. Sometimes it would skip along on the ground, and bury the men in the Ditch, but in general they would not be hurt. I was often in these Ditches when they were working at their batteries.[1]

John Royal was twenty years old when his militia group reached Yorktown. He stated in his pension application [R9054], "His company was stationed on the South-east or lower side of the town. After their arrival his company was employed in the ditches and erecting batteries, the ditches were about thirty feet wide, waggons passed each other in them, the bateries were placed at the angles of the ditches. The brittish fired from their batteries in the Town incessantly on the American troops whilst they were opening the entrenchments and raising the bateries there was no fighting with small arms, after he arrived, on the side where he was stationed, except at the redoubts, which were taken by the French troops. He does not know what accured on the Glocester side of the Town."

Joseph Plumb Martin described in his book the start of the digging on the first trench and General Washington breaking the first ground,

> The next night, which was the sixth of October, the same men were ordered to the lines that had been there the night before. We this night completed laying out the works. The troops of the line were there ready with entrenching tools and began to entrench, after General Washington had struck a few blows with a pick-axe, a mere ceremony, that it might be said "Gen. Washington with his own hands first broke ground at the siege of Yorktown." The ground was sandy and soft, and the men employed that night eat no "idle bread," (and I question if they eat any other) so that by daylight they had covered themselves from danger from the enemy's shit, who, it appeared, never mistrusted that we were so near them the whole night: their attention being directed to another quarter.

There was upon the right of their works a marsh; our people had sent to the western side of this marsh a detachment to make a number of fires, by which, our men often passing before the fires, the British were led to imagine that we were about some secret mischief there, and consequently directed to their whole fire to that quarter, while we were entrenching literally under their noses.[2]

Fourteen year old John Hudson gave a very detailed description of digging a trench at night in a rain storm,

We marched over the causeway to the batteries which I have already stated were stormed by Lafayette. I saw two embrasures to each battery, which proved that there had been the same number of cannon. These, with the dead, had been all removed, and the batteries being thirty feet apart, we marched between the two. Everything that I could see there was covered with blood.

We passed these batteries a short distance, the night approaching, when we were halted, every man directed to sit down, and neither to talk nor leave his place. As I had been sick through that day, and had, like the rest, my knapsack on my back, I laid my cartouch box under my head, and with my musket in my arms, soon fell asleep. During my repose a sudden and violent rain came on, falling in torrents, which failed, however, to wake me, such had been my fatigue. In the course of the night—I cannot tell at what time—the noncommissioned officers came along the ranks, and without saying a word, woke us all and got us to our feet. I rose up with the rain dripping from my clothes. We were directed to shift our arms to the right shoulder, and each man to put his right hand on the shoulder of his file leader, marching in two ranks, the right in front. The road being clear of all obstructions, our progress was uninterrupted, although nothing was visible—no man being able even to see his comrade. We finally halted, and every man had a spade put into his hands. Shortly afterwards—the rain still pouring down—a party of men, with gabions, came along. I will describe them, for the better comprehension of my narrative. Sticks are cut about five feet in length, of the thickness of a man's wrist; one end is sharpened and set in the ground, in a circle of perhaps three feet diameter. Flexible brush, about the size a hoop-pole, with such branches as adhere to them, are interlaced as in making a basket, working upwards from the bottom. The gabion this made is thrown on its side, a long pole run through it, and passed on the shoulders of as many men an can get beneath it. These were placed, when brought to the ground for use, in such position as the engineer judged proper, the stakes being, as before, pressed into the earth. We were then directed, and as at first, merely by signs, to commence three feet inside of where they had been placed, and shovel up earth sufficient to fill the gabions. The ground was of sand, which being thoroughly wet by the rain, was very easy digging. We shoveled until we filled these gabions, and finished by throwing up a bank in front, when the work was completed. The gabions being side and side the earth formed a solid line of breast works, through which a cannon ball could not pass. From what I afterwards saw of the efficacy of this description of defense in repelling cannon balls, there is no doubt that it is a better protection than a stone wall six feet thick, and has this advantage, that it can be made in a few hours. Not a single cannon ball penetrated this defense during the whole siege.[3]

St. George Tucker wrote that the British had found a way to disrupt the American workers without firing a shot,

Last night a discharge of Musketry was heard on the Enemys Lines succeeded by Cannon rather more frequent than in the Day—the cause was probably the same as the night before. Yesterday we had one Man mortally wounded at our Works by a Cannon Ball which carried off part of his Hips—The Enemy have for some days had recourse to an Expedient for interrupting our Men at work without wasting their Ammunition, by flashing a small Quantity of Powder near the Muzzles of their Cannons, which is frequently mistaken for the fusing at the Touch-hole. It is worth Observation that a Man was kill'd by a Cannon Ball a day or two past without any visible Wound—He was lying with his Knapsack under his head which was knock'd away by the Ball, without touching his Head—A Sentry was yesterday kill'd on his post.[4]

As the men dug, the heavy guns were brought up by teams of horses and oxen. Once in place the cannon balls would not only be able to reach the British lines but also the British ships anchored near Yorktown.

On this night when the men were sent out to dig, Doctor James Thacher was sent to the rear with instructions to be ready in case the diggers were attacked. Thacher wrote about his interesting evening in his journal,

> My station on this occasion was, with Dr. Munson, my mate, in the rear of the troops, and as the music was not to be employed, about twenty drummers and fifers, were put under my charge to assist me in case of having wounded men to attend. I put into the hands of a drummer, a mulatto fellow, my instruments, bandages, &c. with a positive order to keep at my elbow, and not lose sight of me a moment; it was not long however, before I found to my astonishment that he and left me and gone in pursuit of some rum, and carried off the articles which are indispensable in time of action. I hastened with all speed to the hospital, about one mile, to procure another supply from Dr. Craik; and he desired that if the Marquis de la Fayette should be wounded I would devote to him my first attention.
>
> On my return I found Dr. Munson and my party waiting, but the troops had marched on and we knew not their route. We were obliged to follow at random, and in the darkness of night, hazarding our approach to the enemy. Having advanced about half a mile, of a sudden a party of armed men in white uniform rose from the ground, and ordered us to stop; they provided to be the rear guard of the French. The officer demanded the countersign, which I was unable to give, and as we could not understand each others' language, I was detained under considerable embarrassment till an officer who could speak English was called, when producing my instruments and bandages, and assuring the French officer that I was surgeon to the infantry, he politely conducted me to my station.[5]

Later during the night, Dr. Thacher entered a small hut to escape from the cold rain. A man came to the door and saw the doctor and drew his sword. The doctor cried out, "friend, friend." The man stopped, put away his sword, and replied, "Ah, Monsieur, friend!" The man then turned and left. Thacher wrote in his journal that it was "doubtful whether he or myself was the most frighten."

Doctor James Thacher {{PD-US}}

That evening Colonel Lamb, of the artillery, wrote to Governor Clinton of New York, "You may depend on its being a night of business."[6] It did prove to be a night of business, but it was not as exciting as anticipated.

General Washington's aid, Lieutenant Colonel Tench Tilghman, wrote in his journal,

> The 6th at night the trenches were opened between 5 & 600 yards from the Enemy's works and the 1st parallel Run, commencing about the Centre of the Enemy's works opposite the secretary's House and running to the right to York River. The parallel supported by 4 Redoubts, These approaches are directed against the 4 works on the Enemy's left. The Enemy kept up a pretty brisk fire during the night but as our working parties were not discovered by them, their shot were in a wrong direction. This same night M.S. Simons began to throw up a work upon the left against a detached Redoubt of the enemy on this side the mouth of the Creek. A false attack was made in the night upon the left to draw the Enemy's attention that way only one officer and one man upon the Right were wounded of Marquis St. Simons command one officer wounded and 15 privates killed and wounded.[7]

Colonel John Laurens, an aid of General Washington, wrote in his diary about the false attack to draw the attention of the British, "The false attack under the orders of the Marquis de St. Simon on the enemy's right was not so fortunate. The desertion of a Hussar at the very moment in which the Gabions were placing drew the whole attention of the enemy towards that Quarter. The batteries on their right, the Guadeloupe frigate and her Tender, uniting their fires of round shot, grape and shells killed and wounded an artillery officer and fifteen of the covering party."[8]

Claude Blanchard visited the French trench and the area near it, where some French wounded were sitting. He could see very well the English flag in their fortifications and in the city.

Washington was impressed that the parallel was built without knowledge of the British forces. He wrote in his journal,

> 6th. Before morning the Trenches were in such forwardness as to cover the men from the enemy's fire. The work was executed with so much secrecy & dispatch that the enemy were, I believe, totally ignorant of our labor till the light of the morning discovered it to them; our loss on this occasion was extremely inconsiderable not more than one officer (French) and about 20 men killed and wounded, the officer & 15 of which were on our left from the corps of the Marq de St. Simon, who was betrayed by a deserter from the Huzzars that went in and gave notice of his approaching his parallel.[9]

Washington's Orderly Book, for the 6th of October, contained fifty-five paragraphs of regulations for the Service of the Siege. These regulations were to prevent confusion during the siege. They provided for every variety of service and precaution. Extracts of the more interesting parts of the regulations are as follows:

> 1st. The service of the Siege will be performed by divisions alternately, the fatigue men will first be detailed out of the division and the remainder will form Battallions under their respective commanders to guard the Trenches.

> 4th. The Major General of the division which mount will be Major General of the Trenches—the Bridadiers will mount their Brigades.

5th The General officers of the Trenches will reconnoiter carefully all the avenues, places of arms & advantageous of the troops in case of attack.

17th. The Trenches shall be relieved every 24 hours unless a particular order to the contrary by the General in which case the relief shall be in the rear of the others.

26th. When the troops shall have taken their post in the trenches the standard bearers will plant their Standards upon the Epaulements & Centries will be posted with proper intervals with orders to give notice of whatever they may see coming out from the place & of the shells that may be thrown by the Enemy but no notice to be given or any movements to be made for cannon shot.

29th. No honours to be rendered in the trenches when the Commander in chief & general officers of the Trenches visit them, the soldiers will stand to their arms facing the Epaulement & ready to mount the Banquet.[10]

During the day, many of the troops learned that Colonel Alexander Scammell died from wounds received on September 30. It must have been especially hard for General Washington, because the Colonel had been his adjutant general for over two years. Scammell also had a talent for telling funny stories, and he was one of the few men that could make Washington laugh.

Doctor James Thacher wrote in his journal his concern that the army would be exposed to smallpox, "The British have sent from Yorktown a large number of negroes sick with the small pox, probably for the purpose of communicating the infection to our army; thus our inhuman enemies resort to every method in their power, however barbarous or cruel, to injure and distress, and thus gain as advantage over their opposers."[11]

Sunday October 7, 1781

(Clear and cool)

British forces:

During the morning, the British were astonished, when the sun came up revealing the American trench so close to the British lines. They were also surprised at how fast the Americans threw up the entrenchments. Since they were out of range of musket fire, they opened fire with cannons on the workers, but the Americans were well protected and continued to work.

Johann Conrad Dohla wrote in his diary of a sleepless night and a possible attack,

At the defenses in the morning and in the reserve in the evening, which each evening drew one hundred men from our regiment, plus a captain and a lieutenant. The first was posted at the wall in front of our line, with sixty men in order to be ready at a moment's notice should an alarm be raised. The latter, with forty men, went into the redoubt assigned to us with the object of providing support to our forward picket should the enemy attack. The rest of the regiment had to remain dressed throughout the night and be vigilant, because of constant small-arms fire against the outposts and pickets of both sides, and the enemy's constant harassament of our outpost.

The riflemen, or American jaegers, approached so close at night that the balls from their long rifled weapons flew in over our lines, but did do damage. This night Private Rossler from Wunsiedel, of the Colonel's Company, deserted from his post with the Ansbach regimental picket.[12]

Colonel Tarleton reported on the parallel being built,

> On the night of the 6th, a large detachment of American and French troops made considerable progress in the first parallel, which extended from the high ground above the river, along the left of the British lines, as far as the ravine that approached the hornwork, occupied by the light infantry. The length of the parallel was about one thousand yards, and its distance from the place, in general, six hundred. The Americans guarded the trenches, and conducted the attack upon the right of the combined forces; the French upon the left: The emulation of the officers communicated zeal to the soldiery.[13]

American/French forces:

For the next two days the allies continued to bring in the artillery and place it in their proper positions. When the British saw the large number of cannons the allies had, they began to reduce the amount of firing from their cannons. They realized their guns would do little harm, and they needed to conserve their shells. At night barrier ditches were placed around the redoubts, and fraises [long wooden poles sharpened at one end] were placed on the outer wall of the redoubts. If the British attacked, they would have a difficult time climbing the outer walls of the redoubts.

A British deserter told the Americans that General Cornwallis had told his men that the Americans had no heavy guns, so they did not need to fear them. He also told his troops that the French fleet was afraid to attack the British ships. The Americans and French soldiers probably shared a good laugh about this news.

The eight hours of digging the day before was satisfactory, but it was not finished. They were high enough to allow the men to keep digging the next day with ample protection. Washington noted in his diary, "Before morning the trenches were in such forwardness as to cover the men from the enemy's fire."[14]

Joseph Plumb Martin had spent the previous night digging the first trench, and the British did not discover it until sunrise the next day. He wrote in his book an interesting story about a British dog,

> As soon as it was day they [the British] perceived their mistake, and began to fire where they ought to have done sooner. They brought out a fieldpiece or two, without their trenches and discharged several shots at the men who were at work erecting a bomb-battery; but their shots had no effect and they soon gave it over. They had a large bull dog, and every time they fired he would follow their shots across our trenches. Our officers wished to catch him and oblige him to carry a message from them into town to his masters, but he looked too formidable for any of us to encounter.[15]

John Hudson had spent all night digging a trench in the rain. That morning he wrote about the British shooting cannon balls at the new fortification with no real effect,

> It ceased raining just as the day was about to dawn, when we observed that our artillery had thrown up a battery a few rods from our right and on the bank of the river; and had raised a lofty flag staff with the star spangled banner streaming to the wind upon it. This was called Matchem's battery, being erected under the direction of a captain of that name, who retained it as his command during the siege. I wish it distinctly understood, that we were so near the British lines with these defenses that there never were any other works erected in our front, in the whole progress of the campaign. After it was fully daylight, the British had the

hardihood to come out with a six pounder, immediately in front of the battery I had assisted to construct, and so near to us that a horseman could have shot any one of these artillerists with his pistol. There they stood firing their piece rapidly for half an hour, battering at the fortification without any apparent effect. After they found that we treated them with silent contempt, for we took no notice of them, they desisted and returned to their own lines. Our allies, the French, who occupied our left, were doubtless busy, what in what way I had no means of knowing.[16]

Wilhelm Graft von Schwerin was a member of the Royal Deux-Ponts Regiment of Germans, who were paid by the French. On October 21, 1781, he wrote to his uncle back home about his adventures with the French Army at Yorktown. The following part of the letter was about the opening of the trench on October 7th,

> When we opened our first line or entrenchment, a lot of cannons were fired at us which did not do great damage to our workers. The work took but three or four days and we already had our fortifications arranged to respond to the first of the enemy, who could respond with but a few bombs and a few small pieces. But one has to admit that our artillery was much superior. We had lots of 24-pounders and an abundance of bombs. Not finding our first siege line close enough to the enemy, our general, Monsieur de Rochambeau, decided that we had to take a position closer to the enemy.[17]

The first Continental troops to man the trenches at noon were Lafayette's Light Infantry. They marched at noon to the trenches under cover of the ravines. They were fired at by the British, but no one was injured. The digging continued on the trenches and construction of redoubts and batteries. Even though the diggers worked under the enemy's fire, there were few casualties. Colonel Tilghman reported that one man was killed, and one man had his foot shot off.

Captain James Duncan wrote in his journal about entering the American trench, "Immediately upon our arrival the colors were planted on the parapet with this motto: *Manus Haec inimca tyrannis.*" [This hand an enemy to tyrants]. What happened next Duncan did not approve of.

Colonel Alexander Hamilton had his men face the British in the open and put them through the manual of arms which exposed them to British cannons. Apparently, he wanted to show the British that they had no fear of British cannons. Captain Duncan wrote in his journal,

> We were ordered to mount the bank, front the enemy, and there by word of command go through all the ceremony of soldiery, ordering and grounding our arms; and although the enemy had been firing a little before, they did not give us a single shot. I suppose their astonishment at our conduct must have prevented them, for I can assign no other reason. Colonel Hamilton gave the orders, and although I esteem him one of the first officers in the American army, must beg leave in this instance to think he wantonly exposed the lives of his men.[18]

Many of the soldiers, especially the French, were taken down with the ague [possibly malaria or some other disease that causes fever and chills.] At the time, the British reported over a 1,000 of their soldiers were on the sick list.

On September 30, Captain Davis bet Lieutenant Feltman a beaver hat, that Cornwallis would be a prisoner by the end of the day. Feltman won his bet, so he in turn bet Captain Davis a pair of silk stockings that Cornwallis would still not be a prisoner in two weeks.

General Washington probably would look the other way, if his men were making bets on the surrender date of Cornwallis. The General had always been opposed to his troops gambling, as he wrote in a letter to Virginia Governor Dinwiddie in 1756, "I have always, so far as was in my power, endeavored to discourage gambling in camp, and always shall while I have the honor to preside there." He wrote to his nephew Bushrod, "Avoid gambling, a vice productive of every possible ill."[19] Reliable rumors did circulate that, earlier in the war Washington at times enjoyed gambling large amounts of money with his officers in his tent.

Joseph Plumb Martin described in his book the very strange death of one of the soldiers from New York,

> In the morning, while the relieves were coming into the trenches, I was sitting on the side of the trench, when some of the New York troops coming in, one of the sergeants stepped up to the breastwork to look about him, the enemy threw a small shell which fell upon the outside of the works, the man turned his face to look at it; at that instant a shot from the enemy passed just by his face without touching him at all; he fell dead into the trench; I put my hand on his forehead and found his skull was shattered all in pieces, and the blood flowing from his nose and mouth, but not a particle of skin was broken. I never saw an instance like this among all the men I saw killed the whole war.[20]

Monday October 8, 1781

British forces:

Bartholomew James wrote in his journal,

> The enemy having learned from one of our deserters the strength and position of our pickets to the left, made an attack on them about midnight and drove them into the works; some time after which a few of them came to the ditch of the hornwork and persuaded the officers they were deserters, who having got on the works to show them the way in, was fired at and two of the officers of the 43rd killed.[21]

American/French forces:

Colonel Richard Butler expressed in his journal criticism and surprise at the British defense, "The enemy seem embarrassed, confused, and indeterminate. Their fire seems feeble to what might be expected, their works, too, are not formed on any regular plan, but thrown up in a hurry occasionally, and although we have not yet fired one shot from a piece of artillery, they are as cautious as if the heaviest fire was kept up."[22]

By now the parallel, redoubts, and batteries that were established had been completed. The French set up a second battery consisting of seven mortars. Von Steuben's division, composed of the Maryland and Pennsylvania Brigades, mounted the trenches. The regiments of Royal Deux-Ponts and Gatinais went into the French sector.

Captain James Duncan wrote in his journal about a very unusual occurrence with a picket placed before their works,

> Some time before daylight this morning we were very much surprised at the conduct of a picket that had been posted some little distance in front of our works. They were fired upon by the enemy, never returned a single shot and retreated into our works in the utmost disorder. Captain Weed, who commanded the picket, was again ordered out, but the enemy had retired. How he will be answerable for his conduct time will discover, as I dare say he will soon be obliged to give an account.[23]

St. George Tucker gave a description of the works that were near completion,

> This Morning the Major of the Regmt. of deux ponts had his Arm shot off as he entered the Trenches—There was a smart Cannonade during a small part of the night, in which the French had seven men kill'd & wounded—I was on Duty in the Trenches to day & sent out a small patrolling party at night under John Hughes who meeting with the Enemys patroles exchanged a few shot with them & was wounded in the Knee. A number of Shot were fired into the Battery during the Evening and between eleven & three at night but without Effect—I now had an opportunity of observing our Works; on the right on the Bank of the River they are engaged in constructing a Battery for twelve heavy Cannon—on the left of these at intermediate Spaces are two Redoubts—opposite the South East End of Secretary Nelsons house we are constructing a Battery for five Cannon—I had not an opportunity of reconnoitering the works further on the left except a single Redoubt which the French are constructing nearly in Front of the Secretary's, at the distance of five hundred yards (as I concieve at most)—We had one Man kill'd & one wounded in the continental Line during the Day & night. The Battery on the right will be finishd before Noon to morrow. One French Soldier was killd sitting down in the Trenches.[24]

Ebenezer Wild wrote in his journal,

> At daylight the enemy appeared with a small field piece a little advanced of their works, from which they fired and wounded several of our men; but were drove into their works again by a small party of men detached from our advanced picket for that purpose. At 11 o'clock we were relieved by the Barron's division, when we marched to camp and were dismissed. Fire from the enemy's works all day as usual.[25]

Now that the trenches were ready, General Knox, who was the commander of the American artillery, ordered his artillery men to parade in the afternoon under Colonel Lamb. They then entered the trenches to prepare the cannons.

Many soldiers described their experiences during the first part of the siege in their pension applications. These are some of their stories,

Thomas Brady was a twenty year old soldier in the Virginia militia. His job was to haul supplies to Yorktown. He stated in his pension application [S4271], "I was constantly engage while at Yorktown in waggoning cannon balls & bomb shells to the batteries of the American Army which was under Genl Washington at that time besieging Yorktown. That said shells & balls were drawn from the landing about a mile & one half to the batteries."

John Deane had served in several early battles and at Valley Forge. He was twenty-three when he and his friend Jonas Garner served at Yorktown. When John applied for a pension [W6998], he had Jesse, a brother of his friend Jonas, write to the pension board to verify his service. Jesse wrote, "I recollect that I heard my Brother Jonas Garner asking John Dean if he Remembered the cannon Ball that came Roling on the Ground at the seige of york there was a man Present saying he would stop the Ball & in attempting to Do so he Lost Both of his Legs, & said John Dean Deceased said he Did, & that he also Recollected many other circumstances which occured During the war."

Twenty-two year old Joseph French was in the militia and stated in his pension application [W79],

> He was under Major Waller, they march'd through various places in Virginia to Petersburg and Cabin Point thence near old James Town cross'd James river at Swan's Point thence Williamsburg and finally went to York we join the militia of Bedford County Virginia at Swanspoint when we arriv'd at york he was under Col Tucker. he was put to the most servile labor at York for many days and was badly straind in in the right arm in carrying and throwing on a pole some thing that we made of Brush for the purpose of Breast works he has never been able to use his said right arm near so well ever since to this day. He was sick at York about the time of the Surrender of Lord Cornwallis.

Walter Evans was eighteen when he was drafted into the militia. He stated in his pension application [R3395], that he saw the British kill many of their horses,

> This declarant enlisted as above at Annapolis in the State of Maryland aforesaid. He first marched from Annapolis to where the city of Washington now stands and from there to York Town in Virginia. Declarant recollects that the Regiment to which he belonged was detained in George Town one day on account of some troops coming from the North who were required to cross over the River in the first place. Some of these troops were French troops. Declarant was at the siege of York Town from its commencement until Cornwallis surrendered his forces to General Washington. During the siege the declarant recollects knowing of the grass tents or hovels thatched with grass of the Virginia militia which produced the discharge of many guns left by the militia who fled from the flames. One or two of the linen tents of the Regiment to which declarant belonged were injured by the fire. Declarant was sick in the house of Gov. Dunmore when it was burnt, it then being used as a hospital which was about Christmas A.D. 1781. During the siege of York Town declarant standing upon the bank of the River saw about five hundred horses, as was supposed, which had been tied together, driven into the river by the British and drowned; some were floating in the river and some had floated upon the beach. It was understood that these horses were drowned by the British on account of forage failing, and the British despairing of supplies, by reason of the fleet of Count De Grasse [Francois Joseph Paul, Comte De Grasse] being at the mouth of the river.

Jane Whiteley was the widow of Robert Whitely, who served in the militia at Yorktown. She filed for a widow's pension [R11459], and she had a friend of the couple state,

> That he Whiteley was at the taking of Lord Cornwallis near Yorktown in Virginia and he had frequently heard him say that he had a messmate by the name of George Vineger and another by the name of Michael Shivertaker that he had heard him say that he assisted in constructing the American breastworks and that he frequently saw all the bombshells from the British position fall very near when they were at work and had seen soldiers put out the matches in the shells and save the powder. That he had heard the said Whiteley say that he saw the French troops pass by where they were in the entrenchments the evening the battle commenced.

Henry Overstreet served a third tour in the militia and was eighteen when he reached the Yorktown area. He stated in his pension [S14069],

That he served a third tour under the command of Capt. Haydon in the year 1781 in September I went down to the armey & joined them in King and Queen County Va. and we marched into Gloucester County and I was called on guard at york river at the mouth of the Peankatank Creek to prevent the negroes from running away to join the enemy whilst they were at york town, from thence we marched down near to Gloucestertown and drove the British further in to prevent them from geting provisions, the Seige commened & held two weeks at yorktown and Corn wallace the British Commander in Chief surrendered to us and we marched down and took possession of Gloucester town & near there I was dismissed or discharged,

Chapness Madding was eighteen when he marched to Yorktown. He stated in his pension application [S4184],

Sometime between the first and middle of September I was again drafted to go to the Siege of York where Cornwallis was fortified, under the command of Captain William Dicks and Lieutenant Clement McDaniel and before we reached York about half way between old James Town and York our Captain took sick or fained to be so (as we had heard some heavy cannonading) turned back, and Lieutenant McDaniel led on the Company, our Company joined six other Companies or Regiment of Virginia troops on our march. we reached the American Army between the first and the 6th of October 1781, then before York and Cornwallis & put up both by land and sea, with the combined American and French armies and the French fleet. After my arrival I was placed under the command of Captain Charles Hutchings of Pittsylvania Virginia and for twelve days and nights was constantly employed in throwing up work and digging ditches and I was one of the fatigue party who helped to erect the last battery that was erected by the besiegers, upon which six guns were to be mounted and would have been ready to have opened a fire the next day had Cornwallis not sent a proposition to cease hostilities until he could arrange the terms of a capitulation, and a day or two afterwards, the British surrendered.

Edward Elley described, in his pension application [S8403], close calls he had with cannon balls flying around,

The third term I was drafted for the service I hired a substitute who filled my place and was in General Lafayette's Army when he passed on by Elleys ford in Culpepper County Va by circuitous rout [route] through Spotsylvania County and into Culpepper in order to strengthen his Army and he joined I think General Morgans Army at the Fork Church in Culpepper County and crossed over the Rapidan River at the Racoon (sic, Raccoon) ford into Orange County and so on down towards Williamsburg on the James River and whilst passing Elleys ford some fifty or sixty of The enemy frequently fired upon us whilst engaged in making preparations for the siege and killed a few of our men. The Militia officers were at this time employed with the soldiers getting brush &c to make watlings required in the fortifications. I was put among the able bodied men to throwing up bumbbatteries. Washingtons grand battery having been previously finished and whilst engaged in throwing up the bumbbatteries night and day we were ordered to squat in the ditch when the enemy fired upon us of which we were notified by the sentinel on guard and Captain Welch ordered the men to hurry with the work else they would not sink dup enough to shelter them from the enemies cannon by morning we who were in the front works were industrious & advanced with the work and in the morning those behind wanted to crowd upon us when fired upon but Captain Welch ordered them to keep their place as it their fault that they were exposed and whilst engaged in this work a cannon ball from the enemy came so near me that the wind of the ball blew my hunting shirt from the bank just by me and another ball came and struck within three feet of us in our work. After throwing up these works I was ordered to the Back where the ammunition was kept put to scraping and cleaning the cannons and Bumbshard to assist in sending off to the battery guns ammunition &c. The works at the battery were thrown up by the Militia Soldiers and whilst they were cutting brush a cannon ball came bounding along on the ground and a youngster put his heel against it and was thrown into lockjaw and expired in a few moments. And I recollect and then circumstances which occred near me a ball came from the enemy struck a man and cut off his leg at the thigh and then struck a stack of arms and rendered them unfit for service after serving at the Park as above stated I was ordered to the works. The works were thrown up by the Militia soldiers the Continentals at this time were encamped about a mile away towards Williamsburg I frequently saw General Washington riding around and directing the operations.

Twenty year old James Fisher joined the militia again in 1780 because of "having little or nothing to do." He was taken prisoner by Tarleton in 1781 and kept in Yorktown, until the Americans got near in September 1781. Cornwallis issued a proclamation, that if the prisoners did not take up arms again they would be released. James was released, and he promptly joined the American army as a waiter to an officer. In his pension application [R3569], James told an interesting story about capturing some British soldiers,

> While we were stationed at said Yorktown an express came to Capt Johnson informing him that a British Man of War had gone up James River & landed a Foraging Party; upon the receipt of this intelligence our Company & about fifty volunteers started off in pursuit. Having ascertained that they had passed on into the interior inland of a Piece of Woods at which we first arrived we were ordered to halt in said woods & await their return. We accordingly tarried in said woods all the remainder of the day & the following night & discovered the enemy on his return on the following morning after our arrival. When the party came within musket range our Corps all discharged our guns at the enemy by which we killed a number of his men & put the whole to flight. Out Capt now gave orders to fire no more, but for the whole Corps to commence pursuit, & for each man to single out some one of the fugitives. We accordingly all hands started off in chase. Now it so happened that between the fugitives & the River was a large field surrounded by a high Virginia Rail Fence, which greatly impeded their progress. The man that I had singled out in the chase reached the Rail but a moment before me, & in his haste to climb & pass it he stumbled & before he could rise again I had reach the fence myself & plunging my musket through one of the lower openings between the Rails I pierced his thigh entirely through with the bayonet, so that the squares of it came out on the opposite side of the poor fellow's thigh, & here it held so strongly into the limb that I had a momentary struggle to disengage it amid the groans & spasams of the sufferer. It was now at this moment that a British Officer who happened to be near the man at the time I wounded him glanced at his situation & turned & sprang to the fence, & made a pass at my head with his Broad sword. The Fence being high barely the point of it reached me cutting through my hat & fracturing my skull slightly – the point of the sword – the rounding part – not having quite penetrated through to the brain. It was this wound the scar of which I now still have & which caused me a vast deal of suffering in after life – that was the cause of my being left behind at the Hospital in Yorktown. We succeeded in capturing every man of the above mentioned Foraging Party amounting to as near as I can recollect sixty or thereabouts.

Sarah Osborn married Aaron Osborn in 1780. He joined the army and talked Sarah into going with him. To obtain a widow's pension [W4458] she gave the following statement (she is referred to as the deponent in the transcript),

> In their march from Philadelphia they were under command of Generals Washington and Clinton, Col. Van Schaick, Capt Gregg, Capt Parsons, Lt Thomas, Ensign Clinton one of the General's sons [this was probably James Clinton, son of General James Clinton]. They continued their march to Philadelphia, deponent on horse back through the streets, and arrived at a place towards the Schuykill where the British had burnt some houses, where they encamped for the afternoon and night. Being out of bread, deponent was employed in baking the afternoon and evening. Deponent recollects no females but Sergeant Lamberson's and Lieutenant Forman's wives and a colored woman by the name of Letts. The Quaker ladies who came around urged

deponent to stay behind, but her husband said, "No he could not leave her behind." Accordingly, next day they continued their march from day to day till they arrived in Baltimore, where deponent and her said husband and the forces under command of General Clinton, Captain Gregg, and several other officers, all of whom she does not recollect, embarked on board a vessel and sailed down the Chesapeake.

There were several vessels along and deponent was in the foremost. Gen. Washington was not in the vessel with the deponent and she does not know where he was till he arrived at Yorktown where she again saw him. He might have embarked at another place but deponent is confident she embarked at Baltimore and that Gen. Clinton was in the same vessel with them as some of the troops went down by land. They continued sail until they had got up the St. James river as far as the tide would carry them, about 12 miles from the mouth, and then landed, and the tide being spent, they had a fine time catching sea lobsters, which they ate.

They, however, marched immediately for a place called Williamsburg, as she thinks, deponent alternately on horse back and on foot. They arrived, they remained two days till the army all came in by land and then marched to Yorktown, or Little York as it was then called. Deponent was on foot and the other females above named and her said husband still on commissary's guard. Deponent attention was arrested by the appearance of a large plain between them and Yorktown and an entrenchment thrown up. She also saw a number of dead negroes lying around their encampment, whom she understood the British had driven out of town and left to starve, or were first starved and then thrown out.

Deponent took her stand back of the American tents, say about a mile from the town, and busied herself washing, mending, and cooking for the soldiers, in which she was assisted by the other females, some men washing their own clothing.

On one occasion when deponent was thus employed carrying in provisions, she met General Washington, who asked her if she "was not afraid of the cannonballs?" She replied "no, the bullets would not cheat the gallows, that it would not do for the men to fight and starve too.

As the sun began to set on the 8th of October, the fortifications were in place and cannons were pointed directly at British lines The Americans had been shot at for the past week without really firing back. Tomorrow it would be their time to rain down cannon balls on the British.

Chapter 6

Artillery of Yorktown

"The English marveled no less at the extraordinary progress of the American artillery, and at the capacity and instruction of the off." -----French General de Chastellux

The Siege of Yorktown was mainly a battle of artillery. Rather than hand-to-hand fighting that took place at other battles, Washington chose to avoid direct contact with British troops. It became a largely one sided battle of long range cannons. No one can say for certain how many pieces of artillery were actually involved. It was reported that the Americans had sixty pieces of different type of artillery, the French had a total of perhaps ninety pieces, and the British a total of 214 of chiefly light weight field cannons.[1]

The Artillery Commanders:

When General Washington selected the units of the American Army that would march to Yorktown, he included only one artillery regiment, the 2nd Continental Artillery Regiment, plus detachments from other regiments. General Henry Knox, American Chief of Artillery, ordered Colonel John Lamb, the commander of the 2nd Artillery, to Yorktown. The regiment marched south and by the 1st of October had guns and supplies ashore at Trebell's Landing. Due to the shortage of horses and oxen, the guns did not reach the artillery park at Yorktown until the 6th.

General Knox from National Archives

Colonel John Lamb---New York Library

The American part of the artillery force consisted of less than 400 men, who were able to perform efficiently because they had been trained so well by Knox and his officers. Knox knew, that for the number of pieces he was bringing to Yorktown, he would need at least 800 men. He added an extra 420 "auxiliaries" from the Virginia Militia, and a Delaware Regiment to bring his total up to 800. The additional men would be able to perform services that would allow the artillery men to remain on the firing line.

On October 1st Brigadier General Henry Knox, American Chief of Artillery, and his French counterpart, Colonel Francois Marie d'Aboville, had surveyed the area and marked positions for the allied batteries.

Francois Marie d'Aboville was fifty-one when he was at Yorktown, and he was a career artillery soldier that had fought in several battles. In 1780, he was sent with Rochambeau's men to join in the American Revolutionary War. At Yorktown under his command he had about 600 artillerymen and around thirty-eight installed cannons.

Even though the British had more artillery pieces, most of what they had were lightweight field cannons that had little effect against the allied earthworks. The allies enjoyed the advantage of siege cannons and very skilled gun crews.

French General de Chastellux, third in command of the French forces, was very impressed with Henry Knox as he wrote,

> We cannot sufficiently admire the intelligence and activity with which he [Knox] collected from different places and transported to the batteries more than thirty pieces of cannon and mortars of large callibre, for the siege….The artillery was always very well served, the general incessantly directing it and often himself pointing mortars; seldom did he leave the batteries….The English marveled no less at the extraordinary progress of the American artillery, and at the capacity and instruction of the officers. As to General Knox, but one-half had been said in commanding his military genius. He is a man of talent, well instructed, of a buoyant disposition, ingenuous and true; it is impossible to know him without esteeming and loving him.[2]

Artillerymen:

A Field officer of artillery was appointed every day to command the trenches. They were to level every artillery piece and attend to the firing. The field officer provided a written report each day to General Knox telling him the amount of ammunition used at each position, and if any men were injured. They were also supposed to include damage reports, but British damage was obvious so none was reported.

The firing of a field cannon required a crew of no fewer than six men and up to ten or more, depending on the size of the piece and how often you needed to fire it. Each person had an important job to do in the twelve step process of firing the cannon. The gun commander of the crew commanded them, and he was in charge of the use and safety of the gun. He would also position the gun and be alert, if the enemy was in position to capture the gun.

A detail of artillerymen was organized to work in the artillery park's tent, where the men made cartridges, cleaned shot, and filled shells. The shells, which came from suppliers in Pennsylvania and New Jersey, had to be tested to assure that the batteries received only high quality ammunition. Part of the artillery men would spend a day at the batteries, while the rest of the men were at the artillery park. The next day the men would switch jobs.

French Artillery Park was where the artillery was stored. Here the artillery could be repaired and ammunition prepared. The Americans had a similar park. Courtesy of the Colonial Historical National Park, NPS.

George Moore described his duties at the artillery park in his pension application [S17593], "Myself & three others from my Company were sent to work in the artillery park with the continental soldiers and were employed in cleaning and trying bombshells cleaning & repairing gun carriages – preparing ammunition & opening roads to carry the cannon to the batteries — when the batteries were finished I continued with the regulars in the battle doing the duty of an artillery soldier during the siege."

During the fifteen day bombardment, over 15,000 rounds were fired by American and French gunners at the British. Because of their destructive power and effectiveness, the British were forced to surrender.

The larger siege guns could only be fired about one an hour. Firing them too quickly could cause the barrels to droop, due to the heat caused by the explosion. Cleaning and preparing the larger cannons also took more time.

Artillery used:

The three types of artillery used by both sides at Yorktown were cannons, mortars, and howitzers. The cannon calibers was based on the weight of the ball used in the gun. A twenty-four pound cannon shot twenty-four pound cannon balls. The smallest cannon was the two pounder, and the largest was the fifty pounder. Most of the British cannons were made of bronze. They could not handle heavier charges of gunpowder, so their range was less.

The Grand American Battery, on the right of the American line near the York River, was completed on the 9th of October. It contained seven eighteen pound siege guns, three twenty-four pound siege guns, eight mortars, and four howitzers.

Cannons:

Cannons included lightweight field guns, mobile pieces, and heavy siege guns. Field guns would fire solid shot [cannon balls], grapeshot, and canister. Since they fired in a flat trajectory, they were most effective in firing into the ranks of infantry but not against the trenches and redoubts that the Americans built. Since most of the cannons the British had were field cannons they had little effect on the American and French positions.

Cannon used by the Americans and French at Yorktown.--Photo by author.

The Americans and French had siege cannons, and the British had none. These cannons were much larger than field cannons, and the wheel might be as tall as or taller than a man standing next to it. They shot twenty-four pound cannon balls and were used to attack fortified positions.

Large Yorktown siege cannon—photo by author

Mortars:

Mortars were mounted on a flat bed, usually made of wood. The barrel could be raised so that it would fire on a high trajectory. The mortar would fire an exploding shell or bomb that would sail above the trench or redoubt and explode while airborne. Many pieces of hot shrapnel would then fall over the troops.

Mortars used by Americans and French. Note that it is mounted on a swivel base.--Photo by author

Howitzers:

The howitzer was a cross between the cannon and the mortar. It was mounted on a field carriage like a cannon. Like a mortar it had a short barrel and could fire a high trajectory using either cannon balls or bombs.

It is hard to determine the exact firing range of the artillery weapons at Yorktown. You have to consider factors such as the size of the cannon, how much was used in the powder charge and the quality of the powder. Black powder was what was commonly used. It consisted of saltpeter, ground charcoal, and sulfur. The cannons at Yorktown may have had a range between 1,000 and 2,000 yards, the mortars 750 to 1,400 yards, and the howitzers 750 to 1,300 yards.

What was fired:

Bombs or shells were projectiles that were filled with gunpowder, and they would explode after a predetermined time. They were hollow shells filled with powder and fused. They were usually shot from mortars and were supposed to burst into flame when they reached their target.

Doctor Thacher described the difference between bombs in the day and bombs in the night, "They are clearly visible in the form of a black ball in the day, but at night, they appear like a fiery meteor with a blazing tail."[3]

Solid round shot were cannon balls of iron that did not explode. You could also use a bar shot, which was two halves of a solid cannon ball connected by a chain, or there was chain shot which was two solid balls connected by a short chain. These would be very effective against infantry soldiers.

Sometimes just the force from the wind of a passing cannon shot could cause injury. Doctor Thacher, was examining a wounded soldier at the Battle of Springfield in 1780, recorded that the soldier's "arm was fractured above the elbow, without the smallest perceptible injury to his clothes, or contusion or discoloration of skin. He made no complaint, but I observed he was feeble and a little confused in his mind. He received proper attention but expired the next day. The idea of injury by the wind of a ball, I learn, is not new, instances of the kind have, it is said, occurred in naval battles, and are almost constantly attended with fatal effects."[4]

Also effective against infantry soldiers was grape or canister shot, which released small pieces of metal or pellets. The canister shot used a closed tin cylinder filled with iron or lead balls. When supplies were short, the gunners would use nails or scrap iron. Once fired the cylinder would open and release the balls inside.

Chapter 7

The Allies Roar Back

"Cornwallis had given out orders to them not to be afraid of the Americans, that they had not any heavy pieces of ordnance except a few pieces of field artillery." ---A deserter from the British army.

According to the rules of siege operations, you should not fire from your batteries until all batteries are operational. By the 9th, the grand French battery would not be ready until the next day. However, Washington broke the rule and ordered any completed battery to open fire. Later according to Colonel Richard Butler, "Lord Cornwallis and the chief officers were burrowed in the ground."

The first night the artillery hit a couple of British ships in the harbor and set fire to one of them. Deserters said that Cornwallis had been astonished at this artillery attack. His men were especially unnerved, because Cornwallis had told them that the enemy was not formidable, and they had no large cannons.

As the firing continued over the next four days, the British soldiers began to feel the effects. Firing day and night prevented the British from escaping the destruction of the guns. In addition, the troops were weaken by sickness and lack of food. Some of the officers in the inner circle of Cornwallis advised the general, "…to evacuate the miserable works of Yorktown; whose every hour both by day and night, was an hour of watching and danger to the officer and soldier. To abandon fortifications that were not tenable, and adopt a design, which, at this juncture, had every probability of success, was equally honorable and judicious."[1]

John Saunders reported in his pension application (S7454), "…the firing was so constant that they could not see the sun and could not tell whether it was clear or cloudy."

Tuesday October 9, 1781

(Pleasant during the day, but cold at night)

With the allied artillery in place, the completed French battery's guns began firing at 3:00 p.m. and the American guns followed at 5:00 p.m. The British defenses were torn apart, and they suffered many causalities which began to dampen their spirits. With the bombardment lasting day and night, the British were not able to make necessary repairs. The British had no place safe to hide, and they began to desert in increasing numbers. Cornwallis still tried to convince his men that they had no need to fear the Americans, because they possessed no heavy artillery.

British forces:

The British frigate, *Guadeloupe*, was making a hostile movement, and the French battery opened up on her with hot shot, so she sought shelter under the town.

Colonel Tarleton gave a depressing account of the British situation later in his book,

> The batteries of the allies opened on the afternoon of the 9th. Two days cannonade clearly demonstrated the badness of the position of the King's troops, and the weakness of the defenses. The circle within the lines presented no place of security except under the cliff, and the fortifications were under soon considerably damaged by the shot and shells of the enemy. Around this time Major Cochrane arrived with a dispatch from the commander in chief [Clinton]. Every line of Sir Henry Clinton's letter described the circumstances which might delay his progress. The situation of the Virginia army becoming every day more critical, and all hopes of relief, which could at no time have been fanguine, having now totally vanished, there appeared no likely measure to rescue the flower of the King's troops from captivity except their own personal execution.
>
> Soon after the arrival of Cochrane, it was offered as advice to Earl Cornwallis to evacuate the miserable works of Yorktown. To abandon fortifications that were not tenable, and adopt a design, which at this juncture, had every probability if success, was equally honourable and judicious.[2]

Hessian soldier Johann Conrad Dohla received interesting information from French deserters,

> At noon I went to help with the defenses. Until today the enemy had not fired a single cannon shot at us, but continued working on the entrenchments, night and day, for nine or ten days, even though we fired at them the whole time, by day as well as night, with cannon, bombs, and howitzers. Nevertheless, they continue to work on their positions.
>
> According to some deserters, they made their positions mostly with fascines and sand baskets, as the French customarily do. They completed batteries and communications trenches, one after the other.
>
> Some deserters, who came over from the French, told us that it was their intent to make their approaches right up to us, and that General Washington had come here through Maryland from Jersey. Having brought eight thousand regular troops across near Baltimore, he had joined General Greene, and both of them had joined the French. (The latter) were between twelve and fifteen thousand men strong, including a corps of hussars, and five German regiments from Alsace, and one French. Marquis de Lafayette and the Prince of Saarbucken-Zweibrucken were their commanders.[3]

Dohla continued in his diary,

> At three o'clock in the afternoon the enemy began to fire on our right wing and from his left wing, where he had set up a battery in the woods and bushes. He fired with 18 and 24 pound cannon on our outermost redoubt, which was about one English mile from our lines, close to the York River on a height. He also threw bombs of one hundred and more pounds at an English frigate that stood in the river as cover for the above mentioned redoubt.
>
> At night, at tattoo [played on drums and used to recall soldiers to their barracks] the enemy began to fire on our left wing, then against our entire line, to fire bombs, cannon, and howitzers. This removed the belief, which we held previously that they had only their regimental cannon there and could not bring up heavy weapons because of the many forests and swamps.
>
> During the night a French bombardier set fire to an English frigate [*Charon*] in the harbor with a heated cannonball. It could be seen burning in the river throughout the night.[4]

Stephen Popp was a German Hessian, and he wrote in his journal, "At 3 p.m. the enemy opened from their left a heavy cannonade on our right, with a battery sheltered in a wooded hill, 18 and 24 pounders."[5]

Captain Samuel Graham of the 76th British Regiment wrote in his memoirs, "on the 9th they fired an eighteen pound ball into the town as a beginning, entering a wooden house where the officers of the 76th Regiment were at dinner."[6] According to Captain Graham the shot wounded two men and killed one man.

British naval officer Bartholomew James wrote in his journal, "It will be impossible to account for the number of killed and wounded in each day's action; therefore I must refer that for the end of the siege, and content myself with observing that the slaughter was great, and that among the killed on this day was the commissary general [Perkins], who with some other officers was killed at dinner."[7]

American/French forces:

During the night some of the Americans played a trick on the British. A deserter had given the Americans the location and strength of a British picket outside the American lines. The Americans sent a patrol out to fire at the picket. This drove the British back inside their works. Then after waiting about an hour, one of the Americans in a hushed voice asked the British, permission for a couple of them to surrender to the British. Two of the British officers got up on their works to show the deserters the way in. Then, the Americans opened fire and killed the two British soldiers. The British thought that this type of conduct was against the wartime code of honor. The Americans probably thought that, if you were dumb enough to fall for the trick, then it was tough luck.

The night of the 8th and 9th, the French sent 800 workmen to finish construction of the batteries and to construct a new one, No. 5, that would contain seven mortars in front of the parallel and to the left.

There was nowhere for a British soldier to hide from the cannons, so rather than manning the lines, some soldiers huddled in the basements of homes. Sometimes they evicted the residents in order to use the basements.

From General Washington's diary, "About 3 o'clock P.M. the French opened a battery on our extreme left, of 4 Sixteen pounders, and Six Mortars & Howitzers and at 5 o'clock an American battery of Six 18s & 24s; four Mortars & 2 Howitzers, began to play from the extremity of our right—both with good effect as they compelled the Enemy to withdraw from their ambrazures the Pieces which had previously kept up a constant firing."[8]

All the batteries were now in place and ready to be fired. The American battery on the right, which joined the river, consisted of six cannons and four howitzers. The battery near the French redoubt consisted of five cannons.

The French battery No. 1 was composed of four 16 pounders, two mortars of 12 inches, four mortars of 8 inches, and two howitzers of 8 inches. No. 2 battery had one of the three 24 pounders, No. 3 had three 24 pounders, and battery No. 4 had one of the three 24 pounders.[9]

At three in the afternoon, Washington gave the honor of firing the first cannons to the French battery on the far left of the first parallel. Some Americans were a little upset, because they thought they should have the honor. The French, however, finished their trench first, and Washington felt the honor should go to them. Their targets were the two British ships in the harbor, the *Formidable* and the *Guadeloupe*. Both of these ships had been supporting the Fusiliers redoubt near the York River. Once under fire, both of the ships sailed toward the Gloucester side and well out of French range.

Washington himself put the match to the first American gun around five in the afternoon, and a furious bombardment followed. The main targets of the batteries were the British artillery. They wanted to either knock them out completely, or at least reduce their firepower. Washington gave orders that the batteries should fire all night to reduce the chances of the British making any repairs.

According to some observers, the cannonball from the cannon that Washington shot, hit a house where a British General and three officers were having an early dinner. Whether or not it was the first shot, the event did occur. General Philip Van Cortlandt reported, "I could hear the ball strike from house to house, and I was afterwards informed that it went thro the one where many officers were at dinner over the tables. I also heard that the gun was fired by the Commander-in-Chief, who was present in the battery for the purpose of putting the first match."[10]

John Hudson wrote in his pension application the excitement of seeing his first cannon fired,

> The generals, as usual, came down, attended with their retinue, and General Washington, not seeing Captain Matchem, inquired where he was. He was shown where the Captain lay asleep upon a plank, in the open air. The General chide him gently for thus exposing himself, asking him why he did not go into his marquee. He answered spiritedly that he would never enter his marquee till he had stopped that bull dog from barking—alluding to a twelve pounder in the wall of the town, which had been playing night and day on his battery, annoying him greatly. Washington then directed him to open his battery immediately, the Generals riding back as customary. There was now a general shout among the soldiers, that we should now see some fun. In my simplicity, I asked "what fun?" Up to this time I had never seen a cannon fired. "Don't you see those matchets burning" they replied. I looked and saw them on staffs, four of five feet long, at the side of the guns.
>
> Captain Matchem accordingly fired his field piece, which was a twelve pounder. The ball, however, had been directed too low, and struck the bottom of the embrasure. He then corrected his aim and threw the second shot, which struck the mouth of his enemy's cannon, in rather an oblique direction, commencing a breach about eighteen inches from the muzzle of the piece, and tore off its side for that distance. This I had the curiosity and opportunity to ascertain exactly, after the surrender of the place. The fire thus opened from the battery, served as a signal to the French on the left, who commenced firing from their whole train of

artillery. I was informed by competent persons at the time, that the combined forces were prepared to fire as much as sixty shot, or shells, at a volley, in less time than once every minute, and frequently did so. Inside the walls of Yorktown, and visible above these walls, were several frame buildings, which soon were battered to pieces under the allied fire, the shattered fragments flying in all directions, and killing and wounding by their fall, without doubt, numbers of the British troops.[11]

Sterling Gunn was seventeen years old when he was in the Virginia militia at Yorktown. He was transferred into the artillery and gave this account in his pension application [S6941],

> This Declarant was marched to old Jamestown under the aforesaid named officers; from thence we marched to Williamsburg and there remained sometime. And from thence he followed in pursuit of the enemy to Yorktown where we besieged the enemy. At this place this Declarant was (by an arrangement of the officers) taken out of the Infantry (into which he had Volunteered at Williamsburg) and was put in the Artillery, and assisted in digging the trenches and building the forts at Yorktown. This Declarant was in the fort and assisted in firing the first Guns that he recollects to have been fired upon the Enemy. Captain Price & Colonel Lamb were his immediate officers in the Artillery who acted under the orders of the brave General Knox. This Declarant also was present at the hoisting of the American flag in the fort. This Declarant continued in the Artillery and fought during the Siege until the capture of Cornwallis

While the artillery was firing away at the British lines twenty-four year old Ebenezer Wild, a 2nd Lieutenant in the 1st Massachusetts Regiment was about a mile away in the woods. He was able to hear quite well the roar of the cannons. He wrote in his diary, "At nine o'clock [a.m.] the Light Infantry moved their tents about half a mile further to the right [toward the York River] and a little advanced of the line of the army. At 2 o'clock turned out and marched into the woods where we were employed in making sausesons, fasciens, &c., till sundown, where we were marched to our tents again."[12] For the next three days in the woods he continued making materials needed for the trenches and batteries.

Edward Elley was drafted into the Virginia militia and was placed in an artillery unit. He wrote a funny story in his pension application (S8403) about how he got a free breakfast from a General,

> After the siege begun my place was at the guns in the battery called Washingtons Grand Battery. There was in this battery four twenty four pounders four eighteen four twelve pounders and twelve mortar pieces was fired in platoons four at a time and the mortars three at a time making four rounds of mortars in order to keep up a constant fire and whilst firing the elevation of the guns got in a violent position because the men in assistance dodged when fired upon by the enemy from their port holes and General Clinton coming up just at that moment put things to rights & I remarked to the men in his hearing come by brave fellows stick to your posts and the day will soon be ours, and for this remark I was very soon rewarded with a good breakfast from the General which was very acceptable, as I had not had a meal for twenty four hours and I never saw men more mortified that were those serving with me at the guns when I received the reward.
>
> Shortly after the siege began thirty three of the enemy deserted and came another in a boat about midnight↓ and joined us and General Clinton them a pass to Genl. Washington. And whilst engaged in firing the guns it appeared to me as if the earth would sink beneath as I continued in this service until within a few days of Wallaces surrender.

My wife having hired a man and sent him down to take my place & so I put the man in my place and took my horse sent for me and set for home immediately and before I reached Fredericksburg on my way home I understood that Wallace had surrendered before I left the service I saw a number of dead horses on the beach which the enemy had drowned I served myself in this term two months myself besides my substitute who served three months and paid him to his satisfaction the amount paid I do not recollect and my substitute who relieved me from the said siege continued in the service and guarded the prisoners from the siege over the mountains to Winchester and then returned and I paid him a suit of good men clothes a blanket a knapsack a cheese & a thousand dollars of Continental paper and thirty silver dollars the price previously agreed upon by my wife.

During one of Washington's visits to the main battery, a soldier of Colonel Lamb's artillery had his leg shattered by the explosion of a shell. As they were taking him to the rear for treatment, the wounded man recognized Washington and he cried out, "God bless your excellency, save me if you can, for I have been a good soldier, and served under you during the whole war." Washington immediately ordered the wounded man taken to Doctor Craik [Washington's personal physician]. However, it was too late and after an amputation was done, the man died.[13]

In his journal Doctor James Thacher noted his concern for the hardships the men were having to endure, "The duty of our troops has been for several days extremely severe; our regiment labors in the trenches every other day and night, where I find it difficult to avoid suffering by the cold, having no other covering than a single blanket in the open field."[14]

Richard Davenport was thirty years old when he joined the Virginia militia. In his pension application [S17914] he wrote of being lucky in two battles, "He was engaged in the battle at Camden, and was under the command of General Stevens, but received no personal injury. Several balls passed through his clothing and his knapsack was cut from his back by a ball and finally lost. He was engaged in active service and witnessed the firing of the first Cannon from the American batteries. He received no wound, but had his hat knocked off by the balls several times. He was present on the occasion of the surrender of the British forces."

Joseph Plumb Martin had helped dig the American trench, and he expressed in his diary great pride when it was time to fire the cannons,

> I was in the trenches the day that the batteries were to be opened; all were upon tiptoe of expectation and impatience to see the signal given to open the whole line of batteries, which was to be the hoisting of the American flag in the ten gun battery. About noon the much wished for signal went up. I confess I felt a secret pride swell in my heart when I saw the 'star spangled banner" waving majestically in the very faces of our implacable adversaries; it appeared like an omen of success to our enterprize, and so it proved in reality. A simultaneous discharge of all the guns in the line followed, the French troops accompanying it with "Huzza for the Americans!: It was said that the first shell sent from our batteries, entered the elegant house, formerly owned or occupied by the Secretary of State under the British government, and burnt directly over a table surrounded by a large party of British officers at dinner, killing and wounding a number of them, this a warm day to the British.[15]

Major Ebenezer Denny, of the 7th Pennsylvania Regiment, wrote in his diary his impressions of the opening of the American bombardment of British lines, "The scene viewed from the camp now was grand, particularly after dark. A number of shells from the works of both parties passing high in the air, and descending in a curve, each with a long train of fire, exhibited a brilliant spectacle."[16]

A French officer wrote about one of his gunners, "A gunner, at one of the embrasures, had his foot carried away by a bullet. I tried to console the unhappy man, when he gave me for an answer, I am less afflicted for the loss of my foot, than for being so unfortunate as not to have had time, before it happen, to discharge the cannon I had pointed with so much care."[17]

Lieutenant Feltman of the Pennsylvania line wrote with pride in his diary how effective their cannons were,

> This morning we completed a very elegant battery for ten pieces of heavy artillery with mortars fixed upon carriages and not on beds in order to throw the shot horizontal into the enemy's works, and there to burst and destroy their works. We have six of those mortars; they were invented by Gen. Knox and proved to be of effect.
>
> This morning 9 o'clock a deserter from the enemy's artillery came to us; he left them just as their piece fired, which was advanced in front of the Governor's house. He informed us that Cornwallis had given out orders to them not to be afraid of the Americans, that they had not any heavy pieces of ordnance except a few pieces of field artillery. He also informed soldiery and inhabitants that the French fleet was inferior to him and were afraid to attack him; that they came to this place to procure a quantity of tabacco, and if they could not be supplied here that the fleet would set sail in eight or ten days at the farthest, and leave the continent. Such are my lord's addresses to his soldiery, but they have more sense than to believe his weak expressions.[18]

It was estimated that around 2,000 runaway slaves were in Yorktown. They were promised their freedom if they would work for the British. However, they were not granted their freedom after the battle. Most of the slaves were sent out of Yorktown by Cornwallis, in order to conserve food needed for his men. The Orderly Book for this date posted an order from General Washington that addressed the slaves that had come from Yorktown,

> The General has been informed that there are in the possession of some officers of the army, negroes who have come out of York. If there are any such, report of them is to made immediately to the Adj. Gen'l; and if any officer should be found, after this notice, keeping in the service, negroes under the above description, he may depend upon being called to the severest account for it. This order is to extend to the officers of the Militia as well as to the Continental troops.[19]

As the allied guns fired throughout the night, the French were busy completing work on their batteries. To haul heavy siege cannons to their station took a team of a dozen or more horses and many men.

Wednesday October 10, 1781

(Pleasant during the day and cool at night)

During the bombardment, gunners spotted a large house in Yorktown and believed that Cornwallis might be in it, so they destroyed it. The British sank some of their merchant ships at the mouth of the York River. This created a barrier that prevented the larger French ships from landing troops on the beach behind the British lines. French gunners destroyed several British ships with hot cannon balls. Clinton was still in New York and was planning to send relief troops to Yorktown on the 12th. Cornwallis told Clinton that his chances of holding out for very long were slim.

British forces:

Major Charles Cochrane was sent by Sir Henry Clinton to deliver dispatches to General Cornwallis. He went in a ship to the Capes, and then he got in an open boat and was able to sneak by the French fleet and land at Yorktown on the 10th during the bombardment. Once the dispatch was delivered, he was appointed an aides-de-camp to General Cornwallis.

Cornwallis knew that Gloucester was his only chance for escape, so he sent a large force of flatboats to Gloucester in an attempt to push out the force that had been sent there by the allies. The French and American forces were not taken by surprise and began firing their artillery at the flatboats. The British promptly turned around and returned to Yorktown.

All along the British lines they were attacked by American and French gunners. The hornwork was the only British works that projected outward toward the allied trenches. As a result, they took the brunt of allied firepower.

Johann Conrad Dohla wrote in his diary about the devastating effects the bombardment was having on the English troops,

> We had to change our camp this morning and set up our tents in the communication trenches, because of the enemy's heavy cannonade. He threw bombs at us of 100 and 150 pounds, also of 200 pounds, and his howitzer and cannonballs were of 18, 24, 36, and a very few of 12 pounds. It was impossible to avoid the frightfully many balls in or outside the city. Most of the inhabitants who were still to be found here fled eastward with their best possessions on the waters of the York River, and dug into the sand cliffs, but even there they were not uninjured. Many were seriously and fatally wounded by the broken pieces of the bombs that were exploding, partly in the air, partly on the ground, which broke arms and legs, or killed them. The ships in the harbor also suffered great damage because the cannonballs flew across the river as far as the land at Gloucester.
>
> At nine o'clock in the morning our Sutler Johann Wilhelm Seewald, of Quesnoy's Company, was fatally wounded by a cannonball that struck him in the right side while he was in a small house immediately behind the front of our camp, near Yorktown, where he had his store. At noon Grenadier Dorrer, of Molitor's Company, was dangerously wounded on the left leg by a bomb, and during the evening the leg had to be amputated above the knee. During the evening the French, with bombs, set fire to a warship and a transport ship in the river. The first was saved. The latter, however, burned completely.[20]

Stephen Popp described in his journal the intense bombardment by the French and Americans,

> The heavy fire forced us to throw our tents in the ditches, the enemy threw bombs, 100, 150, 200 pounders, there guns were 18, 24, and 48 pounders, we could find no refuge in or out of town, the people fled to the water side and hid in hastily contrived shelters on the banks, but many of them were killed by the bursting bombs. More than 80 were thus lost, besides many wounded and their houses utterly destroyed. Our ships

suffered too, under the heavy fire, for the enemy fired in one day 3,600 shot from their heavy guns and batteries. Soldiers and sailors deserted in great numbers.[21]

Bartholomew James was a naval officer aboard the *Charon*, when it was set on fire by French guns. He gave this account in his journal,

> The enemy having opened fresh batteries on this day, and also commenced an additional fire on the Charon with re-hot shot, she was set on fire at half-past six o'clock in three different places, and in a few minutes in flames from the hold to the mastheads. From our being quartered at the guns in front of the army, that timely assistance could not be given her which was necessary to extinguish the fire, and she broke adrift from here moorings and drove on board a transport to which she also set fire, and they both grounded on the Gloucester side, where they burnt to the water's edge. The loss of our things in the Charon are so very trivial when compared to the more distressing scenes of the garrison, that I shall say no more on this head, than that we saw with infinite concern one of the finest ships in the navy of her rate totally destroyed on this day.
>
> On this evening the enemy, having mounted some more of their artillery, totally silenced No. 5 battery, commanded by the first lieutenant of the Charon, who with his men were obliged to quit it, the shot and shell having dismounted his guns and tore up his platforms. At ten o'clock a general attack was made from the center to the left, under cover of their cannon, and the enemy again repulsed. The Hessians gave way twice in front of my works on this night; and the cannonade continued with a degree of warmth seldom equaled and not to be described. The remainder of the night passed in a dreadful slaughter, and we were occasionally employed in throwing up the works the enemy knocked down. Several parts of the garrison was in flames on this night, and the whole discovered a view awful and tremendous.[22]

American/French forces:

During the night, the French heated cannonballs over a fire until they were red hot and then shot them at the few remaining ships outside of Yorktown. The forty-four gun *Charon* caught fire. A French officer reported, "Never could a more horrible or more beautiful spectacle be seen. On a dark night, the ships with all their open port-holes discharging sheafs of fire, the cannon shots that were going off, the appearance of the whole roadstead, the ships under topsail flying from the burning vessels, all that formed a terrible and sublime spectacle."[23]

William Glidewell first joined the Virginia militia in 1778, at the age of eighteen. He wrote in his pension application [S6941], "The American Army laid there [Yorktown] some time firing hot balls and log chains into the town for the purpose of setting it on fire. They set a number of houses on fire."

Colonel Henry Lee noted in his memoirs, "So powerful was the effect of our first parallel, that our shells and red-hot balls in this range of destruction reached even the small navy in the harbor, setting fire to and destroying the Charon, the largest ship, a forty-four gun frigate, with three transports."[24]

At this time Lee felt that Cornwallis would probably surrender, except he still held out hope of relief forces from Clinton. He also believed that Washington would not have started a second parallel, if he could have been positively assured that the French navy would not leave. If they stayed Washington thought the current bombardment in time would force Cornwallis to surrender.

The Grand French battery was finished in the morning and started firing, which brought the number of cannons firing to around forty-six. The firing became so heavy that the British withdrew their cannons for protection.

The first headquarters of Cornwallis was the house of William Nelson, father of Governor Thomas Nelson. Cornwallis remained in the house, until his steward was killed by a cannon ball while carrying a bowl of soup to the general's table. Cornwallis then left the house and occupied the house of Governor Thomas Nelson.

When Governor Thomas Nelson saw the destruction of his father's home in Yorktown during the bombardment, he grew concerned for the safety of his father, William. He appealed to Washington to halt the firing long enough for a messenger to be sent to Cornwallis to request that his father be allowed to come to the American lines. Washington halted the bombardment, and just before one in the afternoon the Americans saw an old man walking past the town's gates. Cornwallis had been kind enough to release William, and he even allowed William's servant, Louis, to take the family silver and plate.

Due to a case of the gout, William had to be carried the rest of the way to the tent of Washington. The officers gathered around the old man wanting to hear news of what was going on inside the British fortification. What William told the officers did not disappoint them. He revealed that the bombardment was very effective and forced the British officers to seek shelter. He also said that Tarleton and Simcoe had been forced to kill over 1,000 of their horses due to lack of fodder.

Colonel St. George Tucker of the Virginia Militia gave an account of the day's activities in his journal,

> Last night & this Morning a very smart Cannonade & Bombardment has been kept up from our Batteries & those of the French—Several Bombs have been thrown into the Enemy's works, where they have bursted, apparently with some Effect. The Enemy last night shut up the Embrasures of their Battery opposite to ours on the right, & their next Battery is entirely silent the Cannon being drawn in from the Embrasures. Some Shells were thrown at the Shipping this morning but I have not heard with what Effect. A smart firing of Musketry was heard to day at Gloster.—Since writing the above I have rode out—The French have a Battery on the Hampton road about six hundred Yards below the Secry Nelson's House opposite the South West Angle, consisting of four twenty four pounders and six other Cannon which appear to be somewhat smaller, two eight inch Howitz, two twelve Inch Mortars and six eight Inch ones—these have been employ'd incessantly the whole Day—A number of Shells have been thrown into the Enemy's Works, &the shot so well directed in general that many of the Embrasures of the Enemies are wholly rendered incapable of offensive Operations—there are but two Cannon now to be seen in their Embrasures—the large Shells were generally directed for the shipping—I am told the Enemy have sunk twenty or thirty of their Vessels to day in shallow Water. On the left of the above Battery is another not yet finishd constructed for four Guns—Another still further on the left (about two hundred Yards from the principal Battery) for the like number.—On the Margin of the river over the Creek on the upper End of York is a considerable Redoubt or Battery of

the British—The French have also a redoubt in that Quarter which commands both the Enemy's Works on our right & the River, but as I have not seen it I can not precisely determine the Spot where it is—Secry Nelson this Day came out of York I am told he is not restricted by a Parole—I shall insert whatever Information he brings which may hereafter come to my Knowledge.[25]

Washington wrote in his diary,

The French opened two batteries on the left of our front parallel—one of 6 twenty four pounders, & 2 Sixteens with 6 Morters & Hawitzers—the other of 4 Sixteen pounders and the Americans two Batteries between those last mentioned & the one on our extreme right the left of which containing 4 Eighteen pounders—the other two Mortars.

The whole of the batteries kept an incessant fire—the Cannon at the Ambrazures of the enemy, with a view to destroy them—the Shells into the Enemy's Works, where by the information of deserters they did much execution.

The French battery on the left, by red hot shot, set fire to (in the course of the Night) the Charon frigate & 3 large Transports which were entirely consumed.

The French opened two other batteries on the left of the parallel, each consisting of 3 Twenty four pounders. These were also employed in demolishing the Ambrazures of the enemys Works & advancd Redoubts.[26]

Colonel Daniel Trabue wrote about the artillery attack on the British positions in his journal and gave a description of the bombs,

I was there one morning about 10 o'clock and our cannons began to roar. Some of the morters were throwing their bomb shells, and they would go a blaze, then turn a sommersault, and fall down in the fort. The report was so loud when it struck the ground as when it came out; the same also, when it bursted, the bombs flying in a circle. What rejoicing there was with our men and the Batteries that were ready to begin, and before night the most of the morters and small cannons were firing. I think that night they were going every minute and sometimes 10 or 15 at the same time.

The shells were made of pot iron like a jug 1-12 inch thick, without a handle, & with a big mouth. They were filled with powder, and other combustibles in such a manner that the blaze came out of the mouth, and keeps on burning until it gets to the body where the powder is, then it bursts and the pieces fly every way, and wound & kill whoever it hits. There were so many flying and falling in the fort that we had no Doubt that we were paying them well for their mischief to us.[27]

Lafayette was the General Officer of the day, and he invited Thomas Nelson Jr. to watch the bombardment of Yorktown at one of the batteries. Aware that Nelson was familiar with the homes within the range of the gunners, Lafayette asked Nelson, "To what particular spot would your Excellency direct that we should point the cannon." "There to that house," replied Nelson. "It is mine, and, now that the Secretary's [his father] is nearly knocked to pieces, is the best one in the town. There you will be almost certain to find Lord Cornwallis and the British head-quarters. Fire upon it, my dear marquis and never spare a particle of my property so long as it affords a comfort or a shelter to the enemies of my country."[28]

Lafayette, who earlier had felt the governor lacked commitment for the siege before the arrival of Washington, was most impressed with Nelson's response. Legend has it that Nelson offered money to the first gunner to hit his home. The shelling of the Nelson House forced Cornwallis to leave the home and move into an underground dug-out behind the house.

The Nelson House---Library of Congress

The Nelson House was struck several times during the siege and still bears the rough treatment it received. This is a cannon ball about 5 feet from the ground and another one was between two windows in the attic. Photo by author.

Fourteen year old army Private John Hudson enjoyed watching the cannons fire, and he wrote of the Nelson's house that was shot at,

> During the siege there had been remarked conspicuously a large house, built of white marble which Capt. Matchem had spared, knowing it to be the property of Gen Hugh Nelson, whose estate lay in the neighbourhood. The General, on his arrival, which took place a few days after, inquired why he did not fire on that building. Matchem accordingly gave the reason. Never mind my property, replied the Gen.; rap

away at it. Matchen then fired one ball, which made its way through the house. Where the ball entered, it made a small breach, but where it came out if forced a very large opening. After the surrender, I learned that there were a number of the British officers had made it their quarters, but they abandoned it as soon as this shot was fired, fearing more would follow. But this was the first and the last, as I distinctly recollect.[29]

Colonel Jonathan Trumbull, toward the end of the day, wrote in his journal, "All our batteries open early this morning with a terrible roar. Continued till 10 o'clock and slacken. The enemy's fire silenced & they driven from their lines, which can make no opposition to ours. In the evening a heavy fire again from our batteries with little return from the town."[30]

Colonel John Laurens wrote in his journal,

> The Charon, a dismantled 44 gun ship, the artillery of which had been distributed in different batteries of the place, was fired by red-hot shot or shells from the Marquis de St. Simon's battery, and together with her transports was totally consumed this evening. It was allowable to enjoy this magnificent nocturnal scene, as the vessels had been previously abandoned by their crews. The enemy's firing of shot and shells is rather resumed.[31]

Jonathan Trumbull wrote in his diary, "The Charon a 44 Gun Ship took fire in the evening from an hot ball and burned to the water. An elegant appearance tho' the loss is regretted. The Charon being placed in such situation as greatly to annoy our troops in the battery above the town, produced that resentment which was the cause of her unhappy fate."[32]

Doctor James Thacher gave a vivid description of the artillery firing on the *Charon* that night,

> From the bank of the river, I had a fine view of this splendid conflagration. The ships ere enwrapped in a torrent of fire, which spreading with vivid brightness among the combustible rigging, and running with amazing rapidity to the tops of the several masts while all around was thunder and lightning from our numerous cannon and mortars, and in the darkness of night, presented one of the most subline and magnificent spectacles which can be imagined. Some of our shells, overreaching the town, are seen to fall into the river, and bursting, throw up columns of water like the spouting of the monsters of the deep. We have made further approaches to the town, by throwing up a second parallel line, and batteries within about three hundred yards, this was effected in the night, and at day light the enemy were roused to the greatest exertions, the engines of war have raged with redoubled fury and destruction on both sides, no cessation day or night.[33]

Count Axel Fersen wrote in his diary about the effects of the allied cannons on the British positions,

> On the 10th, they [the allies] fired all day. We had forty-guns, either cannon, mortars, or howitzers. Our artillery was marvelously well-served; the quality of the works, which were of sand, did not allow our cannon, though so well directed, to have all the effect they would have had on ground; but we learned by deserters that our bombs had great effect and that the number of dead and wounded was increasing. The besieged fired little; they had none but small cannon, the largest was of eighteen; their mortars were only of six or eight inches, while ours were of twelve. During the day we sent many bombs and royal-grenades; at night the enemy established flying batteries. In the daytime they usually withdrew their cannon and put them behind the parapet.[34]

Count William De Deux-Ponts wrote a very optimistic report in his journal,

One of the batteries of our front of attack, composed of four twenty-four pounders, eight six-teen pounders, four mortars, and two howitzers, has been unmasked, and we have begun to make it play. The superiority of the fire of these different batteries over those of the enemy, silenced the firing from the town. All our guns have been well aimed; several parapets can already be seen with their tops damaged; and we know, from the reports of several deserters, that the enemy has been much astonished at the firing of our batteries, and that our shells, especially, disturb him much. He fires now scarcely six guns an hour, while heretofore he has kept up rather a steady fire, and well directed; nevertheless, we have had no reason to complain of the number of men killed and wounded.[35]

Baron Von Steuben showed humor and devotion to the country as he related an interesting story,

Baron De Viomenil commanded in the trenches on the 10th of October. At four o'clock in the evening he sent Count Deuxponts to tell me that he had observed, while visiting the trenches, that my division was extremely weak, and as it was probable the enemy might make a sortie that night, he wished to reinforce my left wing from five to eight hundred men, if I should think it necessary. In presence of General Wayne I answered Count Deuxponts that I did not think that I wanted any reinforcements, and that if the enemy were to attack me, I should answer for being able to hold the battery until Baron De Viomenil could arrive to support me, and further, that in case he was attacked, he might rely on me to support him with eight hundred men in two columns.

When Count Deuxponts had gone away, Wayne remarked that I had only one thousand men in my entire division. No doubt of it I replied; that in my calculation, too, but if it should happen, I should, on my own responsibility, leave two hundred men to defend the battery, and with the remaining eight hundred men attack forthwith in two columns. I added that if I was guilty of a certain amount of gasconade with regard to the number of men, it was for the honor of his county, whereupon Wayne took me by the hand, and addressing himself to the officers present said: 'Now gentlemen, it is our duty to make good the exaggeration of Baron Steuben, and to support him just as if he had double the number of troops that he has.'[36]

Baron Von Steuben---National Archives

Claude Blanchard spoke highly of his French gunners as he wrote in his journal, "We had artillery of the first class, and the Americans, for their part, had large cannons and displayed great activity; but they did not approach the perfection of our gunners, who were the admiration of General Washington."[37]

Colonel Henry Lee was very pleased the way things were going. He wrote in his memoirs, "The slender defences opposed to us began to tumble under the demolishing fire. The loss of time sustained in bringing our cannon six miles, was amply compensated by the effects of the wise determination to put the issue of the siege on heavy metal."[38]

Chapter 8

Closer to the British Lines

"....the steadily increasing number of American guns were silencing the enemy works and making most noble music." ---Colonel David Cobb, aid to General Washington

Thursday October 11, 1781

(Pleasant during the day and cool at night)

On the night of October 11, Washington ordered the digging of the second parallel closer to the British lines. Without this parallel the siege would go on longer, and Washington, fearful that the French fleet might leave, needed to end this battle soon. General Von Steuben was ordered to have the second parallel dug without the British knowing it. When completed, this would put allied gunners just 400 yards away from the British lines. For the gunners this would be point blank range.

British forces:

Lord Cornwallis wrote to General Henry Clinton and stressed to him that only naval action could save him,

> Cochrane arrived yesterday. I have only to repeat what I said in my letter of the 3rd, that nothing but a direct move to York River, which includes a successful naval action, can save me. On the evening of the 9th the enemy opened their batteries, and have since continued firing without intermission with about forty pieces of cannon, mostly heavy, and sixteen mortars from eight to sixteen inches. We have lost about seventy men, and many of our works are seriously damaged. With such works, on disadvantageous ground, against so powerful an attack, we cannot hope to make a very long resistance.[1]

About five hours later, Cornwallis added a P.S. to his letter to Clinton, "Since the above was written we have lost thirty men."

Johann Conrad Dohla, who was on boat duty, described in his diary the effects the bombardment had on the British ships in the harbor,

> I went on boat watch. Today there was exceptionally heavy firing by both sides. Thirty-six hundred shots by the enemy were counted in this twenty-four hours. These were fired at the city, into our lines, and against the ships in the harbor. These ships are completely ruined and shot up. The bombs and cannonballs also killed many inhabitants and Negroes from the city and marines and sailors, and soldiers. People were to be seen lying everywhere, fatally wounded, with heads, arms, and legs shot off. Also to be seen, by the water, were wounded being dragged and carried, who had been wounded on watch, at posts in the lines, on defense, and on work details, by the terribly heavy cannonade, and also, the burial in the sand, near the river, of soldiers and sailors. I saw bombs fall into the water which often, five, six, or eight, or more minutes lay in the water

and then exploded, which caused such havoc in the water that it was almost unbelievable. It threw sand and soil from the river onto the bank. When one sat there it was as if one witnessed the shock of an earthquake.

The shrapnel and shells from these bombs again fell short and fell into the houses and buildings of the city, and into our camp, where they did much damage and robbed many good soldiers of their lives, or broke their arms and legs. I myself had a piece of shell from an exploded bomb in my hands which weighed more than thirty pounds, and was more than three inches thick.

The marines and sailors who were on the English ships had to move into the defenses and batteries and performed duties there. During the night another English frigate was set afire by an enemy cannonball. It could not be saved and burned completely. Also at night, a fireship, which was ready for use, was sunk in the harbor by an enemy cannonball. This evening as Private Herterich sat before his tent in our camp, he was struck on the right leg by a piece of an exploded bomb, so that he could no longer walk, but had to be carried in the camp by some of his comrades.[2]

Colonel Tarleton wrote in his book about the impact the second parallel had on the British defenses,

The second parallel was considerably advanced before the first: It approached the redoubts, which were placed on the left flank of Yorktown: The places of arms and the communications were judiciously constructed. The King's troops now began to lose men very fast, both by sickness and by the enemy's fire: To reinforce the line, Lieutenant Dundas was ordered with great part of the 80th regiment from Gloucester, and the future command of that post was entrusted to Colonel Tarleton.[3]

Bartholomew James described in his journal the horror and devastation going on in the British lines during the bombardment, even though the soldiers were not ready to give up,

I now want words to express the dreadful situation of the garrison, for it is scarcely possible to describe the calamitous condition we were in during the remainder of the siege. The enemy on this evening began their second parallel, having advanced three hundred yards nearer to us; their fire continued then incessant from heavy artillery and mortars, and we opened fresh embrasures to flank the enemy's works, keeping up a constant fire with all the howitzers and small mortars then in the garrison. Upwards of a thousand shells was thrown into the works on this night, and every spot became alike dangerous. The noise and thundering of the cannon, the distressing cries of the wounded and the lamentable sufferings of the inhabitants, whose dwellings were chiefly in flames, added to the restless fatigues.[4]

American/French forces:

Captain James Duncan commented in his journal about the *Charon* that was hit during the early part of the previous night,

Last night commenced a very heavy cannonade and the enemy returned the fire with no less spirit. Being apprehensive of a storm, they often fired in every direction. The largest of the enemy's vessels was set on fire by the bursting of a shell or red hot ball from some of our batteries, and communicated it to another, both of which were burnt down. They must have lost a considerable quantity of powder in the last, as there was an explosion which made a heavy report. The whole night was nothing but one continual roar of cannon, missed with the bursting of shells and rumbling of houses torn to pieces.[5]

Washington ordered General Von Steuben to have the second parallel to be dug that night. That would place them within 400 yards from the British lines. This line was about 750 yards long, three and a half feet deep, and seven feet wide. This placed the trench within musket range and easy artillery range of the British. Once completed it would bring both wings of the allies within storming distance of the British lines.

The French sent 750 workers to help dig the new trench and fifty workers to finish battery No. 5. At about ten in the evening the French workers heard musket shots, and they thought there was about to be an attack. It turned out to be just a British patrol, so the work continued. To try and conceal the work going on, the American and French batteries fired all night. The British returned fire, but caused little damage.

Colonel Richard Butler was placed in command of 600 men, and he later wrote in his journal, "...the second parallel was within about 250 yards of their [British] works; in many places this was done so secretly that the enemy did not know of it till day."

At dusk the French workers and Von Steuben's men marched out with every second man carrying a fascine, and shovel, and by morning they had the trench dug. Orders by the Baron for soldiers in other trenches were, "The soldiers not to be allowed to lay down in the night, but remain as in the day with their arms in their hands."[6]

The east, or right wing of the works, was made difficult by the presence of British redoubts 9 and 10, which were about 150 yards away. These two redoubts were behind a moat and had many sharp-pointed stakes, or fraise surrounding them. These forts were well defended, and they blocked the continuation of the trench. The French fleet was now just days away from sailing back to the West Indies, which made it necessary for redoubts 9 and 10 to be captured.

While the digging was going on during the night, Von Steuben was there with General Wayne. A shell fired by the British landed near the two men. The Baron threw himself into the trench, and Wayne followed falling on top of him. The Baron, seeing that it was Wayne on top of him, said "I always knew you were brave, general, but I did not know that you were so perfect in every point of duty; you cover your general's retreat in the best manner possible."[7]

Colonel David Cobb, an aid to General Washington, described the firing of the American guns in a very novel way, "....the steadily increasing number of American guns were silencing the enemy works and making most noble music."[8]

In his journal, Major Ebenezer Denny described redoubts No. 9 and 10,

> Second parallel thrown up within three hundred yards of the main works of the enemy; new batteries erected, and additional number of cannon brought forward-some twenty-four pounders and heavy mortars and howitzers. A tremendous fire now opened from all the new works, French and American. The heavy cannon directed against the embrasures and guns of the enemy. Their pieces were soon silenced, broke and dismantled. Shells from behind their works still kept up. Two redoubts advanced of their lines, and within rifle shot of our second parallel, much in the way. These forts or redoubts were well secured by a ditch and picket, sufficiently high parapet, and within were divisions made by rows of casks ranged upon end and filled with earth and sand. On tops of parapet were ranged bags filled with sand-a deep narrow ditch communicating with their main lines.[9]

Colonel John Laurens recorded his last entry in his journal,

> The last battery finished. This night a second parallel supported by a Ravin on the left and properly flanked by redoubts was commenced and happily forwarded undiscovered by the enemy. The position of tow advanced works in the enemy's right forbid our extending this parallel as far to the right as the first.[10]

Claude Blanchard wrote in his journal of the possible escape of Lord Cornwallis to Gloucester, "Some deserters from the enemy came to us, who told us that our fire greatly annoyed the English. According to their account, it was suspected that Cornwallis desired to escape; it would have been possible for him to do so by passing, during the night, across to Gloucester, but where would he have gone? He had a long journey to make to reach Carolina, where the English held some places; he ran the risk of perishing from want."[11]

Lieutenant Feltman wrote in his journal about some mysterious back smoke he saw coming from the British lines, "Last night about seven I was taking a view of the shells we threw into York, which was very pleasing to see. Shortly after I perceived a large black smoke rising which I conjectured was the enemy's burning of some of their vessels, but after inquiring into the matter found that they were set fire by some of our shells."[12]

Also included in his diary entry, Lieutenant Feltman had on this date some information on a General Court Martial held at the camp. Captain P. Duffy was charged with "scandalous and infamous behavior unbecoming the character of an officer and gentleman." Many of these soldiers did not have the background of being raised as gentlemen. They came from a violent and hard environment, and they could be very quick tempered.

It seemed that on the night of the 23rd or the morning of the 24th of September, Duffy tried to stab Captain Bullard with his sword. He was also charged with firing a pistol at the captain with a gun that he took from Lt. Brewer. Duffy faced charges by Colonel Stewart of being drunk, rioting in the street, abusing and threating a French guard on duty at the hospital. He was found guilty and discharged from the service.

Colonel Timothy Pickering took time from his duties on this evening, to give his wife an account, by letter, of the death of Colonel Scammell,

> It may give you some pleasure to be informed of the proceedings of the allied army, especially as the present object of their attention is important, and generally interesting, so that the event of this expedition may capitally affect our negotiations for peace. September 28th, the armies, invested the place…We have had very few men killed; and not one officer, as I recollected, has been hurt, excepting Colonel Scammell, who was unfortunately wounded and taken prisoner on the 30th of September, while reconnoitering a work the enemy had abandoned. It was barbarously done; for after two dragoons had him their prisoner, a third came up and shot him through the side. Of this wound he died the 6th instant, at Williamsburg, lamented by all who knew him and who valued friendship, integrity, and truth. The French have had an officer or tow badly wounded.[13]

Pickering gave his wife no details about what had been going on in October. However, he did give an account, of the recent events in a letter, in the form of a journal to Samuel Hodgdon. He wrote about the parallels being dug and setting up the artillery. He also mention Secretary

Nelson coming out of York and telling them how the British forces were suffering from the bombardment.

He wrote about complaints concerning the shells made in Pennsylvania, "Knox damns the Pennsylvania shells, as not being well cast, varying greatly in weight, and especially for not being proved. As a Proof of the latter, they observed that the cores have not been well cleaned out; so that, if they in fact passed a proof, it is not a full evidence that they are sound, as any holes might be stopped up by the remains of the cores. He and Bowman say, French's are perfect."

He went on to add a personal note, "I am impatient to get nearer to the enemy, that our work may be more speedily accomplished, and our ammunition not thrown away. Cornwallis prudently reserves his till that time. He scarcely answers one shot in fifty."[14]

Also on this date, Timothy Pickering took time to write to Congress about a matter important to him. With all that was going on with the siege, the matter he wrote to Congress about seemed rather trivial. However, in his defense, the man had sacrificed much for his country and placed himself in harm's way, and yet he was treated by Congress the following way,

> Two or three days since, I had the mortification to be refused the letters in the post-office addressed to me, unless I paid the postage. Before that time the postmaster had contented himself with charging me with the postage of letters. Those above referred to were all on public business, and I wished to take them up; but want of money obliged me to leave them in office, where they still remain.
>
> I entreat the attention of Congress on this subject. Certain officers of the army receive their letters free from postage. The letters of the principal staff must generally be at least as necessary and important; I cannot even conjecture one tolerable reason for the distinction. Nor can I discern any public advantage in the regulation obliging the latter to pay for public letters. As the matter now stands, I must either obtain any letters by the post, without payment, or, if this be inadmissible, I shall be obliged to direct all my deputies to cease sending me any paper by the post, and to suspend their communication till other conveyances present.[15]

On October 22nd, the letter was read to Congress, and it was resolved, "That letters to and from the Quartermaster General be carried free of postage."

In his diary Colonel St. George Tucker gave interesting information about what had gone on in the British lines,

> This Evening I walk'd down to the Trenches—The Enemy threw a few shells from five mortars which appear to be in the Battery in front of Secry Nelson's House, at the French Battery near the Clay Hill (a small distance from Pigeon Hill). Most of these burst in the Air at a considerable Height nor do I know whether any one of them fell into, or near the Battery. After this their shells were directed apparently towards the place where we this Evening begun to open our second paralel—One half of them at least burst in the Air; I do not know what Effect the remainder had—A few shot at the Interval of twenty or thirty minutes were all the Annoyance we recieved from their works during the Evening, except the Shells.
>
> I this day dined in Company with the Secretary. He says our Bombardment produced great Effects in annoying the Enemy & destroying their Works—Two Officers were killed &one wounded by a Bomb the Evening we opened—Lord Shuten's Cane was struck out of his Hand by a Cannon Ball—Lord Cornwallis has built a kind of Grotto at the foot of the secretary's Garden where he lives under Ground—A negroe of the Secretary's was kill'd in his House—It seems to be his Opinion that the British are a good deal dispirited

altho' he says they affect to say they have no Apprehendsions of the Garrison's falling—An immense number of Negroes have died, in the most miserable Manner in York. A Whale Boat from New York arrived at York the morning the Secry came out, with two British Major's on board—He could not hear any news from N.Y. except that it was probable that Admiral Digby with his Squadron would shortly make a push at the Count de Grasse however inferior he may be to him in Strength. We may therefore expect some important news from the Fleet soon.[16]

Washington wrote in his diary, "Two Gentlemen, a Major Granchien & Captn. D'Avilion being sent by Admiral de Grasse to reconnoiter the Enemys Water defences, & state of the River at and near York, seemed favourably disposed to adopt the measure which had been strongly urged of bringing Ships above the Town & made representations accordingly to the Count de Grasse."[17]

Friday October 12, 1781

(Pleasant during the day and cool at night)

British forces:

Back in New York City the relief ships of Cornwallis had been loaded with supplies and troops. Prince William Henry traveled to Staten Island to see the troops off. A good show was given for the Prince, as the men marched around and flew their banners. The British soldiers back at Yorktown, hugging the ground and trying not to get blown apart, would have been very proud that the troops in New York took the time to parade around for the Prince.

That morning at Yorktown, the British awoke and were astonished to find that the allies had dug a trench even closer to their lines. To answer this threat, they began firing their cannons at the allied lines and killing several soldiers.

That evening Major Charles Cochrane was having wine with Cornwallis. After dinner they decided to go up to the ramparts to take a look at the allied lines. Others at the table protested, and felt that it was too dangerous. Cochrane insisted that they go, and said he was leaving his glass of wine and would return to finish it.

When they reached the rampart, he decided to fire a ricochet shot at the enemy. He showed poor judgement by peering over the rampart, while under fire, to see the effects of his shot. At that moment a solid shot from the Americans hit him square in the head, as he stood next to Cornwallis. British Major Charles Cochrane became the only British field officer killed at Yorktown.

The following is an extract from a letter sent on October 21, from British Captain Mure to Andrew Stewart. The Captain was somewhat blunt in telling what happened, "I am sorry to tell you your nephew Major Cochrane, suffered among those killed. He had his head carried off by a cannon-shot when standing next to Lord Cornwallis. He came two days before in a most spirited manner. I pity poor Mrs. Cochrane who, I hear, is at New York."[18]

Johann Conrad Dohla wrote that the enemy was getting closer to their lines,

> Today a bomb fell so unfortunately into the camp that it killed four men in a tent and fatally wounded two others. Private Stutzel while on command in the defenses, had his left foot shot off by a piece of shrapnel, so that it three days later his leg had to be amputated at the thick part of the calf. The enemy, as far as we can notice, is working very hard on his batteries, defenses, and communication trenches, and his approaches are advancing very near to our lines. They have also completed a new and very long battery in the middle of their camp, in which they have placed sixteen cannon of 36, 42 and 48 pounds.[19]

Now that the *Charon* had been sunk, Bartholomew James and the rest of the officers waited for General Cornwallis to assign them new positions. Cornwallis believed that the enemy would attack the hornwork, so he assigned the officers and sailors to aid in its defense. James wrote in his journal,

> I immediately offered myself a volunteer to work this battery [hornwork] and set off for it accordingly with a midshipman and thirty-six seamen, to be relieved in eight hours by the first lieutenant. In fifty-two minutes after my arrival in the hornwork the enemy silenced the three left guns by closing the embrasures, shortly after which they dismounted a twelve-pounder with a part of its muzzle shot away, with which I kept up a fire till it was also rendered useless. At six o'clock in the evening, the first lieutenant having been sent to relieve me a shell burst between us and gave me a contusion in my face and right leg, with which I conceived myself very fortunate, having during my stay in the works had nine men killed, twenty-seven wounded, eight of which died as they was removed, and most of the wounded had lost an arm or leg, and some both. In short, myself and the midshipman, both wounded, were the only two that returned out of thirty-six, having stood a close cannonade with the enemy for eight hours, who had ninety-seven pieces of heavy cannon playing on us all that time. I quitted the works about a quarter after six, having received the thanks of Lord Cornwallis, who was in the redoubt during the greatest part of the time.[20]

American/French forces:

Washington knew that to complete his siege line he would need to capture British redoubts No. 9 and 10. Once they were taken, British defenses would be severely weakened. The allies began to send reconnoiter teams to study the redoubts. Washington met with Rochambeau to discuss strategy on taking them.

Lieutenant Feltman wrote in his diary that on the previous night he had been given command of eighty-two men to work on the second parallel. He described the dangerous work that took place,

> Every second man of the whole detachment carried a fascine and shovel or a spade, and every man every man a shovel, spade or grubbing hoe. Just at dusk we advanced within gunshot of the enemy, then began our work. In one hour's time we had ourselves completely covered, so we disregarded their cannonading; they discharged a number of pieces at our party, but they had but little effect, they only wounded one of our men. We were in the center of two fires, from the enemy and our own, but the latter was very dangerous; we had two men killed and one badly wounded from the French batteries, also a number of shells bursted in the air above our heads, which was very dangerous to us. We dug the ditch three and a half feet deep and seven feet in width. In the morning [the 12th] before daylight we were relieved by the militia.[21]

After Feltman was relieved from duty, he was able to rest for a few hours. That afternoon there was much artillery fired from both sides, and he and his men were sent out to cut down trees for more fortifications. The following day he did the same job all day.

During the night, the French batteries in the first parallel stopped firing in order to elevate the cannons. The British immediately began to fire at the workers of the second parallel and wounded several men. The French cannons started firing again, and the British guns went silent.

Claude Blanchard had spent the night, of the 11th and 12th at Williamsburg, caring for the sick and wounded. He had been assigned the work of carrying men to the hospital by ambulance. He was overwhelmed with the number of patients he attended to and expressed his frustration in his journal,

> I was at Williamsburg, always busy about our sick men; I had four hundred of them and thirteen officers. Besides there was always the same want of assistance, for Monsieur de Choisy's division, encamped in front of Gloucester; I found myself in the most cruel embarrassment and on the eve of seeing the service fail which was especially entrusted to me. And that would have happen if we had not had at this period from two to three hundred wounded; that might be. Therefore I could not think without distress of M. de Chastellux's remarks, of whom I had required vehicles from the North river, only for carrying some effects, at the rate of 250 sick persons, "We shall not have fifty sick!" And already at the beginning of the siege we had four hundred of them.[22]

Blanchard was in much better spirits on the 13th, when some supplies to treat the men with, reached him. He soon returned to the batteries at Yorktown.

Washington wrote in his diary,

> Began our second parallel within abt. 300 yards (& in some places less) of the enemys lines and got it so well advanced in the course of the Night as to cover the Men before morning. This business was conducted with the same secresy as the former & undertaken so much sooner than the enemy expected (we should commence a second parallel) that they did not by their conduct, & mode of firing, appear to have had any suspicion of our Working parties till day light discovered them to their Picquets; nor did they much annoy the Trenches in the course of this day (the Parallel being opened last Night from the ravene in front, and on the right flank of the Enemy till it came near to the intersection of the line of fire from the American 4 Gun Battery to the enemy's advanced redoubts on their left. The french Batteries fired over the second parallel.[23]

By morning the allies were in position in the new trench. Now they were at point blank range, and their cannon could pound the British lines to rubble.

Colonel Jonathan Trumbull, toward the end of the day, wrote an optimistic note in his journal,

> Second parallel completed. Batteries are constructing for the removal of the Artillery nearer the town. Enemy begin to increase their fire. Some small shells are thrown by them, and we experience more annoyance, but if no more effectual opposition is experience the town must soon be too hot for his Lordship and his troops. Some loss this day.[24]

Josiah Atkins, of the 5th Connecticut Regiment, left his regiment in New York with a group of men taking supplies to the infantry in the south. The men joined with General Anthony Wayne's troops in Pennsylvania. Josiah was taken ill with "a violent pain in his head" on September 17th, while about twenty miles north of Williamsburg. He kept getting worse, and his medication had little effect. On October 2nd, he made an application to return to his regiment in New York.

To be released, he had to go to his regiment that had already marched on. He got his release signed on the 4th, and he began his long walk home even though he was very ill. He made it as far as Hanover, which was about 60 miles north of Williamsburg. Near the age of thirty-two, he died in the hospital at Hanover Virginia around October 15th. In the open pages of his diary, which he began in April 1781, was his will,

> My Dear Friends and Fellow Soldiers—As we are engaged in a bloody war, the fate of which is uncertain; as we are drawing near the enemy and can expect nothing but fighting; as in any action some may fall, and as my life is as uncertain as any others; so should it be my fate to drop and yours to survive, you may chance to light on this book and its contents, with the other things I may happen to have about me, which 'tis probable will be a watch, a pair of silver shoe buckles, knee buckles, stock buckle, brooch, stone sleeve-buttons, and perhaps some money. These I freely I give to you. Yes, I bid you welcome to them on your gaging to grant me this request. To use best your upmost endeavor to send this book with its contents to my dear wife, whom have left at home to mourn my misfortune. Should this fall into the hands of our enemies I have no expectations of its ever reaching [her]. But should any of you, my friends and fellow soldiers, take this, I expect, I request, Yes I reason to exact it at your hands.
>
> You may think this of small importance. However, You must suppose that it will be satisfactory to her (on whose account it is written) to hear my fate. You may think the matter is difficult, but I assure you 'tis not. If you convey it to any of the infantry belonging to Waterbury in Connecticut (my wife and friends living in that town), or any who belong in Woodbury or Watertown or any of the towns adjacent, it will hardly fail to reach my house, Josiah Atkins in Waterbury, or in the Society of Farmingbury. Give them some of your bounty to induce them to be faithful in discharging their trust in delivering this to my wife. This is a thing I so anxiously desire, that if you do not use your utmost endeavor for this purpose, I cannot forgive you, neither will God (unless by bitter repentance—but the things you have taken will rise in Judgment against you). This I entreat you by those powerful inducements, and I could use many more—but relying on your goodness, generosity and benevolence, I shall ass no more, assuring you, I ever while in life, the friend and well-wisher of all the soldiers.   Josiah Atkins
>
> P.S. Should this fall into the hands of any other person than a soldier, I do request and expect the same kind treatment at their hands, and though I nor mine should not be able to reward you, yet God will.[25]

It is unknown how the diary made its way back to his wife. A letter addressed to his wife inside the diary encouraged her to marry again. He and his wife Sally had a daughter named Sally and a son named Josiah.

Colonel Alexander Hamilton wrote to his wife and playfully scolded her for not writing. His wife Elizabeth was pregnant with their first child, a son they would name Philip. He would be born in a little over three months,

> I wrote you two days since My Dear Betsey, but as I am informed by one of the Gentlemen at Head Quarters that there is an opportunity for Philadelphia, I embrace it with that pleasure which I always feel in communicating with you. You complain of me my love, for not writing to you more frequently, but have I not greater reason to complain of you? Since I left Kings ferry, I have received three letters from you, that is three in seven weeks. You have no occupations to prevent your writing; I am constantly employed. Yet I am sure I have written to you during that period more than twenty letters. Don't imagine that this neglect will go unpunished. I hope to see you in three or four weeks from this time, and you may then expect to be called to a severe account. I know you rely upon your power over me. You expect that your usual blandishments will have the usual charm. You think you have only to smile and caress and you will disarm my resentment; but

you are mistaken. The crime is of too serious nature to be forgiven; except with one atonement which I am sure it will not be easy for you to make. This is to love me better than ever. If upon deliberate examination you should find this impossible, I may compound for one substitute. You shall engage shortly to present me with *a boy*. You will ask me if a girl will not answer the purpose. By no means. I fear, with all the mothers charms, she may inherit the caprices of her father and then she will enslave, tantalize and plague one half (the) sex, out of pure regard to which I protest against a daughter. So far from extenuating your offence this would be an aggravation of it.

In an instant my feelings are changed. My heart disposed to gayety is at once melted into tenderness. The idea of a smiling infant in my Betseys arms calls up all the father in it. In imagination I embrace the mother and embrace the child a thousand times. I can scarce refrain from shedding tears of joy. But I must not indulge these sensations; they are unfit for the boisterous scenes of war and whenever they intrude themselves make me but half a soldier.

Thank heaven, our affairs seem to be approaching fast to a happy period. Last night our second parallel commenced. Five days more the enemy must capitulate or abandon their present position; if they do the latter it will detain us ten days longer; and then I fly to you. Prepare to receive me in your bosom. Prepare to receive me decked in all your beauty, fondness and goodness. With reluctance I bid you adieu.

Adieu My darling Wife My beloved Angel Adieu[26]

Unfortunately Alexander's son would die in a duel in 1801, and three years later Alexander would die, also in a duel, at the same place. Alexander was never quite the same after the death of his son.

Elizabeth & Alexander Hamilton-National Archive

General Washington wrote to Congress and gave them an update of what had been happening since October 7. He ended his letter with, "I cannot but acknowledge the infinite obligations I am under to Count de Rochambeau, the Marquis de St. Simon, commanding the troops from the West Indies, the other general officers, and indeed the officers of every denomination in the French army, for the assistance which they afford me. The experience of many of those gentlemen, in the business before us, is of the utmost advantage in the present operation."[27]

This sounded like a man about to achieve a long sought victory. Washington showed his greatness by not praising himself for achieving what was once thought to be impossible, instead he gave credit to the leaders around him.

Saturday October 13, 1781

(Pleasant during the day and cool at night)

British forces:

Bartholomew James wrote in his journal that their situation looked hopeless even though they were promised relief from Clinton. "….the garrison becoming every hour more defenceless from the fire thereof, it was now we begun to despair of any relief capable of saving the garrison from a surrender, though all the expresses from the commander-in-chief flattered us with their speedy arrival."[28]

American/French forces:

Cornwallis's cave is located on the beach below Yorktown. Inside the metal door on the left is two small rooms. It is very unlikely that Cornwallis spent time here during the siege. Some inhabitants of Yorktown may have stayed here during the siege. Photo by author

As the allied artillery fire continued, a few sources later reported that Cornwallis had moved and was hiding in a cave on the beach. This was probably just local lore. The cave the locals referred to as Cornwallis's Cave, would have been too small and far from the action for him to stay there. Also, Cornwallis was not the type of leader that would hide in a cave, while his men were engaged in a battle. The General was famous for the way he was willing to share the sufferings of his troops. While marching to Yorktown he had slept in the open and ate the same rations as his men. Cornwallis, like Washington, took an active part in the battle.

Doctor James Thacher, in his journal, gave a good description of the artillery shells used and the damage they caused,

> It is astonishing with what accuracy an experienced gunner will make his calculations, that a shell shall fall within a few feet of a given point, and burst at the precise time, though at a great distance. When a shell falls, it whirls round, burrows, and excavates the earth to a considerable extent, and bursting makes a dreadful havoc around. I have more than once witnessed fragments of the mangled bodies and limbs of the British soldiers thrown into the air by the bursting of our shells, and by one from the enemy, Captain White, of the 7th Massachusetts regiment, and one soldier were killed, and another wounded near where I was standing. About twelve or fourteen men have been killed or wounded within twenty four hours; I attended at the hospital, amputated a man's arm; and assisted in dressing a number of wounds.[29]

Captain James Duncan was sent to the second parallel, and he wrote in his journal, "We lost several men this night, as the enemy by practice were enabled to throw their shells with great certainty. About noon this day our division relieved the trenches, and about 2 o'clock advanced to the second parallel."[30]

Chapter 9

The Noose Tightens

"During this attack they made such a terrible screaming and loud hurrah shouting that there was nothing otherwise to believe than all hell had broken loose." ---Hessian soldier Johann Conrad Dohla in redoubt No. 9

Sunday October 14, 1781

(Mild day, at night a thick fog rolls in and later rain)

Up until now there had been just a few skirmishes and a couple of men killed and wounded each day. The main action had been the artillery duels between by the two armies. As long as the British controlled redoubts No. 9 and 10, the siege line could not be completed, and Cornwallis could hold out longer and perhaps even until help arrived.

Washington did not have the luxury of waiting the British out, because he could lose the backing of the French fleet very soon. He told his staff that redoubts No. 9 and 10 must be taken at once.

Redoubt No. 10 was a square redoubt and smaller than the No. 9. It was located within twenty feet of the river bank overlooking a bluff and manned by about seventy troops. Redoubt No, 9 was about a quarter mile inland and manned by 120 British and Hessian troops.

The two redoubts could not be taken by artillery, but it would require troops to charge the forts and capture them in hand-to-hand fighting. As one Frenchman said, "The capture of these redoubts had become indispensable." Count William De Deux-Ponts wrote in his journal, "as long as these two works belong to the enemy, our [French] parallel will be imperfect; and we all hope that they will be attacked at once."[1]

John Boudy, who first joined the army in 1776, explained why they needed to capture the redoubts in his pension application (W5858), "General Washington ordered us to storm to breastworks of the enemy which were galling us very much."

On the 12th of October, General Washington had ordered the artillery to pound the two British redoubts. By the 14th he felt that the British forts had been sufficiently damaged by the shelling. He had Lafayette gather 400 of his infantry men for the attack. French General Rochambeau was allowed to choose the men he wanted to lead and take part in their attack.

Washington wanted information about the assault kept a secret so that the British would be taken by surprise. Rumors began to spread among the allies, but the British were kept in the dark. American Lieutenant Feltman was not aware that the redoubts were going to be attacked, but there were rumors of something going on. He wrote in his diary on the 14th, "This evening it is reported there is something grand to be done by our Infantry."[2]

Alexander Hamilton heard a rumor of the attack, and he protested the fact that the Chevalier de Gimat had been selected by Lafayette to lead the American assault. Hamilton made the point that he was a senior officer to the Chevalier and by right should lead the attack. Lafayette told his friend the decision had been made and it was too late to change commanders.

Hamilton was not about to take no for an answer, so he took his case to General Washington and demanded that he be given command. Washington and Lafayette met and reviewed who was the senior officer and found that Hamilton was correct. So, Hamilton was given the command he sought. Back then to lead the men in battle meant that he would be leading from the front. Hamilton, who had been married less than a year, with a baby due in a few months, was willing to put his life at great risk by accepting this command. To lead an attack was not only an honor, but he knew it could also be very beneficial to his political career after the war.

Around noon Washington rode to the French camp to discuss the assault with French General Baron de Viomenil. He found that the Baron had at least a dozen officers who requested to lead the assault. Washington may have laughed to himself that the French army also had a few "Hamiltons." The honor to lead the French attack went to Colonel William de Deux-Ponts.

One redoubt was to be stormed by Colonel Alexander Hamilton under the command of General Lafayette and the other redoubt by Colonel William de Deux-Ponts under the command of Baron de Viominel. The troops of the two nations were excited for each to show the greatest courage.

On the eve of the attack, Baron de Viomenil showed Lafayette open contempt for the unseasoned militia led by Lafayette. Lafayette replied, "We are young soldiers, it is true; but our tactics on such an occasion are to unload our guns and go straight ahead with the bayonet."[3]

About a half hour before the two assaults, a false attack by Saint-Simon's men was made on the British right. At eight o'clock six rockets were fired as a signal, so that the attacks could be made at the same time.

British forces:

A Hessian soldier, Johann Conrad Dohla a private in the Fourth Company, of the Bayreuth Regiment, gave his account of the attack on redoubts No. 9 and 10 and the panic that followed,

> Today in the city, below the bank at the water's edge, a cannonball of more than one hundred pounds was found, which had been fired by the enemy. Between seven and eight o'clock at night the enemy attacked the outer redoubts, Numbers 7 and 8 [this may refer to the times of the attack which was between 7 and 8], on the left flank, in which were assigned one captain and two lieutenants with one hundred English and Hessian privates. The enemy, under the cover of a thick fog, crept up to the abatis completely unnoticed, and before anyone was aware, they had quickly and silently made a few openings. A great number of French grenadiers, of which part had long storming pikes, made an assault with the greatest determination, sprang into the

trenches, tore out the palisades, and after a hard-fought defense, and heavy small-arms fire from the command in the positions, successfully entered the two redoubts without firing a shot. A few of the command fled during the attack and came into the lines. The others were captured, and also some killed and wounded. The enemy also had many dead and wounded. He immediately occupied these two positions, made them secure, and planted the French white flag on which were three lilies. [Dohla was not aware that the Americans attacked one of the redoubt.]

During this attack they made such a terrible screaming and loud hurrah shouting that there was nothing otherwise to believe than all hell had broken loose. Supposedly three thousand men, French and American, took part in this storming operation, mostly volunteers. During this incident, there was an alarm in our entire camp. All troops had to move out and onto the wall. The entire left wing fired their small arms. It. Was believed they would break in our left wing in order to storm our entire line. However, after taking the two redoubts, they were completely quiet during this night, except that the exchange of fire continued from both sides.

During this storming the following stratagem was employed. In the middle of our lines, loud German commands were heard. "The entire column or brigade, forward march! Halt! Cannons to the front!" And that, two or three times. Also, a few rifle balls flew over the wall and into the middle of our line. By this means they created a false alarm and we believed that they would attack us in the middle.

During this night, 14 October, two men of the Bayreuth Regiment, deserted from a picket. On the whole, since the siege began, many of our troops, the English and the Hessians, have deserted to the enemy.[4]

Stephen Popp, a Hessian soldier, also heard allied orders given in German during the attack on the redoubts. He claimed that the troops that were wounded or refused to surrender were killed,

Heavy attack in force, the enemy seized one of our redoubts and made an attack on our right wing, but were forced back with heavy loss, then attacked our left, and the French grenadiers stormed our line, without firing a shot, captured a hundred of our men on the advanced line, killed and wounded those who refused to surrender,---made a great noise with their shouting, seized our lines and turned them, and with 3 or 400 men held them. Our whole force was sent forward to strengthen our left, for a general attack was ordered and we could distinctly hear and understand the orders given in German to the enemy's German troops,--we did our best to save our guns and to keep the enemy at bay.[5]

Stephen claimed that some soldiers were killed or wounded after they surrendered. A few defenders refused to surrender according to the journal of Jean Baptiste Antoine de Verger, a French sub-lieutenant that was there, "Several wishing to continue the fight with bayonets paid with their lives."[6]

Naval officer Bartholomew James gave an account of what went on during the entire day and he was very impressed with the infantry attack that evening. He also acknowledged that they were running short of ammunition,

Our works having become too feeble to resist the force of the enemy's heavy artillery, and as also, from the want of ammunition, we could not to any degree impede their operations, considerable breaches were made in our strongest batteries and redoubts, and the whole became so very weak and defenceless that they were scarcely tenable. On this morning they sunk another fireship and two transports, and at seven in the evening attempted to storm the flanking redoubt to the right, and was repulsed with great loss. At nine o'clock they stormed from right to left with seventeen thousand men, advancing with drums beating and loud huzzas, when the whole garrison was a scene of fire throughout the lines, which added to the thunder of the heavy artillery and the blaze of musketry from so prodigious an army within a few yards of each other, opened to view a scene which I cannot attempt to describe. In this storm the enemy carried two of our flanking redoubts to the left which had hitherto retarded their approaches, and most of the unhappy fellows [were] put to the bayonet, as usual in cases of storms.[7]

Captain Samuel Graham of in the British 76th Foot Regiment wrote a brief account of the attack in his memoir,

> On the evening of the 14th the two redoubts on our left flank were attacked, and carried after a gallant resistance; that next to the river was taken by the Americans, and the other by the French. The French general who commanded the attack found fault with his aid-de-camp who led for dismounting his horse, the works being so much battered and destroyed. The two redoubts were soon included in the enemy's lines.[8]

Colonel Tarleton wrote of the attack in his book, and he was very complementary of the courage of the Americans and French. Since he was stationed across the York River at Gloucester, he could hear the sounds of battle and see the flashes of cannon fire. He may well have believed that a major attack was going on,

> On the evening of the 14th, General Washington directed a detachment from each army to attack, after dark, the two outward redoubts upon the left of the British lines at York. The Marquis de la Fayette commanded the assault made from the American works, and the Baron de Viomenil that which proceeded from the French trenches. The Americans headed by a number of officers and volunteers, performed their duty with vigour and courage; The British redoubt, which had been much damaged by the fire of the batteries, was soon carried, and the commanding officer, with many of his detachment, was made prisoner. Colonels Hamilton, Lawrance, and De Gimat, distinguished themselves on this occasion. The Baron de Viomenil was not less successful in his attempt. The French chasseurs and grenadiers met with more difficulties and greater loss; but they entered with fixed bayonets, and made themselves masters of the redoubt.
>
> The Count de Deux Points, the Count Charles de Damas, and several other French officers of distinction, were amongst the foremost of the assailants. No trial was made by the King's troops to repossess the redoubts; and the working party of the combined army included them within their parallel before morning. The loss of men sustained by the British was not great, or nearly so important as the loss of the ground covered by the redoubts. The enemy's works were pushed forwards with skill as well as assiduity, and, by their nearer approach to the body of the place, the situation of the besieged became every hour more disadvantageous. The batteries of the first parallel had silenced the cannon of the town, and made considerable impression on the fortifications; Those of the second parallel were nearly finished on the 15th.[9]

Captain Johann Ewald, a Hessian officer, wrote in his diary about the redoubt assault. He also told a chilling story of an encounter with a groups of slaves that had been forced out of Yorktown,

> [Note: the first part of this entry is missing some words] An hour before sunset, the besieged doubled their fire, and at seven o'clock in the evening a false attack was made on the redoubt on the right. About eight o'clock General Baron Viomenil attacked the detached redoubt on the left with French soldiers, and the Marquis de Lafayette attacked the adjacent one with the Americans. Both redoubts were taken with the bayonet after a fight of _____. The Hessian Lieutenant Anderson of the Erb Prinz Regiment and the English Captain Tailor were seized with swords in hand by the enemy. Both officers were wounded by bayonets or swords and won the _____ of the enemy. Most of the garrison is said to have saved itself too _____ people make long faces and say, "Who would have thought this _____?" I have heard these words so often

from a soldier that I would gladly sent the faithful sleeper to "Doctor Schwift's Little House" [probably a privy] _____ him of his complaint.

_____ would just as soon forget to record a cruel happening. On the same time of the enemy assault, we drove back to the enemy all of our black _____ds, whom we had taken along to despoil the countryside. We had tem to good advantage and set them free, and now, with fear and trembling, they had to face the reward of their cruel masters. Last night I had to make a sneak patrol, during which I came across a great number of these unfortunates. In their hunger, these unhappy people would soon devoured what I had; and since they lay between two fires, they had to be driven on by force. This harsh act had to be carried out, however, because of the scarcity of provisions, but we should have thought more about their deliverance at this time.

Moreover, all the artillery and baggage horses, for which there was no forage, were killed and dragged into the York River [there may have been up to 1,200 horses destroyed]. Several days after their death these poor animals came back in heaps with the tide, nearly up to the sunken ships. The sight of these horses was saddening to a person of feeling. But what should we have done if we did not want the enemy to have them? Voltaire says, "La raison de guerre, c'est las raison de guere." [The reason for war is but little reason.][10]

A few hours after the two redoubts were captured by the allies, Cornwallis wrote a letter to Clinton,

Experience has shown that our fresh earthen works do not resist their powerful artillery, so that we shall soon exposed to an assault in ruined works, in a bad position, and with weakened numbers. The safety of the place is, therefore, so precarious, that I cannot recommend that the fleet and army should run great risqué in endeavouring to save us.[11]

Americans/French forces:

Before the attack:

Washington had the cannons bombard the redoubts to destroy the abatis which defended them, to make the attack much easier. Baron Viomenil was very impatient and wanted to start the attack. He felt that all the cannon fire was a waste of ammunition and the assault should start at once.

General Rochambeau, to calm Viomenil, descended alone into the ravine which separated him from the enemy, mounted the other side, entered the abatis within pistol-shot of the English batteries, and returned to assure Viomenil coolly that the abatis was not sufficiently destroyed. He told the commander he must wait until the parapet was more leveled, in order that his grenadiers should be exposed as little time as possible.[12]

The grenadier regiment of Gatenois was a good regiment, and at one time they had the honored title of Royal Auvergne sans tache [the spotless]. Some of the grenadiers had served during the past with that title of honor. However, years earlier the title of honor had been taken from the regiment. General Rochambeau approached the men of his old regiment, which he had

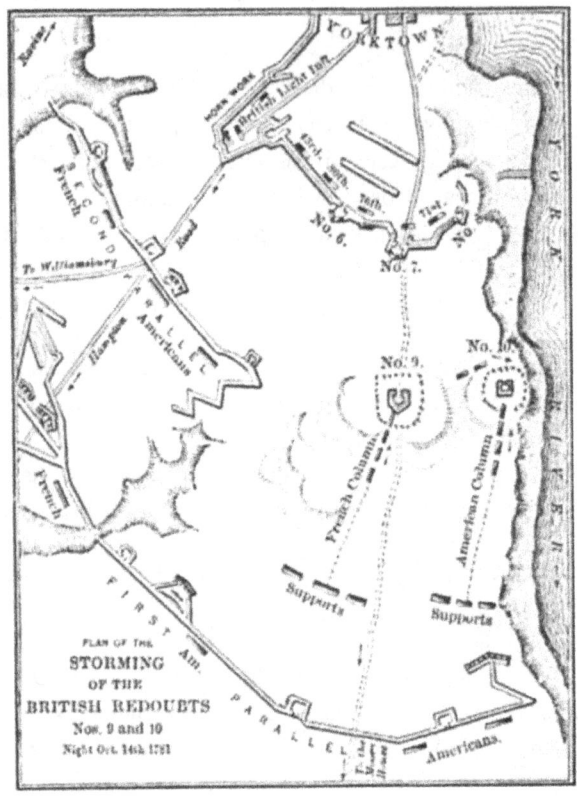

led into battle many times. He said, "My children, if I have need of you to night, I hope you have not forgotten that we have served together in your brave regiment of Auvergne, to call it by the honourable title which it has borne since its formation."

One of the sergeants stepped from the ranks of the regiment and said to the general, "General, we will all willingly get killed for you, if you will promise to allow our regiment definitely and officially to bear the name of the Royal Auvergne, which has always been given us, and of which we are all proud."[13]

Storming of the Redoubts. Map from *The Yorktown Campaign and The Surrender of Cornwallis* by Henry P. Johnston, 1881, page 144.

Rochambeau promised it would be granted if the redoubt was captured. As the men were leaving the trench, Baron de Viomenil said to the men, "Above all things, men, not a word, not a shot, till you are in the enemy's entrenchment, and there, only when the drums beat, march forward and show the English how you can use the bayonet."[14]

As Colonel William de Deux-Ponts and his men moved out, others around him wished him success and glory. He later wrote in his journal, "That moment seemed to me very sweet, and was very elevating to the soul and animating to the courage. My brother, especially, my brother—and I shall never forget it—gave me marks of tenderness which penetrated to the bottom of my heart."[15]

Americans attack redoubt No. 10:

Before the attack, John Kercheval, who had joined the army in 1776 at the age of 13, stated in his pension application (W3023) that he asked Colonel Hamilton if he could join the attack. Hamilton refused, but he was granted permission to join the French unit in their attack.

Lafayette knew that the redoubt was defended by experienced British troops. He also knew that most of his men were young and inexperienced soldiers. He had all the men unload their arms and form in a column, that he would led them himself quickly across the field. A quick surprise attack he believed was the key to success. If the men had loaded weapons there would be the chance of someone firing early and alerting the British.

General Lafayette---National Archives

Samuel McNeill wrote in his journal, "Our division arrived at the deposite a little before dark while every man was ordered to disencumber himself of his pack. The evening was pretty dark and favored the attack."[16]

Before the American troops moved, Washington made a brief address admonishing the men to act the part of firm and brave soldiers. He expressed the necessity of accomplishing the object, as the attack on both redoubts depended on their success. Captain Stephen Olney said, "I thought then, that his Excellency's knees rather shook, but I have since doubted whether it was not mine."[17] Captain Olney was no stranger to battle. At the Battle of Princeton on January 3, 1777, he had saved the life of the future President, James Monroe.

For Washington to give this speech was unusual, because this was not the sort of thing he felt comfortable doing. It was obvious that this attack worried Washington, and its success was very important.

When Colonel Hamilton was with his troops, he made a short address that was heard by General Washington in the main battery. "Did you ever hear such a speech?" remarked a Lieutenant in the battery. Another other man said, "With such a speech I could storm hell!"[18]

At redoubt 9 the soldiers would have to create an opening through the abates. ---Library of Congress

A fog rolled in from the York River, settled over the battlefield, and blended in with the smoke of the cannon fire. Hamilton got his men ready to move toward the redoubt about 400 yards away. They faced around seventy British and Hessian troops, and the Americans were going to attack them with unloaded guns. As they laid on the ground waiting for the signal to advance, some of the men probably thought to themselves that this might be their last night on earth. Some may have worried that if they should fall in battle, what would become of their families. Then the order was given, "Up! Up!"

As the Americans crept through the fog and smoke, they stopped about half way and each company was asked to give a volunteer for the forlorn hope. [This was a group of soldiers chosen to take the lead in the military operation. They would be at great risk, because they would be the first to enter the redoubt.] The leader of the twenty man group was Lieutenant John Mansfield of the 4th Connecticut Regiment. As one of the first to enter the redoubt he was seriously wounded by a bayonet but survived.

Colonel Hamilton ordered his close friend, John Laurens, to take his eighty men around to the back of the redoubt to prevent any of the enemy escaping. As the Americans were mounting the redoubt, Lieutenant Colonel Laurens, appeared suddenly on their flank, at the head of two companies. Major Fish, not aware that Laurens had joined the attackers said, "Why, Laurens, what brought you here?" Colonel Laurens replied, "I had nothing to do at headquarters, and so came here to see what you all were about."[19]

The soldiers in the front dropped thick bundles of sticks into the dry moat surrounding the redoubt. This allowed the soldiers to easily cross the ditch. Then the men carrying ladders placed them on the sides of the redoubt, which allowed the men to climb them to the top of the wall.

The Americans rushed forward, tore away part of the abatis with their own hands, and climbed over the rest without waiting for the snappers to remove it in the usual manner. Hamilton, at 5 feet 7 inches, at the head of his men, climbed on the shoulder of one of his soldiers, who knelt for the purpose and mounted the enemy's works. As they mounted to the assault, the cry of the Americans was, "Remember New London."[20] The men rushed after Hamilton, and soon they captured the redoubt at the point of the bayonet.

The attack and capture of the redoubt took about ten minutes. Causalities on both sides were light; nine Americans killed and thirty-two wounded, and the British had eight killed and about 20 captured.

Redoubt 9, stormed by the French---Library of Congress

The three young officers, Lafayette, Hamilton, and Laurens, had achieved the glory they knew might be the last for this war. They each had joined Washington in their early twenties to fight for freedom. They shared a common goal even though they came from varied backgrounds. Lafayette was the wealthy French Aristocrat, and Laurens was the son of a wealthy slaveholder in the south, while Hamilton was the bastard child born in the West Indies. All three still in their twenties can now see the final victory at hand.

Joseph Plumb Martin took part on the attack of redoubt 10. He was told to march to the trench and was given no other information. He felt that "something extraordinary, serious or comical, was going forward, but what, he could not easily conjecture." He wrote a detailed description of the attack in his book,

> We arrived at the trenches a little before sunset; I saw several officers fixing bayonets on long staves. I then concluded we were about to make a general assault upon the enemy's works; but before dark I was informed of the whole plan, which was to storm the redoubts, the one by the Americans and the other by the French.

The Sappers and Miners were furnished with axes, and were to proceed in front and cut a passage for the troops through the abates, which are composed of the tops of trees, the small branches cut off with a slanting stroke which rendered them as sharp as spikes. These trees are then laid at a small distance from the trench or ditch, pointing outwards, and the butts fastened to the ground in such a manner that they cannot be removed by those on the outside of them;----it is almost impossible to get through them. Through these we were to cut a passage before we or the other assailants could enter. At dark the detachment was formed and advanced beyond the trenches, , and lay down on the ground to await the signal for advancing to the attack, which was to be three shells from a certain battery near where we were lying. All the batteries in our line was silent, and we lay anxiously waiting for the signal. The two brilliant planets, Jupiter and Venus, were in close contact in the western hemisphere, (the same direction that the signal was to be made in) when I happened to cast my eyes to that quarter, which was often, and I caught a glance of them, I was ready to spring on my feet, thinking that they were the signal for starting. Our watchword was Rocjambeau, the commander of the French forces' name, a good watchword, for being pronounced Ro-sham-bow, it sounded, when pronounced quick, like rush-on-boys. We had not lain there long before the expected signal was given, for us and the French, who were to storm the other redoubt, by the three shells with their fiery trains mounting the air in quick succession. The word up, up, was then reiterated through the detachment. We immediately moved silently on toward the redoubt we were to attack, with unloaded muskets. Just as we arrived at the abatis, the enemy discovered us and directly opened a sharp fire upon us. We were now at a place where many of our large shells had burst in the ground, making holes sufficient to bury an ox in, the men having their eyes fixed upon what was transacting before them, were killing us off at a great rate. At length one of the holes happen to pick me up, I found out the mystery of the huge slaughter. As soon as the firing begin, our people began to cry, "the fort's our own!" and it was "rush on boys."

The Snappers and Miners were ordered not to enter the fort, but there was no stopping them, "We will go," said they, "then go to the devil," said the commanding officer of our corps, "if you will." I could not pass at the entrance we had made, it was so crowded; I therefore forced a passage at a place where I saw our shot had cut away some of the abatis; several others entered at the same place. While passing, a man at my side received a ball in his head and fell under my feet, crying out bitterly. While crossing the trench, the enemy threw hand grenades, (small shells) into it; they were so thick that I at first thought then cartridge papers on fire; but was soon undeceived by their cracking. As I mounted the breast work, I met an old associate hitching himself down the trench; I knew him by the light of the enemy's musketry, it was so vivid. The fort was taken, and all was quiet in a very short time. Immediately after the firing ceased, I went out to see what had become of my wounded friend and the other that fell in the passage—they were both dead. In the heat of the action I saw a British soldier jump over the walls of the fort next the river and go down the bank, which was almost perpendicular, and twenty or thirty feet high; when he came to the beach he made off for the town, and if he did not make good use of his legs I never saw a man that did.

All that were in the action of storming the redoubt were exempted from further duty that night; we laid down upon the ground and rested the remainder of the night as well as a constant discharge of grape and canister shot would permit us to do; while those who were on duty for the day completed the second parallel by including the captured redoubts within it. We returned to camp early in the morning all safe and sound, except one of our Lieutenants, who had received a slight wound on the top of the shoulder by a musket shot. Seven or eight men belonging to the Infantry were killed, and a number wounded.[21]

Captain Olney, of the Light Infantry Company of the Rhode Island Regiment, was a member of the Americans that attacked redoubt 10, and he was severely wounded. He provided the following explicit description of the battle,

The column marched in silence, with guns unloaded, and in good order. I had a chance to whisper to several of my men (whom I doubted,) and told them that I had full confidence that they would act the part of brave

soldiers, let what would come; and if their guns should be shot away, not to retreat, but take the first man's gun that might be killed. When we had got about half way to the redoubt we were ordered to halt, and detach one man from each company for the forlorn hope. My men all seemed ready to go. The column then moved on; six or eight pioneers in front, as many of the forlorn hope next, then Colonel Gimatt with five or six volunteers by his side, then my platoon, being the front of the column. When we came near the front of the abatis, the enemy fired a full body of musketry. At this, our men broke silence and huzzaed; and as the order for silence seemed broken by every one, I huzzaed with all my power, saying, see how frightened they are, they fire right into the air. The pioneers began to cut off the abatis, which were the trunks of trees with the trunk part fixed in the ground, the limbs made sharp, and pointed towards us.

This seemed tedious work, in the dark, within three rods of the enemy; and I ran to the right to look a place to crawl through, but returned in a hurry, without success, fearing the men would get through first; as it happened, I made out to get through first; as it happened, I made out to get through about the first, and entered the ditch; and when I found my men to the number of ten or twelve had arrived, I stepped through between two palisades, (one having been shot off to make room,) on to the parapet, and called out in a tone as if there was no danger, Captain Olney's company, form here! On this I had not less than six or eight bayonets pushed at me; I parried as well as I could with my espontoon, but they broke off the blade part, and their bayonets slid along the handle of my espontoon and scaled my fingers; one bayonet pierced my thigh, another stabbed me in the abdomen just above the hip-bone. One fellow fired at me, and I thought the ball took effect in my arm; by the light of his gun I made a thrust with the remains of my espontoon, in order to injure the sight of his eyes; but as it happened, I only made a hard stroke in his forehead. At this instant two of my men, John Strange and Benjamin Bennett, who had loaded their guns while they were in the ditch, came up and fired upon the enemy, who part ran away and some surrendered; so that we entered the redoubt without further opposition.

My sergeant, Edward Butterick, to whom I was much indebted for his bravery, helped me nearly all this affray; and received a prick of the enemy's bayonet, in his stomach. Sergeant Brown was also in time, but attempting to load his gun, received a bayonet wound in his hand. Colonel Gimatt was wounded with a musket ball in the foot, about the first fire of the enemy; and I suppose it took all the volunteers to carry him off, as I never saw any of them afterwards. When most of the regiment had got into the redoubt, I directed them to *form in order*. Major Willis's post being in the rear; I supposed he got in about the time I was carried away with the wounded.[22]

During the short time Olney was on the parapet, a pistol was aimed at his head by one of the British close by, which, had it discharged, might have caused his death. A private soldier named John Strange, who was a drummer in the company, was the third soldier that entered the redoubt and he struck down the arm of the person who held the pistol. The blow was given with such force that the English soldier lost his arm.

The bayonet wound, which Captain Olney received, was so severe that he had to hold his bowels in by pressing both his hands over the wound. When he was examined the next day, his left arm had turned black about three or four inches in length but the skin was not broken. The stab in his thigh was slight, but the stab in the hip was thought to be mortal by the surgeons. He was carried to the hospital at Williamsburg, and in about three weeks he rejoined the regiment. He was disappointed that he missed the surrender ceremony, for which he said he had fought so long and hard. He did receive a personal letter from Lafayette mentioning his bravery, which was passed on to Washington.

Royal Jennings was in the militia at the age of eighteen and wrote about the assault in his pension application (S154), "We advanced so near them that if we could see a small opening we could go shoot a rifle ball into the fort."

French attack on redoubt No. 9:

As the French left their trench, Colonel Deux-Ponts was joined by several uninvited officers. They were Chevalier de Lameth, Comte Charles de Damas, and Comte de Vauban. Colonel Deux-Ponts tried to get them to return to the French lines, but the chance for glory was too great and the three men refused.

The French troops advanced quietly under cover of darkness and reached the first entrenchments without alerting the enemy. The snappers, with hatchets in hand, went to work on the stakes guarding the redoubt. Soon British gunfire opened up on the French troops.

At redoubt No. 10, Lafayette sent an aid, eighteen year old militia Lieutenant Mordecai Barbour, through the terrible fire of the whole British line to the Baron de Viomenil with the message, "I am in my redoubt; where are your?" It is possible that in the back of Lafayette's mind he remembered how Baron de Viomenil spoke with contempt of his militia. Major Barbour was wounded before he reached the French attackers, but he still delivered his message. Barbour would later lead a regiment in the War of 1812.

The French officer, at the head of his column, waited patiently under fire of the enemy waiting for his snappers to clear away the abatis. "Tell the marquis I am not in mine, but will be in five minutes."[23]

Charles de Lameth reached the parapet first, as he turned to cheer the men on two bullets struck him. One ball shattered his right knee, and the other ball passed through his left thigh. The second man to reach the top was Baron de l'Estrade, who was knocked down by a wounded soldier. The Baron rose again and led his men into the redoubt.

As promised, the French troops entered the redoubt in five minutes by the beat of the drum and in order, as if they were marching down the street. This action showed discipline, bravery, and coolness, but it cost them in the number of their men killed and wounded.

The enemy gathered themselves behind a sort of entrenchment composed of casks, which offered them little protection. The French officers were about to order a charge with bayonets, when the English laid down their weapons and surrendered. A great cry of "Vive le Roi" [Long live the King] echoed through the dark night.

"Never did I behold a more majestic spectacle. I did not stay there long; I had to attend to the wounded, to have order preserved amongst the prisoners, and to make arrangements for holding the post I had just captured," said Guillaume de Derux-Pontsd.[24]

George Daniel Flohr was a German who joined for an eight year enlistment in the French Royal Deux-Ponts Regiment. He was one of the soldiers that attacked redoubt 9, and in his journal he wrote of the confusion inside the redoubt,

> Anyone can imagine what happened once we were inside the redoubt. People of four nations were thrown together: Frenchmen, English, Scots, and Germans ... the soldiers ... were so furious that our people were killing one another: The French were striking down everyone in a blue coat. Since the Deux-Ponts wore blue, many of us were stabbed to death. Some of the Hessian and Anspach troops [German units in the British army] wore uniforms almost identical to ours, and the English wore red that in the dark of night seemed blue as well, so things went very unmercifully.[25]

The casualty numbers for the attack were: fifteen killed and seventy-seven wounded for the French; and eighteen killed and about fifty captured and wounded for the British. The attack took about ten minutes.

Jean-Baptgiste Antoine de Verger was a French officer in the Royal Deux-Ponts Regiment. He kept a journal of his time at Yorktown, and he was also noted for his drawings of what he saw. He was with the soldiers that assaulted redoubt No. 9,

> The attack ordered on the two advanced redoubts of the enemy, one resting on the river, the other on its left, was executed at nightfall. The American light infantry, supported by two of their trench battalions, under the command of the Marquis de La Fayette, attacked the river redoubt [British No. 10] and captured it at bayonet point with the loss of 4 officers wounded and 20 men killed or wounded. The French troops were ordered to attack the other redoubt [British No. 9]. The overall commander was the Baron de Viomenil, who debouched with the troops and led them in perfect order and absolute silence.
>
> The enemy discovered the column early and opened a very lively musket fire upon it. We found their abatis in far better condition than we had anticipated, since much of our artillery had been battering the redoubt for several days. Ignoring the enemy fire and slashing those that resisted with their axes, our pioneers had opened passages for us through which the grenadiers and chasseurs of the Royal Deux-Ponts and Gatinais regiments entered the fosses together with the aforementioned pioneers, who were still obliged to cut through several palisades to open the fraises of the redoubt. These same grenadiers and chasseurs took advantage of the openings to mount the parapet, where they formed up and soon forced the surviving enemies to surrender. Several, wishing to continue the fight with bayonets, paid with their lives.
>
> We captured 3 officers and 40 men, after counting 18 dead. Another 120, under a lieutenant colonel, escaped. During the attack our loss in officers and men was about 80 killed or wounded. The enemy at once commenced a lively cannonade on the redoubt we had just captured, killing and wounding many men
>
> The moment the redoubt was taken, the men cried "Vive le Roi!" [Long live the King] which was echoed along our whole line. This the English took to be the signal for a general assault and rained on us a volley of musketry accompanied by quantities of bombs and shells from all their redoubts and batteries.[26]

Count William de Deux-Ponts led French troops attacking redoubt 9. British Colonel Tarleton in his book mentioned the assault, and he wrote that Count William was "amongst the foremost of the assailants." This statement coming from a British officer would indicate that the Count's bravery must have been conspicuous. This is part of what happened that the Count wrote in his journal,

The Baron de Viomesnil ordered me to come to him on our arrival at the beginning of the trenches. I was not mistaken as to the object for which he intended me. A moment afterwards he confirmed my opinion, telling me that I should make the attack on one of the redoubts which obstructed the continuation of our second parallel. The General ordered me at once to form my battalion, and to lead it to that part of the trenches nearest to which we ought to come out. I called together the captains of my battalion, and told them the duty with which we were honored. I had no occasion to excite their courage, nor that of the troops whom I commanded; but it was my duty to let them know the wishes of the General, and the exact order in which we were to attack the enemy.

We then started to go into the trenches; we passed by many troops, either of the trenches, of workmen, or of the auxiliary grenadiers and chasseurs. Everybody wished me success and glory, and expressed regrets at not being able to go with me. That moment seemed to me very sweet, and was very elevating to the soul and animating to the courage. My brother,—especially, my brother, and I never shall forget it,—gave me marks of a tenderness which penetrated to the bottom of my heart. I reached the place that the Baron de Viomesnil had indicated to me; I there awaited nightfall; and shortly after dark, the General ordered me to leave the trenches, and to draw up my column in the order of attack. He informed me of the signal of six consecutive shells, fired from one of our batteries, at which I was to advance; and in this position I awaited the signal agreed upon.

Before starting, I had ordered that no one should fire before reaching the crest of the parapet of the redoubt; and when established upon the parapet, that no one should jump into the works before receiving the orders to do so. The six shells were fired at last; and I advanced in the greatest silence; at a hundred and twenty or thirty paces, we were discovered; and the Hessian soldier who was stationed as a sentinel on the parapet, cried out "Werda"? [Who comes there?] (* The English officers taken in the redoubt have told me since, that the moment we were discovered was seized by the English commander, named MacPherson, and by thirty men, to save themselves ignominiously) to which we did not reply, but hastened our steps. The enemy opened fire the instant after the "Werda." We lost not a moment in reaching the abatis, which being strong and well preserved, at about twenty-five paces from the redoubt, cost us many men, and stopped us for some minutes, but was cleared away with brave determination; we threw ourselves into the ditch at once, and each one sought to break through the fraises, and to mount the parapet (That was not an easy thing to do. I could not have succeeded without aid. I had fallen back into the ditch after a first attempt. M. de Sillegue, a young officer of the chasseurs of Gatinois, who was ahead of me, saw my difficulty, and gave me his arm to assist me iu getting up. He received at nearly the same time a musket shot in the thigh.)

We reached there at first in small numbers, and I gave the order to fire; the enemy kept up a sharp fire, and charged us at the point of the bayonet; but no one was driven back. The carpenters, who had worked hard on their part, had made some breaches in the palisades, which helped the main body of the troops in mounting. The parapet was becoming manned visibly.

Our fire was increasing, and making terrible havoc among the enemy, who had placed themselves behind a kind of intrenchment of barrels, where they were well massed, and where all our shots told. We succeeded at the moment when I wished to give the order to leap into the redoubt and charge upon the enemy with the bayonet; then they laid down their arms, and we leaped in with more tranquillity and less risk. I shouted immediately the cry of Vive le Roi, which was repeated by all the grenadiers and chasseurs who were in good condition, by all the troops in the trenches, and to which the enemy replied by a general discharge of artillery and musketry.

The Baron de Viomesnil came to give me orders to be prepared for a vigorous defence, as it would be important for the enemy to attempt to retake this work. An active enemy would not have failed, and the Baron de Viomesnil judged the English general by himself. I made my dispositions to the best of my ability; the enemy showered bullets upon us. I raised my head above the parapet, and at the same time a ball, which ricochetted in the parapet, and passed very near my head, covered my face with sand and gravel. I suffered much, and was obliged to leave the place, and to be con- ducted to the ambulance.[27]

The French learned from some of the prisoners that before the assault British Major McPherson, the commanding officer of the redoubt, had left with thirty men. This may have been the reason the British surrendered so quickly and did not fight to the last man.

While the battle was being fought:

Washington watched the assault from the grand battery with his staff, and with General Lincoln, General Knox, and their staffs. While the assault was going on, the English kept up a very heavy fire of cannon and musketry along the whole line. One of Washington's aids, Colonel Cobb, said to him, "Sir, you are too much exposed here. Had you not better step a little back?" "Colonel Cobb," answered Washington, "if you are afraid, you have the liberty to step back."

Dr. Munson was at the main battery with Washington watching the assault. Munson reported, "While the attack was progressing a musket ball rolled along a cannon, and fell at the feet of Washington. General Knox seized him by the arm, and said; 'My dear General, we can't spare you yet!' Washington replied, 'It is a spent ball, and no harm is done.' When the attack was over, Washington turned to Knox and said, 'The work is done, and well done, William, hand me my horse.'"[28] Soon after the final assault the sky clouded over, and it began to rain.

American Captain James Duncan was in the trench hundreds of yards from redoubt No. 9 and 10. He was not aware that the redoubts were being attacked that evening. He wrote in his journal about his brush with death.

> The enemy last night kept up a continual blaze from several pieces of cannon of nine royals [royal was a small mortar carrying a shell with a diameter of 5.5 inches.] and some howitzers. Early in the night the fire was directed against the French, who were just to our left, but about 10 o'clock our people began to erect a battery. They soon discovered us, and changed the direction of their fire. It happen to be our lot to lie in the trenches just in the rear of the battery exposed to all their fire; and now ere I to recount all the miraculous escapes I made that night; I would almost be incredible. I cannot, however, but take notice of a remarkable and miraculous one indeed. About midnight the sentry called "A shell!" I jumped up and immediately to watch the direction, but had no suspicion of its coming so near until it fell in the center of the trench, within less than two feet of me. I immediately flung myself on the banques among some arms, and although the explosion was very sudden, and the trench as full of men as it could possibly contain, yet not a single man was killed and only two of my own company slightly wounded. [29]

Colonel St. George Tucker was on duty in the trenches and did not take part in the assault on the redoubts. He described some close brushes with enemy artillery shells,

> Last night I was on Duty again. The party under my Comand was employ'd in erecting a Battery opposite the South East End of Secry Nelsons house, at the distance of about two hundred Yards from one of the Enemies Batteries and a Redoubt from which they discharged Shells. The French at the same time were constructing two considerable Batteries further on the left, the furthest is about one hundred & fifty Yards in front of the Enemies Battery in Front of Secry Nelson's house. The other about one hundred and seventy Yards & on the Flank of the same Work, between our Battery and these is a Redoubt which I apprehend is intended as a Bomb Battery. The Enemy kept up an extremely hot fire during night but with no other Injury in the Battery

where I was employd than the wounding two men by the bursting of a shell. As soon as it was so light as for them to discover our situation (for the work was begun after Dark) they annoyd us excessively with round and Grape Shot as well as Shells of all which there was an incessant Fire untill twelve OClock when I was relieved. We lost one Man killd & eight wounded after day Light, the Continental Troops. had an Officer & nine or ten Men killd or wounded in the same Battery.As we march'd out of the Trenches a Shell fell in among the first plattoon of my Men, and wounded three men very badly & Several others slightly, tho' within ten Foot of it I was happy enough to escape without Injury as I did from five others which burst within that or near the same. Distance in the Course of the Morning. The Enemy have continued a very galling Fire from their Works the whole Day. In the morning several Yagers or Rifle men fired at us for some time—A few rifle men being posted to return their Fire soon silenc'd it.[30]

After the capture of the redoubts:

About fifteen minutes after both redoubts had been captured, firing broke out on the far left of the French line. Monsieur de Custine had gotten the times of the fake attack mixed up and began the firing after the attack was over. Baron von Closen later learned from a friend that de Custine had been drunk during and after the orders to fire were given.

As soon as the redoubts were secured, 500 workmen began working to continue the parallel between the two newly captured redoubts. They were nearly finished by the time the sun rose. Lieutenant John Bell Tilden was in a unit that provided cover for the attackers. He wrote in his journal,

> Our line at the commencement of ye attack marched up as a covering party through a very heavy fire. The enemy lost Major Campbell, two captains, two subalterns and upwards of a hundred men killed, wounded and prisoners. The same night drew a parallel from the river to the batteries in ye second line, including ye two redoubts we i.e. Penna. Line lay a foundation for a ten gun battery on our line, between the two redoubts in front of ye enemy fire gun battery, ye distance not two hundred yards. The enemy threw a number of shells among us but fortunately did no damage.[31]

Washington made a brief note of the assault in his diary,

> The day was spent in compleating our parallel, and maturing the Batteries of the second parallel. The old batteries were principally directed against the abattis & salient angles of the enemys advanced redoubts on their extreme right & left to prepare them for the intended assault for which the necessary dispositions were made for attacking the two on the left and,
>
> At half after Six in the Evening both were carried, that on their left (on the Bank of the river) by the Americans and the other by the French Troops. The Baron Viominel commanded the left attack & the Marqs. de la fayette the right on which the light Infantry were employed.
>
> In the left redoubt (assaulted by the Americans) there were abt. 45 men under the command of a Major Campbell; of which the Major a Captn. & Ensign, with 17 Men were made Prisoners. But few were killed on the part of the Enemy & the remainder of the Garrison escaped. The right Redoubt attacked by the French, consisted of abt. 120 Men, commanded by a Lieutenant Colo. of these 18 were killed, & 42 taken Prisoners, among the Prisoners were a Captain and two Lieutenants. The bravery exhibited by the attacking Troops was emulous and praiseworthy, few cases have exhibited stronger proofs of Intripidity coolness and firmness than were shown upon this occasion. The following is our loss in these attacks and since the Investiture of York.[32]

Major Ebenezer Denny of the 4th Pennsylvania Regiment was in a battery and did not take part in the assault on the redoubts. He gave his account of the attack in his journal,

On the night of the 14th, shortly after dark, these redoubts were taken by storm; the one on our right, by the Marquis, with part of his light infantry-the other, more to our left, but partly opposite the centre of the British lines, by the French. Our batteries had kept a constant fire upon the redoubts through the day. Belonged this evening to a command detailed for the purpose of supporting the Marquis. The night was dark and favorable. Our batteries had ceased-there appeared to be a dead calm; we followed the infantry and halted about half way-kept a few minutes in suspense, when we were ordered to advance. The business was over, not a gun was fired by the assailants; the bayonet only was used; ten or twelve of the infantry were killed. French had to contend with a post of more force-their loss was considerable. Colonel Hamilton led the Marquis' advance; the British sentries hailed them-no answer made. They also hailed the French, "Who comes there?" were answered, "French grenadiers." Colonel Walter Stewart commanded the regiment of reserve which accompanied the Marquis; they were immediately employed in connecting, by a ditch and parapet, the two redoubts, and completing and connecting the same with our second parallel. The British were soon alarmed; some from each of the redoubts made their escape. The whole enemy were under arms-much firing round all their lines, but particularly toward our regiment, where the men were at work; the shot passed over. In about three quarters of an hour we were under cover. Easy digging; light sandy ground.[33]

Colonel Richard Butler of the 5th Pennsylvania Regiment wrote in his journal,

The two attacks commenced almost at the instant, and were conducted with spirit and bravery, the dispositions military, the redoubts were both carried in ten minutes, with trifling loss on all side. The prisoners were secured, and immediately the second parallel was completed. After these were carried, an alarm was spread around the British line in order to ascertain what weight of fire they would produce, which proved very faint.[34]

The following account of this attack was taken from the Boston Evening Post, November 17, 1781,

Copy of the report of his Excellency the Count de Rochambeau:

On the night between the 14th and 15th instant, the trench was mounted by the regiments of Gatinois and Royal Deuxponts, commanded by the Baron de Viomesnil, to which were added our companies of auxiliary grenadiers. We had resolved to attack as soon as dark, the two redoubts on the left of the enemy, that were detached from their other works. The Marquis de la Fayette undertook that on our right, with the American troops; the Baron de Viomesnil that on the left, with the French. Four hundred grenadiers, commanded by the Count William Deuxponts and M. de L'Estrade, lieut. colonel of Gatinois, opened the attack; they were supported by the regiment of Gatinois. The Marquis de la Fayette, and the Baron Viomesnil made so vigorous and strong disposition of their troops, that they carried two redoubts sword in hand, and. killed, wounded, or took the greater part of those who defended them. The number of prisoners amounts to seventy-three, one major and five other officers included.

The troops, both American and French, have shown the most distinguished courage. The Count William Deuxponts was slightly wounded by a cannon ball; he is not in the least danger. The Chev- alier de la Methe, Adjutant Quarter-Master-General, has been severely wounded in both knees by two different musket balls. M. de Sireuil, captain of the chasseurs of the regiment of Aginois, and two other officers of the same regiment have been wounded. 'Tis the third time that M. de Sireuil, though very young, has been wounded; un- luckily, this time, the wound is very dangerous. We have had ten men killed or wounded. The troops are full of the highest praises of the Baron de Viomesnil, who likewise is exceedingly pleased with their courage and firmness.

I have ordered two days' pay to be distributed to the four companies of grenadiers and chasseurs of the regiment of Gatinois and Royal Deuxponts, besides a considerable reward to the ax-bearers and carpenters, who open the way for the troops through the abattis and pallisadoes.[35]

After the battle, General Rochambeau filed his report for the King of France. Once the King read the report, he signed an order which restored to the Grenadier Regiment of Gatenois the honored name of "Royal Auvergne sans tache."

For his conduct during the battle Count William De Deux-Ponts, received the title of Chevalier in the Military Order of St. Louis. In his journal he gave his men praise, "With troops so good, so brave, and so disciplined as those I have the honor to lead against the enemy, one can undertake anything, and be sure of succeeding."[36]

The Continental Congress forbid General Washington from granting commissions and promotions in rank to recognize merit. Washington wanted to honor merit, especially among enlisted soldiers, so he established the Badge of Military Merit on August 7, 1782. This badge was given to three men along with a brace of silver-mounted pistols.

On May 3, 1783 a badge was presented to William Brown of the 5th Connecticut Regiment. No record of his citation exists, but it is believed that he was given the badge because of his bravery on the assault of redoubt No. 10 at Yorktown. Years later the badge of Military Merit was replaced with the Purple Heart Medal.

Doctor James Thacher knew that after the assault on the redoubts, he was going to be a very busy man. He was sent for even before the firing had stopped. He wrote in his journal,

> I was desired to visit the wounded in the fort, even before the balls had ceased whistling about my ears, and saw a sergeant and eight men in the ditch. A captain of our infantry, belonging to New Hampshire, threatened to take the life of Major Campbell, to avenge the death of his favorite, Colonel Scammel, but Colonel Hamilton interposed and not a man was killed after he ceased to resist. During the assault, the British kept up an incessant firing of cannon and musketry from their whole line.[37]

It should be noted here that later a small controversy arose over who was in command of the Americans that attacked redoubt 10. Hamilton commanded the regiment that breached the redoubt, and he was given most of the credit for its capture. However, it was later pointed out in a book on the life of General Peter Muhlenberg, written by his nephew, that the General was actually in command. The regiment led by Hamilton was part of a light brigade under the command of Muhlenberg.

General Muhlenberg, after entering the redoubt, was slightly wounded; the only dispatch, therefore, reporting its capture, was the one written by Colonel Hamilton.[38] Major Isaac Heydt said in 1840 that General Muhlenberg advanced at the head of Barber's regiment and in person led the storming party. Many accounts reported that Hamilton's regiment was the first over the walls of the redoubt.

Hamilton was happy to take any credit for actions during the siege that would help advance his political career. Muhlenberg was content to remain in the shadows concerning his actions at redoubt 10. Both men showed their bravery that night on October 14th and deserved any glory thrown their way.

Hospitals:

The American wing of the army had a hospital on the field in the rear of General Lafayette's headquarters. The chief doctor and surgeon was De. James Craik, and one of the doctors serving with him was Dr. James Thacher.

The French wing also had a field hospital, which was used for immediate problems. The main hospital was located at Williamsburg, and the wounded were taken there in ambulances. These were two or three wheeled horse drawn wagons. On the night of the assault on the redoubts there were already around 500 sick troops in the hospital due to malaria.

Claude Blanchard Commissary of the French Auxiliary Army had for several days helped with the sick and wounded wrote in his journal, "I spent two or three hours at the ambulance in the midst of these wounded, a part of whom I despatched to Williamsburg. At this time I had more than five hundred sick, of whom twenty were officers."[39]

Now that redoubts 9 and 10 were captured, the army of Lord Cornwallis was completely hemmed in, and the allies could send in cannon shells at very close range [less than 300 yards].

It must be noted here that in several early publications of the American Revolution, both in Europe and America, for example; Gordon's *History of the American War*, and Shepherd's *A History of the American Revolution*, both published in the early 1800's, slander was made of two of the American leaders. These authors suggested that Generals Washington and Lafayette ordered the Americans to give no quarter to the British, when they stormed redoubt No. 10.

Shepherd wrote in his book, "It must be to the honor of the American soldiers, that though in revenge for a massacre recently committed at New London, in Connecticut, by a body of troops under the command of the renegade Arnold, they had been ordered to take no prisoners, they foreborn to comply with this requisition, and when they had penetrated into the redoubt, spared every man who ceased to resist."[40]

The authors that wrote these comments have given no proof of it occurring. It is claimed that the orders were given to Alexander Hamilton. Twenty years after the event Alexander Hamilton wrote to the editor of the Evening Post in New York City, "Positively, and unequivocally, I declare that no such or similar order was ever by me received, or understood to have been given, nor any intimation or hint resembling it."[41]

Chapter 10

A Desperate Attempt to Escape

"Thus expired the last hope of the British army." ---Colonel Tarleton on the failure of the escape to Gloucester

Monday October 15, & Tuesday October 16, 1781

(Turning cold and heavy storms)

Now in command of redoubts 9 and 10, Washington was able to bombard the town on three sides. Cornwallis had his batteries open fire on the allied positions and then ordered a storming party to attack allied lines. During the night of the 16th at about four in the morning, the British attacked two unfinished allied batteries, one French and one American. They moved quietly from the hornworks into a French communication trench that took them to the French battery. The French soldiers were asleep and were bayonetted by the English troops. Then they spiked the four cannons in the battery.

During this time, another group of the attackers went to an American battery. They slipped pass the sentries by posing as French soldiers. They charged the Americans, of Colonel Henry Skipwith's Virginia Militia, defending the battery. The Americans had left their weapons in the trench behind them, so they immediately fled. The British used their bayonets to spike the three cannons.

Once discovered, an alarm went out and French reinforcements rushed to the batteries. The British retreated back to their lines and left behind eight dead and twelve captured. The British attackers returned to their lines and claimed to have spiked eleven cannons and killed over 100 Frenchmen.

By morning all the spiked cannons were repaired. The French and American gunners then engaged in a friendly competition to see who could do the most damage to the British positions. As the bombardment continued during the day, Cornwallis ordered boats brought to the shore for a daring escape.

All day on the 16th the allies worked on finishing the new line. They continued to bombard the British at close range, and that evening they increased their security in case the British were going to send out raiding parties again. The allies now had nearly 100 cannons, both large and small, compared to perhaps a dozen British guns. The firing of the new batteries brought great interest from the troops. Many of them flocked to the new trenches to watch the bombardment. This made it necessary to issue orders that no one could enter the new trenches without a pass from the commander of them.

Cornwallis knew that his defense would not be able to hold against this new bombardment, so he began to plan for an escape.

British forces:

General Cornwallis wrote to General Clinton in New York to give him the news that his situation in Yorktown had gone from bad to worse,

> Last evening the Enemy carried my two advanced Redoubts on the left by Storm, and during the Night have included them in their Second Parallel, which they are at present busy in perfecting. My Situation now becomes very critical. We dare not shew a Gun to their old Batteries, and I expect their new ones will be open to-Morrow Morning. Experiences has shewn that our fresh earthen Works do not resist their powerful Artillery, so that we shall soon be exposed to an Assault in ruined Works, in bad position and with weakened Numbers.
>
> The Safety of the Place is therefore so precarious that I cannot recommend that the Fleet and Army should run great Risque, in endeavouring to save us.[1]

Bartholomew James wrote in his journal, "The enemy lost no time in throwing up a line of communication between the two flanking redoubts, which they perfected before daylight, and from which they could now rake the whole garrison. The fire continued as usual without intermission."[2]

Some of Cornwallis's officers were not happy with his inactivity to the allied threat. They encouraged the general to make some sort of an attack upon the enemy. Around five in the morning Cornwallis ordered 350 men [a few sources reported that 600 men were used] of the 80th foot guards under the command of Colonel Lake, and a detachment of Light Infantry, under Major Armstrong to attack the advanced posts of the French and Americans. During the charge on the allied position Major Armstrong urged his men on by crying, "Push on my brave boys, and skin the bastards!"[3]

The British were forced to retreat to the safety of their own lines when Chevalier de Chatelus marched toward them with reinforcements. In all, the British claimed to have killed about 100 French troops, and spiked eleven cannons. According to some allied accounts there were thirteen British troops killed, one wounded, and ten captured. The attack was daring but had little effect on the allied operations.

Captain Johann Ewald, a Hessian officer, was the only source that described an improper spiking of the allied guns. He wrote in his journal a critical account of the action,

> Since the accomplishment of a plan is seldom completely successful in this war, the English artillerists, who had been ordered to spike the guns, had brought along wheel nails to serve for spiking, which were too large, instead of the proper steel spikes. For that reason the English soldiers had to stick their bayonet points in the vents and break them off to spike the guns. Now it was thought, the guns had been made useless, and there was rejoicing over the stroke. A great many fops [a dandy] assured me: "This stroke will save us. This will take a great amount of time until the enemy can repair this loss. By God, eleven cannons is a fine thing!"
>
> In their joy, the poor benighted devils forgot that such a loss is easily replaced through the reserve train, and that all this merely amounts to a respite for the besieged.

> It was about ten o'clock in the morning, when I was standing near the water with my eyes turned toward the redoubts. I had listened to this foolish talk with annoyance, for everything irritated me now since, I had to endure daily the most severe attacks of fever, during which my nerves suffered extremely. Suddenly the spiked guns began to play frightfully. Within an hour they battered our works so badly in the flank and rear that all our batteries and works were silenced within a few hours. Thereupon Lord Cornwallis thought of nothing else but to cut his way through on the Gloucester side, because he had to fear being taken by storm with each passing hour. As soon as night fell, a number of boats were brought to the shore in which a part of the best men who were still healthy were to be passed over to Gloucester.[4]

Hessian soldier Johann Dohla wrote in his diary, "I went on watch in our defenses as lance corporal. The bombardment continued on both sides throughout the day and night, however, the enemy was very quiet and fired only a few bombs at us. But our continued firing throughout the entire night."[5]

Preparing for escape:

Tarleton wrote in his book, "A retreat by Gloucester was the only expedient that now presented itself to avert the mortification of a surrender, or the destruction of a storm. Though this plan appeared less practicable than when first proposed, and was adopted at this crisis, as the last resource, it yet afforded some hopes of success."[6]

Faced with increasing losses from the allied artillery, Cornwallis decided that crossing over to Gloucester with the majority of his troops, and leaving a small group behind to surrender, was his best option. If he could attack and defeat Lauzun's Legion at Gloucester, he could capture his horses and then move rapidly away from the allied forces. With a little luck he might be able to join forces with Clinton in New York. The plan was very risky and had little chance for success, but Cornwallis had run out of options.

Just before midnight of the 16th, the British were able to salvage sixteen boats that were seaworthy. They determined that it would require at least three roundtrips to carry the men across the York River and to Gloucester. Cornwallis sent Lord Chewton to Gloucester with instructions for Tarleton to prepare for an attack upon De Choisy at daybreak.

There was a good chance that an attack on De Choisy would take him by surprise. There was a spy in Gloucester that could have taken the Queen's Rangers to the rear of the allied post by a secret path.

In Yorktown British troops were relieved by German Hessians, who then manned the trenches. The Germans, combined with some Navy gunners, kept up fire against the allies to cover the rest of the army's retreat across the river. Cornwallis decided to go on the second wave across the river, so he could have time to write a letter to Washington. In the letter he asked Washington to show mercy to the men left behind.

As the first group of men rowed across the York River, the winds began to pick up and a thunderstorm blew in. The boats began to bounce around in the high waves, heavy rain fell, and the winds grew in intensity. Two of the boats were blown off course and landed back on the

Yorktown side shore where the frightened men were taken prisoner by the Americans. Fourteen boats made it across the river, and the water soaked men went ashore safely. It was impossible to bring any more men across until the storm blew itself out.

The weather did not break until around two in the morning. Cornwallis knew this would not be enough time to gather the scattered boats, so the escape was called off. Around noon the next day, he had the men that crossed earlier to Gloucester brought back. It was now clear to the British that their choice was annihilation or surrender.

Hessian Captain Johann Ewald probably described the worst night of his life due to the weather and his illness,

> As soon as night fell, a number of boats were brought to the shore in which a part of the best men who were still healthy were to be passed over to Gloucester. But such a violent storm arose that several boats capsized, whereupon the entire praiseworthy plan came to a standstill.
>
> I will not forget this past night in all my life. Choisy threatened to seize us with sword in hand. I had to command two redoubts and a battery for which I was responsible. It was as dark as a sack, and one could neither see nor hear anything because of the awful downpour and heavy gale. Moreover, there was a most severe thunderstorm, but the violent flashes of lightning benefited us, since we could at least see around us for an instant. And to make me really feel the harshness of my wretched life, the fever suddenly attacked me at midnight in the most horrible manner. I was driven to take the most dreadful remedy in the world: two tablespoons full of China powder mixed with the strongest rum. In this desperate situation, I asked for nothing more from nature than to keep my head up during this night—or death. It helped. The fever subsided, and I was quite lively afterward. I thanked God and left everything in His Hands.[7]

Cornwallis sent a letter to Clinton on the 20th and described the failure of the escape attempt to Gloucester,

> At this time we knew that there was no part of the whole front attacked on which we could show a single gun, and our shells were nearly expended. I therefore had only to choose between preparing to surrender next day, or endeavoring to get off with the greatest part of the troops, and I determined to attempt the latter.
>
> Sixteen large boats were ordered to be in readiness to receive troops precisely at ten o'clock. With these I hoped to pass the infantry during the night, abandoning our baggage, and leaving a detachment to capitulate for the towns-people, and the sick and wounded, on which subject a letter was ready to be delivered to General Washington. With upmost secrecy the light infantry, greater part of the guards, and part of the Twenty-third regiment landed at Gloucester; but at this critical moment, the weather, from being moderate and calm, changed to a most violent storm of wind and rain, and drove all the boats, some of which had troops on board, down the river.
>
> In this situation with my little force divided, the enemy's batteries opened at daybreak; the passage between this place and Gloucester was much exposed; but the boats now returned, they were ordered to bring back the troops, and they joined us in the forenoon without much loss. Our works were in the meantime going to ruin. We had at that time could not fire a single gun, only one eight-inch and a little more than one hundred cohorn shells remained. I therefore proposed to capitulate.[8]

When it became apparent that the escape to Gloucester was not possible, Tarleton wrote, "Thus expired the last hope of the British army."[9]

Americans/French forces

In his diary Baron Cromot de Bourg said that during the early morning hours 100 men were used to protect the batteries, while 400 men were used to improve the parallel and redoubts. He also wrote, "Towards five o'clock in the morning the enemy made a sortie; they entered a redoubt and our batteries where they imperfectly spiked four guns which again fired six hours afterwards."[10]

Count William de Deux-Ponts gave an account in his journal as to why the British attack on a battery was successful, "The trenches were not guarded with all desirable precaution; many slept; there were few sentinels; a picket that distrusted nothing; some batteries, where there were nobody."[11]

Axel de Fersen wrote in his journal about the attack on the French redoubt, "They were repulsed at once, and we had about twenty men killed and wounded. Our soldiers, who have been extremely tired since the beginning of the siege, were asleep and surprised."[12]

Colonel John Lamb wrote in his memoirs about the attack, "A force under Col. Abercrombie was sent against two of the French redoubts, without the discharge of a gun. The war cry of the Scottish Colonel, as he reached the trenches, was distinctly heard in the American batteries, 'skiver the beggars' was better understood there, than by those in the disputed redoubts."[13]

Major Ebenezer Denny wrote in his diary, "Just before day the enemy made a sortie, spiked the guns in two batteries and retired. Our troops in the parallel scarcely knew of their approach until they were off; the thing was done silently and in an instant. The batteries stood in advance of the lines, and none within but artillery. This day, the 16th, our division manned the lines-firing continued without intermission. Pretty strong detachments posted in each battery overnight."[14]

Private John Hudson wrote about the British attack and the precautions taken by the allies afterwards,

> One night during the siege a major of the 43d regiment, sallied our on the besiegers with his command of several hundreds, and actually captured one of the French batteries, spiking their guns. By this time the whole line had taken the alarm, and he met with so warm a reception, that he was glad to regain the town, with such of his troops as he was not obliged to leave behind dead and wounded upon the field.
>
> After this, and as a consequence of this incident, we had a piquet guard placed in advance of our batteries, and just under the muzzle of the enemy's guns. I was myself one of that guard one night. We had double centinels placed all along under the line of the British works, who were stationed each with one knee to the ground and the gun cocked lying on the other, our hail being to give three smart taps on our cartouch boxes. Our instructions were to fire instantly when the same signal was not repeated.
>
> Those taps resembled greatly the flapping of the wings of the turkey buzzard, which abounded from the number of the unburied dead lying on the neighborhood, and would have been ascribed by the enemy to these birds, if the din of the cannon had permitted the signal, during any interval of their discharges, to be heard and noticed.[15]

Colonel Richard Butler in his diary gave a description of the French counterattack that killed several British troops, "He [Count de Noailles] ordered the Grenadiers to charge bayonet and rush on, which they did with great spirit crying Long live the King, and to use the British phrase skivered eight of the Guards and Infantry, and took twelve prisoners, and drove them quite off."[16]

St. George Tucker gave an account of the early morning British attack in his journal,

> Just at Daybreak this Morning the Enemy made a Sally & attack'd the Redoubt which the French had taken the night before—[Major Henry] Skipwith with one hundred Men was in the Redoubt; their Arms were deposited in the Trenches behind—As soon as the Enemy were discoverd he march'd his Men out of the Redoubt to take their Arms—by this time the Enemy had gained the parapet but the French Troops who formed the covering party rushing in immediately, soon repulsed them. At the same time the Enemy attackd another Redoubt further on our left and scaling the Works with great Alacrity Spiked up eight pieces of Cannon which were intended for a Battery on which we were at that time employ'd. They were immediately after repulsed—The Cannon were cleared again before the Battery was in readiness to mount them, So that they effected no good purpose by the Sally & lost some Men; six or eight were killed in the Redoubt where Skipwith was stationed. This Afternoon one of our Batteries on the second parallel was opened—All those on the first I believe are dismantled—At least the two principal ones are. As the Genl. Orders of to day prohibit any officer from entering the Trenches I must write by Guess hereafter except when I go upon Duty.[17]

George Washington made a passing mention of the British attack in a letter he sent to Thomas McKean,

> The enemy last night made a sortie for the first time. They entered one of the French and one of the American Batteries on the second parallel which were unfinished. They had only time to thrust the points of their Bayonets into four pieces of the French and two of the American Artillery and beat them off, but the strikes were easily extracted. They were repulsed the moment the supporting Troops came up, leaving behind them seven or eight dead and six prisoners. The French had four officers and twelve privates killed and wounded, and we had one serjeant mortally wounded.[18]

Henry Dearborn wrote in his journal, "During the day sixteen deserters came out this morning who say the Troops are very much fatigued, with excessive hard duty, & that they are very sickly."[19]

The General Orders of Washington, for October 15, praised the repelling of the British attack, and it also contained some very good news for hungry troops,

> Major General the Marquis de la Fayette's division will mount in the Trenches tomorrow.
>
> The Commander in Chief congratulates the Allied Army on the Success of the Enterprize last evening against the two important works on the left of the enemys line: He requests the Baron Viomenil who commanded the French Grenadiers and Chasseurs and the Marquis de la Fayette who commanded the American Light Infantry to accept his warmest acknowledgements for the excellency of their dispositions and for their own Gallant Conduct upon the occasion and he begs them to present his thanks to every individual officer and to the Men of their respective Commands for the Spirit and Rapidity with which they advanced to the Attacks and for the admirable Firmness with which they supported themselves under the fire of the Enemy without returning a Shot.

> The General reflects with the highest degree of pleasure on the Confidence which the Troops of the two Nations must hereafter have in each other. Assured of mutual support he is convinced there is no danger which they will not chearfully encounter—no difficulty which they will not bravely overcome.
>
> The troops will be supplied with fresh beef to thursday next inclusive, they will receive three pints of salt to every one hundred rations for the allowance of Wednesday and Thursday.[20]

Joseph Plumb Martin was given the day off after the attack on redoubt 10. He never mentioned in his diary about the British attack of the 16th. He spent his day off exploring the woods away from the battle,

> Being off duty one day, several of us went into the woods and fields in search of nuts; returning across the fields, which lay all common, we came across a number of horses at pasture; thinking to make a little fun for myself, I caught one of the horses and mounting him, as the Dutchman did his bear, without saddle or bridle, set off full speed for camp, guiding my nag with a stick. After I had proceeded thus for nearly a mile, my charger appeared to possess a strong inclination to return to his associates. He at length set off back with himself and me too, at full spring, I clung to him till I found he was directing his course under the limbs of a large spreading oak tree, I accordingly jumped off.[21]

On this day, Alexander Hamilton wrote to Lafayette to give him a report of his actions in the taking of redoubt 10. He passed on praise for several of his officers,

> I have the honor to render you an account of the corps under my command in your attack of last night, upon the redoubt on the left of the enemy's lines.
>
> Agreeable to your orders we advanced in two columns with unloaded arms, the right composed of Lt. Col Gimat's batalion and my own commanded by Major Fish, the left of a detachment commanded by Lt Col Laurens, destined to take the enemy in reverse, and intercept their retreat. The column on the right was preceded by a van guard of twenty men let by Lt. Mansfield, and a detachment of sappers and miners, commanded by Capt Gilliland6 for the purpose of removing obstructions.
>
> The redoubt was commanded by Major Campbell, with a detachment of British and German troops, and was completely in a state of defence.
>
> The rapidity and immediate success of the assault are the best comment on the behaviour of the troops. Lt Col Laurens distinguished himself by an exact and vigorous execution of his part of the plan, by entering the enemy's work with his corps among the foremost, and making prisoner the commanding officer of the redoubt. Lt Col Gimat's batalion which formed the van of the right attack and which fell under my immediate observation, encouraged by the decisive and animated example of their leader, advanced with an ardor and resolution superior to every obstacle. They were well seconded by Major Fish with the batalion under his command, who when the front of the column reached the abatis, unlocking his corps to the left, as he had been directed, advanced with such celerity, as to arrive in time to participate in the assault.
>
> Lt. Mansfield deserves particular commendation, for the coolness firmness and punctuality with which he conducted the van guard. Capt Olney, who commanded the first platoon of Gimats batalion is intitled to peculiar applause. He led his platoon into the work with exemplary intrepidity, and received two bayonet wounds. Capt Gilliland with the detachment of sappers and miners acquitted themselves in a manner that did them great honor.
>
> I do but justice to the several corps when I have the pleasure to assure you, there was not an officer nor soldier whose behaviour, if it could be particularized, would not have a claim to the warmest approbation. As it would have been attended with delay and loss to wait for the removal of the abatis and palisades the ardor of the troops was indulged in passing over them.
>
> There was a happy coincidence of movements. The redoubt was in the same moment inveloped and carried on every part. The enemy are intitled to the acknowlegement of an honorable defence.

> Permit me to have the satisfaction of expressing our obligations to Col Armand, Capt Segongne, The Chevalier De Fontevieux and Captain Bedkin officers of his corps, who acting upon this occasion as volunteers, proceeded at the head of the right column, and entering the redoubt among the first, by their gallant example contributed to the success of the enterprise.
>
> Our killed and wounded you will perceive by the inclosed return. I sensibly felt at a critical period the loss of the assistance of Lt. Col Gimat, who received a musket ball in his foot, which obliged him to retire from the field. Capt Bets of Lauren's corps, Capt Hunt and Lt. Mansfield of Gimats were wounded with the bayonet in gallantly entering the work. Capt Lt. Kirkpatrick of the corps of sappers and miners received a wound in the ditch.
>
> Inclosed is a return of the prisoners. The killed and wounded of the enemy did not exceed eight. Incapable of imitating examples of barbarity, and forgetting recent provocations, the soldiery spared every man, who ceased to resist.[22]

Hamilton then turned his attention toward his wife, and he wrote to her about the attack on the redoubts two days before, "Two nights ago, my Eliza, my duty and my honor obliged me to take a step in which your happiness was too much risked. I commanded an attack upon one of the enemy's redoubts; we carried it in an instant, and with little loss. You will see the particulars in the Philadelphia papers. There will be, certainly nothing more of this kind; all the rest will be approach and if there should be another occasion, it will not fall to my turn to execute it."[23]

Seventeen year old Asa Gillett from Connecticut first joined the army at the age of thirteen. He may have been one of the last American soldiers to be wounded at Yorktown during the battle. He stated in his pension application [S34898], "I was again wounded in the thigh of the left leg on the last day of the battle of Yorktown by a musket ball passing through the thigh yet without injury to the bone. The surgeon stated that I bled so profusely that I would have bled to death had no appliance been at hand."

On the 15th, Captain Stephen Olney was in the hospital recovering from the serious wounds he received storming redoubt 10. Some of his fellow officers informed him of a statement sent out by Lafayette that brought Olney even more pain. Lafayette had said that he was sorry for the misfortune of Captains Hunt and Olney.

What was upsetting to Olney was that he had suffered wounds during combat with the enemy soldiers. Hunt was in the rear and hit his ankle against a bayonet fixed to a gun that was laying on the ground. The statement implied that both men were wounded by accident. Onley immediately wrote to Lafayette to explain how he was wounded. Lafayette wrote back explaining how the mistake happened. He also wrote, "I have the highest regard for your gallantry on the occasion, and shall be always happy to render you for your services, and a testimony to the merit you are so justly entitled to."[24]

Comments about the attempted escape by the British:

Lafayette later wrote about the attempted escape by Cornwallis, "The plan was a bold one, and worthy of such a man as Cornwallis. His boats were all in readiness, and part of his troops had already landed on the opposite side of the river, when a violent tempest suddenly rendered it impossible for his to continue his operations."[25]

The aide-de-camp to Rochambeau, Axel de Fersen, wrote in his journal about the bold attempt to escape to Gloucester by Cornwallis,

> Lord Cornwallis sent two thousand men to Gloucester to force a way through for him, intending to march two hundred leagues through enemy's country to reach York [New York]. The enterprise was bold, but crazy; it might have succeeded with two hundredmen. The only fault committed by Lord Cornwallis was that of having stopped at Yorktown; that fault, however, Was not his, it was that of General Clinton, who ordered him to stay there, and he could only obey.[26]

Chapter 11

Capitulation

"Lord Cornwallis at length realizing the extreme hazard of his deplorable situation, and finding it in vain any longer to resist, has this forenoon come to the humiliating expedient of sending out a flag, requesting a cessation of hostilities for twenty four hours." ---Journal of Doctor James Thacher

Wednesday October 17, 1781

(Clear and cold at night)

The allied artillery could now bombard the British fortifications with ease. The British had practically exhausted their supply of shells and barely returned fire. Many houses in the town were greatly damaged or in complete ruin. Dead men and horses were lightly covered with dirt, which gave the British camp the smell of rotting flesh. Half of the forces were ill or too weakened to fight, and there was no hope for escape.

Bombardment of the British lines began at daybreak. Suddenly at 10 a.m., a young boy, wearing a red coat and carrying a drum, climbed up on a British parapet and beat the signal for a parley. Behind him an officer soon appeared holding a white flag. The two moved outside the British fortification. Because of the heavy cannon fire, the boy's drum could not be heard, but when the Americans saw the two moving toward them, the firing ceased. An American soldier met the British officer, blindfolded him, and sent the drummer boy back to the British lines. He then led the officer to a house at the rear of the American parallels.

Drummer for parley from Frank Leslie's Popular Monthly Vol. XII July to December, 1881, page 653.

Men on both sides watched the soldier with the white flag cross across the shell-torn ground between the two lines. Each man knew what it meant, and each felt a sense of relief.

Meanwhile, back in New York, General Clinton received a letter from Cornwallis warning that Yorktown probably could not be saved. However, Clinton continued to make plans to sail a relief force there.

British forces:

Around seven o'clock in the morning, Cornwallis and General Charles O'Hara were at the hornwork studying the allied lines. Cornwallis reluctantly called a council of war to assess the situation. It was reported in the meeting that their artillery ammunition was gone, and only 100 mortar shells were left. The medical staff reported that more and more men were reporting sick or wounded. The British knew that there was only one thing left to do, and that was to surrender.

About 10 o'clock in the morning Cornwallis sent a letter to General Washington and proposed stopping hostilities for twenty four hours to settle the terms of surrender. Back in New York, General Clinton was starting to sail down the Bay of New York with a convoy of twenty-five ships and seven thousand choice troops.

James Robertson, a British officer and the governor of New York, wrote a letter on the 17th to the Commander-in-Chief of the Forces in England, Lord Amherst. He gave Lord Amherst an update of the situation at Yorktown. He was not very optimistic about the future, "Our fleet consisting of 25 Ships of the line are now getting under way, they take on Board Sir Henry Clinton, Generals Leslie, Paterson, Lord Lincoln, with nearly seven thousand of our choice troops, while I dread this coming too late, and can turn my thoughts to no other subject."[1]

A little after two in the afternoon Cornwallis received a reply from Washington that granted a suspension of hostilities for two hours. Cornwallis sent the reply back at 4:30 in the afternoon, in which he gave an outline of the conditions under which he hoped that some agreement could be reached.

Colonel Simcoe mentioned in his journal that he proposed to Cornwallis for Loyalist and American deserters in the British lines be allowed to escape from Yorktown,

> It was understood that Earl Cornwallis had proposed a cessation of hostilities, for the purpose of settling the terms on which the posts of York and Gloucester were to be surrendered. On the first confirmation of this supposition, Lt. Col. Simcoe sent Lt. Spencer to his Lordship, to request that his corps consisted of loyalists, the objects of the enemy's civil persecution, and deserters, if the treaty was not finally concluded, that he would permit him to endeavor to escape with them in some of those boats which Gen. Arnold had built; and that his intention was to cross the Chesapeake and land in Maryland, when, from his knowledge of the inhabitants of the country and other favourable circumstances, he made no doubt of being able to save the greatest part of the corps and carry them into New York. His Lordship was pleased to express himself favourably in regard to the scheme, but said he could not permit it to be undertaken, for that the whole of the army must share one fate.[2]

The Hessian soldier, Stephen Popp, wrote in his journal that the men apparently knew that they would be surrendering, "Lord Cornwallis himself visited the works and saw how near the enemy had some. He returned to his headquarters and at once sent the first flag of truce, which was very civilly treated. The English troops at once began to destroy their tents, ruin their arms, and prepare for surrender. We were are heartily glad the fighting was over."[3]

In the early evening a terrible accident occurred that could have compromised the cease fire. The British artillery commander had ordered his men to fill some shells with powder, in case the firing would resume in the morning. Stephen Popp wrote in his journal about this accident, "Towards 7 p.m. there was a violent explosion of one of our magazines, some of the English soldiers sent to fill bombs with powder there had drunk too much brandy, were careless, and set fire, which cost 28 lives."[4]

Another Hessian soldier, Johann Conrad Dohla also wrote of the terrible event in his diary,

> Toward evening everything became still, and no further shots were fired by either side. During the evening several flags of truce went back and forth, and work on the surrender accord was conducted in earnest.
>
> At nine o'clock at night a powder magazine in the city blew up and killed thirteen people, of whom part flew into the air in pieces, but part were horribly crushed and covered with earth. Among those killed was an Ansbach grenadier who was on watch there, and also three English cannoneers who wished to take out powder and munitions and who apparently touched it off.[5]

Hessian Captain Johann Ewald described the condition of the troops at Yorktown, "Now that all the batteries were dismantled, the works destroyed, munitions and provisions wanting, the wounded and sick living helpless without medicine. The army melted away from 7,000 to 3,200, among whom not a thousand men could be called healthy. Lord Cornwallis decided to call for a parley on the afternoon of the 17th."[6]

Americans/French forces

In the morning several new batteries were opened in the second parallel, which began to pour in cannon fire. French and American commanders celebrated the fourth anniversary of British General John Burgoyne's surrender at Saratoga, with the heaviest amount of cannon fire they could send.

Count William De Deux-Ponts wrote in his journal, "On the 17th of October, we began at ricochet with so much success, that a large part of the fraises of the works of the place were knocked down, and in several places breaches were begun."[7]

A messenger was sent to Washington who was still back at his camp. The general had spent the morning catching up on letters to various people. Washington was surprised at the sign of the white flag, because he expected it to appear much later. He thought that Cornwallis would hold out for another week until his supplies ran out.

Washington's camp. He had 2 large tents, one for meetings with staff and for dinning, a smaller tent was his private quarters and for sleeping. The house on the left may have been used for additional shelter. To the right and just over a small hill is a shallow creek for fresh water. Photo courtesy of the Colonial Historical National Park, NPS

Washington received the letter from Cornwallis and broke the seal. He read, "I propose a cessation of hostilities for twenty four hours, and that two officers may be appointed by each side, to meet at Mr. Moore's house, to settle terms for the surrender of the ports of York and Gloucester."[8]

Washington finished a letter he started to Count De Grasse. He told him of the good news he had just received and asked him to join in the peace process,

> I do myself the honor to transmit the copy of a letter, which I have just received from Lord Cornwallis. I have informed him in answer thereto, that I wish him, previous to the meeting of the commissioners, to send his proposals in writing to the American lines, for which purpose a cessation of hostilities for two hours will be allowed.
>
> I should be anxious to have the honor of your Excellency's participation in the treaty, which will according to present appearance shortly take place. I need not add how happy it will make me to welcome your Excellency in the name of America on this shore, and embrace you upon an occasion so advantageous to the interests of the common cause, and on which it is so much indebted to you.[9]

Washington met with his aids to discuss the note from Cornwallis. Jonathan Trumbull Jr. wrote a reply, and the aids discussed it. The men could hear their cannons fire in the distance, which indicated that the flag of truce had been returned to the British lines.

John Laurens suggested that the line, "a cessation of Hostilities" be changed to read, "a suspension of Hostilities." The men all agreed to this change and the note was signed.[10]

The reply that was sent back to Cornwallis,

> An ardent Desire to spare the further Effusion of Blood, will readily incline me to listen to such Terms for the Surrender of your Post & Garrisons at York & Gloucester, as are admissible.
>
> I wish, previous to the Meeting of Commissioners, that Your Lordships Proposals in Writing, may be sent to the American Lines: for which Purpose, a Suspension of Hostilities during two Hours from the Delivery of this Letter will be granted—I have the Honor to be My Lord Your Lordship's Most Obedient and most humble Servant.[11]

About two in the afternoon, the cannons ceased, and the same British officer approached the allied lines under a white flag. The note was given to the officer, and he returned to the British lines. For the first time in many days the battlefield was silent. It was now up to Cornwallis to make the next move.

Cornwallis was not happy with the two hour cease fire. He had hoped to delay the surrender as long as possible in hopes that Clinton would come to his rescue. In fact, while this drama was being played out, the British fleet in New York was putting to sea. Having no choice, the British general began to write out his surrender terms.

Cornwallis, with very little fire power left and nothing to really bargain with, hoped that Washington would give him favorable concessions. Cornwallis sent his reply to Washington around 4:30 in the afternoon. Again, an officer was sent out under a flag of truce, and the message was taken to General Washington. It read,

> The time limited for sending my answer will not admit of entering into the detail of articles; but the basis of my proposals will be that the garrison of York and Gloucester shall be prisoners of war, with the customary honors; and for the convenience of the individuals which I have the honor to command, that the British shall be sent to Britain, and the Germans to Germany, under engagements not to serve against France, America, or their allies, until released, or regularly exchanged. That all arms and public stores shall be delivered up to you; but that the usual indulgence of side-arms to officers, and of retaining private property, shall be granted to officers and soldiers; and that the interest of the several individuals in civil capacities and connected with us, shall be attended to.
>
> If your excellency thinks that a continnance of the suspension of hostilities will be necessary to transmit your answer, I shall have no objection to the hour that you propose.[12]

The last paragraph in Cornwallis's statement was a roundabout way of saying that he would like the cannons to cease firing. After eight days of firing, the British were definitely ready for it to stop.

Cornwallis requested that he be given the same generous term that General Gates had given Burgoyne at Saratoga. Cornwallis asked that the surrendering troops be returned to England or Germany if they pledged not to rejoin the fighting. General Gates had been criticized for approving that same provision at Saratoga. Even if the soldiers did not return to America, they would ease England's military burden by relieving her forces elsewhere. Washington had no intention of being as lenient as Gates, so he rejected the British terms. Also, Washington was concerned that the

British fleet from New York would arrive at any time and break up the French blockade of Yorktown. He did, however, extend the cease fire for the night.

For the first time in eight days the British would be able to sleep at night in peace. The British soldiers would not be in fear of a shell landing on them in camp. While the men on both sides rested in the stillness of the night, General Washington and his staff worked through the night to prepare an answer for Cornwallis.

General Washington wrote in his journal about the events of the day,

> 17th. The French opened another Battery of four 24s. & two 16s. and a Morter Battery of 10 Morters and two Hawitzers. The American grand Battery consisting of 12 twenty fours and Eighteen prs.—4 Morters and two Hawitzers.
>
> About ten Oclock the Enemy beat a parley and Lord Cornwallis proposed a cessation of Hostilities for 24 hours, that Commissioners might meet at the house of a Mr. Moore (in the rear of our first parallel) to settle terms for the surrender of the Posts of York and Gloucester. To this he was answered, that a desire to spare the further effusion of Blood would readily incline me to treat of the surrender of the above Posts but previous to the meeting of Commissioners I wished to have his proposals in writing and for this purpose would grant a cessation of hostilities two hours—Within which time he sent out A letter with such proposals (tho' some of them were inadmissable) as led me to believe that there would be no great difficulty in fixing the terms. Accordingly hostilities were suspended for the Night & I proposed my own terms to which if he agreed Commissioners were to meet to digest them into form.[13]

Chaplain Israel Evans wrote in his diary, "General Washington informed them [the British] what terms he would give them, and has allowed them only two hours to consider them, and to give an answer. This day four years, Burgoyne and his whole army surrendered to the United States; that signal instance of the smiles of heaven, and what we now have in prospect, should make us very thankful to Almighty God."[14]

Claude Blanchard, the Commissary-in-Chief under General Rochambeau, wrote in his journal of hearing of the truce, "M. de la Cheze had the kindness to send me word of it immediately; I greatly rejoiced at it as a citizen, and also for this reason, that I perceived in this capitulation the end of our uneasiness respecting the service of the hospitals." [15]

Virginian Daniel Trabue, who was peddling goods to the soldiers at Yorktown, described the battlefield and the flag of truce,

> The Flag was received by the officer of this place. The officer that brought the flag said he had a letter for General Washington. The officer that commanded sent him with one of our officers to headquarters. This was a mile away, and about the center of our Line. As quick as they were gone the cannon fired again, and continued to beat Down the Wall. The conclusion among us all was that Lord Cornwallis was about to surrender.
>
> We started back and went through the Field as the Enemy had stopped firing. We went a little back of our Ditch and there we saw another sight. The Old Field was all torn up with balls from the enemy's cannon; it looked as though large bar sheer ploughs had been running there, only they would skip in places. When we got our Wagon & tent we told about the flag.
>
> They all said they expected it, as they did not see how the Enemy could stand so much fire, as we had given them. About this time the Flag had reached Gen'l Washington, and in a very few minutes the fire

ceased near headquarters, and continued to cease along the line each way. As quick as it could go down the River, by orders it ceased there also; so in about an hour all was still and calm, and the storm was over. A great many hands make light work.[16]

Colonel St. George Tucker wrote of the evening in his journal,

> Lord Cornwallis being allow'd but two hours sent out another Flag to request further time to digest his proposals—It has been granted and Hostilities have ceased ever since five OClock. It was pleasing to contrast the last night with the preceeding—A solemn stillness prevaild—the night was remarkably clear & the sky decorated with ten thousand stars—numberless Meteors gleaming thro' the Atmosphere afforded a pleasing resemblance to the Bombs which had exhibited a noble Firework the night before, but happily divested of all their Horror.[17]

Jonathan Trumbull wrote in his diary,

> Expect to begin our new roar of cannon, mortars, &c. but are prevented by the appearance of a flag from his Lordship, which bears a letter proposing a sessation of hostilities & a conference of commissioners to consider on terms of surrender of the ports of York & Gloucester. This produces a correspondence; --the more honourable to our General as it was the first message or letter that had every passed between the two Commanders, and was begun on the part of the British hero.[18]

Lieutenant Ebenezer Wild wrote,

> At daylight we found the enemy had stopped up the embrasures of the most of their batteries, and the fire from their cannons became almost silenced; but they continued to throw small shells very brisk. By this time the fire from our works became almost incessant, as new batteries are opening from almost every part of the line. About nine o'clock a drummer appeared and beat a parley on the rampart of the enemy's hornwork; in consequence of which hostilities ceased till a flag came from their works to ours and returned again, when the firing commenced on both sides as usual. About 11 o'clock an answer to the enemy's flag was returned, and a cessation of arms granted them. At 12 O'clock we were relieved by the Barron's division as usual..[19]

Lieutenant John Bell Tilden made a casual mention of the day in his journal, "Our division at 11 o'clock went to the trenches. British send out for terms of Capitulation; flags pass and repass all day. Attend ye Baron Steuben as his aid this day."[20]

Major Ebenezer Denny wrote in his journal about seeing the British drummer and the first truce flag of the day,

> In the morning, before relief came, had the pleasure of seeing a drummer mount the enemy's parapet, and beat a parley, and immediately an officer, holding up a white handkerchief, made his appearance outside their works; the drummer accompanied him, beating. Our batteries ceased. An officer from our lines ran and met the other, and tied the handkerchief over his eyes. The drummer sent back, and the British officer conducted to a house in rear of our lines. Firing ceased totally.[21]

Doctor James Thacher, of the Massachusetts 16th Regiment, wrote a very descriptive account of the events of this day in his journal,

> The whole of our works are now mounted with cannon and mortars, not less than one hundred pieces of heavy ordinance have been in continual operation during the last twenty four hours. The whole peninsula trembles under the incessant thunderings of our infernal machines; we have leveled some of their works, and even see the men in their lines torn to pieces by the bursting of our shells. But the scene is drawing to a close. Lord Cornwallis at length realizing the extreme hazard of his deplorable situation, and finding it in vain any longer to resist, has this forenoon come to the humiliating expedient of sending out a flag, requesting a

cessation of hostilities for twenty four hours, that commissioners may be appointed to prepare and adjust the terms of capitulation. Two or three flags passed in the course of the day, and General Washington consented to a cessation of hostilities for two hours only, that his Lordship may suggest his proposals as a basis for a treaty, which being in part accepted, a suspension of hostilities will be continued till tomorrow. [22]

Joseph Plumb Martin mentioned in his memoir that it was a rather unlucky day for the British troops,

After Lord Cornwallis had failed to get off, upon the seventeenth day of October, (a rather unlucky day for the British) he requested a cessation of hostilities for, I think, twenty-four hours, when commissioners from both armies met at a house between the lines, to agree upon articles of capitulation. We waited with anxiety the termination of the armistice, and as time drew nearer our anxiety increased. And now we concluded that we had obtained what we had taken so much pains for, for which we had encountered so many dangers, and had so anxiously wished. Before night we were informed that the British had surrendered and that the siege was ended.[23]

Colonel Pickering was excited to write to his wife about the good news of the proposed surrendering by General Cornwallis,

On this memorable day, in 1777, Burgoyne surrendered. On this present day, Lord Cornwallis has proposed a surrender. A suspension of hostilities has, in consequence, taken place. The negotiation is not yet settled, nor do I know the terms proposed. This event is unexpected, and can be accounted for only on supposition that the enemy want provisions or warlike stores, for their works would admit of yet many days' defence; though, on the 14th, in the evening, we took two of their most detached redoubts, which gave us great advantage, and at once brought our batteries near the enemy's, Cornwallis has made a very feeble resistance; one sally only be attempted, and that a trivial one. I congratulate you, my dear Becky, on the near prospect of the success we wished for. I trust the treaty will soon be closed. This great event will give you a happy turn to our affairs, and perhaps by next spring procure peace to America.[24]

Colonel Henry Dearborn of Washington's staff recorded the events of the day in his journal,

We had a number of very warm Batteries opened this morning in our advanced Parallel, which made the Enemies situation so very disagreeable.—that about the middle of the day his Lordship was induced to send out a flag, with some proposals for a Capitulation.—soon after, a Cessation of Hostilities took place, & the evening was taken up in negotiation between two Officers of our Army, & two of the Enemies, on the Terms of capitulation.[25]

A letter from David Forman was sent to Washington to give him an update of the British fleet in New York,

The British Fleets are now Completely Repaired Twenty five or 26 Ships of the Line including the Prince William of 74 and The Torbay of 64 Guns Arrived from the West Indies, They have also Three Ships of 50 Guns which they Intend taking in The line. enclosed your Excly has an acct handed me from New York on which I think dependance may be made it comes through a person who has it in his power to know their intended operations.

Your Excly will I hope excuse my sending the Original paper without any Observations on it When I inform Your Excly that I this day had my Good Friend Doct. Scudder killed by my side on the Banks of Black point in Shrewsbury and that my particular Attention is demanded to his Widow and Children.

I have a Very Strict look out kept in Their Shipping and will Your Excly may relye on it send forward the moment they sail. [26]

That night General Washington received a letter from Samuel Bradford. Bradford was a Captain of Artillery in the Virginia Continental line, and he also served as an aid-de-camp to General Weedon. Samuel sent a letter to George Washington that gave him information about what was going on at the Gloucester side,

> Genl Weedon being unwell, had retired at Sunsett about 3 Miles from Camp, till Morning. I therefore took the liberty of opening Col. Trumbull's Letter of this date. The Intelligence of today from Deserters are that the Enemy crossed over (by the accts he collected in Town) near 1000 Men last Night & had deliver'd out Cloathing to their Troops, but made no mention of Lord Cornwallis being over in person. The reports from our Hussars station'd at Perrins House for intelligence, are, that the Enemy have been crossing & recrossing the whole day, but it appeared that more went to York, than crossed to this side & between 4 & 5 this Evening 7 Large Boats loaded supposed to carry 50 Men in each crossed from this Side to York..[27]

Chapter 12

Agreeing to Terms of Surrender

After looking over the articles that were written Colonel Ross said, "This is a harsh article." ---British Colonel Ross to American Colonel Lauren about article three of the surrender

---

Thursday October 18, 1781

(Clear, but a chilly night)

At dawn the French and Americans were serenaded by the Scottish bagpipers of the Seventy-sixth Regiment. They were answered by the Royal Deux-Ponts Regimental Band. As the sun began to rise the parapets on both sides were crowded with soldiers facing each other. None of the former enemies spoke, but they just stood silently looking at each other. On the Gloucester side the frigate *Guadeloupe* was scuttled during the night, and she laid in the water at an angle.

That afternoon two men from each side met and discussed the terms of the British surrender. They talked late into the night until a draft of surrender was written and given to General Washington for his approval. Men on both sides spent another peaceful night in the trenches.

British forces:

Hessian soldier Stephen Popp recorded in his journal, "Quiet all day, while flags of truce were coming and going, negotiating terms of surrender. 2 French ships took positions near the Hessian lines."[1]

Private Johann Conrad Dohla of a Hessian Regiment wrote about the excessive amount of chocolate the troops had,

> The entire day was quiet with no cannonading on either side. At noon two Frigates and one schooner from the French fleet entered the harbor. All troops during the last fourteen days have received much sugar and chocolate, or cocoa, as the English call it, with the daily ration. These were taken from a Dutch merchant ship that the English captured and divided among the regiments. We drank chocolate three, four, or even more times a day. Also, we ate it with sugar on bread, but still could not use it all. It served us well during the present sleepless work and fatigue, which we had day and night with the greatest danger to our lives.[2]

Both Popp and Dohla wrote about the ships that dropped anchor just off the town. They were the ships that Washington had previously requested from Admiral de Grasse. They were finally sent, even though now they were not needed. On board one of the ships was Admiral de Barras who brought a message for Washington, that he would represent the French fleet because de Grasse was down with an asthma attack.

Twenty-nine year old Bartholomew James of the Royal Navy wrote, "At four o'clock in the afternoon we sent a second flag with less favourable proposals, and which produced a cessation of arms for four hours which was afterwards increased to the 29th."[3]

Colonel Tarleton wrote in his book,

> General Washington answered that the garrisons of York and Gloucester should be received as prisoners of war; that the annexed condition of sending the British and German troops to the parts of Europe to which they respectively belonged was inadmissible; that the same honours would be granted to the surrendering army, as were granted to the garrison of Charlestown; and that the shipping, boats, artillery, arms, accoutrements, and military chest, were to be delivered to the heads of departments, who would be instructed to receive them. Two hours were allowed to consider these and other proposals, and to appoint commissioners to digest the articles of capitulation, otherwise hostilities would be recommenced.[4]

Americans/French forces

During the night George Washington and his aids worked on a reply to the letter to Cornwallis that would lay out the surrender terms. The request for the British and German troops to be sent back to Europe was totally rejected.

The day before in his trenches, Baron Von Steuben received the first flag of truce bearer from Cornwallis. During the morning, Lafayette approached with his division to relieve von Steuben and his men. The baron refused to be relieved, and claimed that the etiquette in Europe said that the offer to capitulate was made during his guard. It was now a point of honor that he would remain in the trenches with his men until the capitulation was signed, or hostilities began. The dispute between the two generals was taken to Washington, but Steuben remained until the British flag was struck.[5] Lafayette accepted Washington's decision, although privately he was annoyed at von Steuben since he was not very fond of the German.

Colonel Richard Butler was a member of the 5th Pennsylvania Regiment that served under Baron von Steuben, and he wrote,

> The troops in the trenches being entitled to the honor of closing the siege, we therefore remained unrelieved in the trenches. This day the whole army were ordered to hold themselves in readiness for any service requisite. Two Commissioners from the American and two from the British army, to draw up the capitulation in form. This being a day of negotiation, every thing appeared to be in suspense.[6]

Major Ebenezer Denny was very happy to hear the young British drummer, "Several flags pass and repass now even without the drum. Had we not seen the drummer in his red coat when he first mounted, he might have beat away till doomsday. The constant firing was too much for the sound of a single drum; but when the firing ceased, I thought I never heard a drum equal to it- the most delightful music to us all."[7]

St. George Tucker of the Virginia militia described the area on the morning of the 18th of October,

> At dawn of day the British gave us a serenade with the Bag pipe, I believe, & were answered by the French with the Band of the Regiment of deux ponts. As Soon as the Sun rose one of the most striking pictures of

War was display'd that Imagination can paint—From the point of Rock Battery on one side our Lines compleatly mann'd and our Works crowded with soldiers were exhibited to view—opposite these at the Distance of two hundred yards you were presented with a sight of the British Works; their parapets crowded with officers looking at those who were assembled at the top of our Works—the Secretary's house with one of the Corners broke off, & many large holes thro the Roof & Walls part of which seem'd tottering with their Weight afforded a striking Instance of the Destruction occasioned by War—Many other houses in the vicinity contributed to accomplish the Scene—On the Beach of York directly under the Eye hundreds of busy people might be seen moving to & fro—At a small distance from the Shore were seen ships sunk down to the Waters Edge—further out in the Channel the Masts, Yards & even the top gallant Masts of some might be seen, without any vestige of the hulls. On the opposite of the river the remainder of the shipping drawn off as to a place of security. Even here the Guadaloupe sunk to the Waters Edge shew'd how vain the hope of such a place. On Gloster point the Fortifications and Encampment of the Enemy added a further Variety to the scene which was compleated by the distant View of the french Ships of War, two of which were at that time under sail—A painter need not to have wish'd for a more compleat subject to imploy his pencil without any expence of Genius.

This was the Scene which ushered in the Day when the pride of Britain was to be humbled in a greater Degree than it had ever been before, unless at the Surrender of [British general John] Burgoyne [in 1777]—It is remarkable that the proposals for a surrender of Lord Cornwallis's Army were made on the Anniversary of that important Event—At two o Clock the Surrender was agreed on & Commissioners appointed to draw up the Articles of Capitulation—They are now employed on that Business—The Guadaloupe or some other Frigate was sunk two night ago—we know not whether by Design or Accident—I can not omit one Anecdote which happened during the Siege—Baron Viominit at the Attack on the Enemy's redoubts on Monday Evening observing two Sargeants distinguish themselves by their Intrepidity, sent for them to dine with him the next Day & placed them at his right hand where he treated them with the highest Respect and Attention.[8]

Thirty-eight year old Sylvanus Seely was a colonel in the New Jersey Militia. He had been ordered to guard New Jersey with his men, when Washington marched to Yorktown. Seely wrote to Washington on the 18th of October about the movement of the British fleet from New York. "The Fleet I mentioned in mine of the 14th Consisting of 24 Ships of the line two 40 & a number of Frigates, sailed from the Hook yesterday about Ten in the Morning whether they have taken all the Troops I mentioned with them is uncertain but I believe they have, & they have undoubtedly taken between two & three thousand of their best Troops on board their Ships of War."[9]

Lieutenant William Feltman enjoyed the cease fire by taking a walk and he wrote, "Flags passing and repassing this whole day. This day our fleet have in sight with a detachment from Penna. This afternoon Lieuts. Martin, Henley and self took a walk to the left of our lines, where we found the following batteries all ready to be opened at one moment's time."[10]

Doctor James Thacher wrote in his journal about the flags passing back and forth and the meeting of each side to discuss terms,

They have this day held an interview with the two British officers on the part of Lord Cornwallis, the terms of capitulation are settled, and being confirmed by the commanders of both armies, the royal troops are to march out tomorrow and surrender their arms. It is circumstance deserving of remark, that Colonel Laurens who is stipulating for the surrender of a British nobleman, at the head of a royal army, is the son of Mr. Henry

Laurens, our ambassador to Holland, Who being captured on his voyage, is now in lose confinement in the tower of London.[11]

Lieutenant Ebenezer Wild of the 1st Massachusetts Regiment noted the peace talks in his journal,

Cessation of arms still continues. At 9 o'clock I mounted the camp guard. About 11 two Commissioners from the allied armies met two more from the British at Moors House (which is on the right of the American lines), where the articles Capitulation were agreed on & signed. At 4 o'clk P.M. detachments of the allied armies took possession of the enemy's works in York and Gloucester.[12]

Alexander Hamilton wrote a letter to his wife Elizabeth to tell her the good news from Yorktown,

Your letter of the 3d. of September my angel never reached me till to day. My uneasiness at not hearing from you is abated by the sweet prospect of soon taking you in my arms. Your father will tell you the news. Tomorrow Cornwallis and his army are ours. In two days after I shall in all probability set out for Albany, and I hope to embrace you in three weeks from this time. Conceive my love by your own feelings, how delightful this prospect is to me. Only in your heart and in my own can any image be found of my happiness upon the occasion. I have no time to enlarge. Let the intilligence I give compensate for the shortness of my letter. Give my love to your Mama to Mrs. Carter to Peggy and to all the family.

Adieu My Charming beloved wife, I kiss you a thousand times, Adieu, My love, A Hamilton[13]

Negotiations:

The reply to Cornwallis was sent back, and again the British general was given only two hours to accept or reject it. Washington did not want Cornwallis to drag this negotiation out in hopes of being rescued by Clinton,

My Lord Cornwallis,

To avoid unnecessary discussions and delays, I shall, at once, in answer to your Lordships letters of yesterday, declare the general Basis upon which a definitive Treaty and Capitulation may take place.

The Garrisons of York & Gloucester, including the Seaman, as you propose, will be received prisoners of War. The condition annexed, of sending the British and German Troops, to the parts of Europe to which they respectively belong is inadmissible. Instead of this, they will be marched to such parts of the Country as can most conveniently provide for their subsistence, and the benevolent treatment of Prisoners, which is invariably observed by the Americans, will be extended to them. The same honours will be granted to the surrendering Army as were granted to the Garrison of Charlestown.

The Shipping and Boats in the two Harbours with all their Guns, Stores Tackling, Furniture and Apparel, shall be delivered in their present State, to an Officer of the Navy, appointed to take possession of them.

The Artillery Arms, Accoutrements Military Chest, and public Stores of every denomination, shall be delivered, unimpaired to the Heads of departments to which they respectively belong.

The Officers will be indulged in retaining their side Arms of the Officers & Soldiers may preserve their Baggage and Effects with this reserve, that property taken in the Country, will be reclaimed.

With regard to the Individuals in civil Capacities whose interest your Lordship wishes may be attended to; untill they are more particularly described, nothing definitive can be settled.

I have to add that I expect the sick and wounded will be supplied with their own Hospital Stores, and be tended by British Surgeons, particularly charged with the care of them.

Your Lordship will be pleased to signify your determination either to accept or reject the proposals now offered, in the course of two Hours from the delivery of this letter, that Commissioners may be appointed to digest the Articles of Capitulation, or a renewal of Hostilities may take place. I have the honor to be My Lord Your Lordships Most obedient and humble servant.[14]

Cornwallis read the terms, and he realized that there was not a lot in the proposal that he objected too. Washington had left open the question of what to do with the British sympathizers within the British lines. The general thought that this was a point that could be taken up later. He replied to Washington's terms,

> I agree to open a treaty of capitulation upon the basis of the garrisons of York and Gloucester including seamen, being prisoners of war, without annexing the condition of their being sent to Europe; but I expect to receive compensations in the articles of capitulation for the surrender of Gloucester in its present state of defence. I shall in particular, desire that the Bonetta sloop of war may be left entirely at my disposal from the hour that the capitulation is signed, to receive an Aid-de-camp to carry my dispatches to Sir Henry Clinton. Such soldiers as I may think proper to send as passengers in her, to be manned with fifty men of her own crew, and to be permitted to sail without examination, when my dispatches are ready; engaging, on my part, that the ship shall be brought back and delivered to you if she escapes the dangers of the sea, that the crew and soldiers shall be accounted for in future exchanges, that she shall carry off no officer without your consent, nor public property of any kind; and I shall likewise desire that the traders and inhabitants may preserve their property, and that no person may be punished or molested for having joined the British troops.
>
> If you choose to proceed to negotiation on these grounds, I shall appoint two field officers of my army to meet two officers from you at any time and place that you think proper, to digest the articles of capitulation.[15]

Cornwallis believed that if the negotiations to save the Loyalist from being hung fell through, then he could cram as many as possible onboard the *Bonetta* and save them. Perhaps he was aware, that it had been reported, that Washington once remarked, "The best thing that the Loyalist could do was to commit suicide."[16] Washington was not seeking revenge, so he agreed to negotiations on those grounds.

Washington appointed Colonel John Laurens to represent him, and Rochambeau chose Vicomte de Noailles, the brother-in-law of Lafayette, to represent the French commander. Cornwallis appointed his aide, Major Alexander Ross, and Lieutenant Colonel Thomas Dundas. On the Gloucester side the allies appointed Duc de Lauzun to discuss terms with Colonel Banastre Tarleton.

The Moore house was chosen for the meeting place, which was about one and a half miles east of Yorktown on Temple Farm. The house was owned by Augustine Moore, a leading landowner in the area.

Meeting at the Moore House:

During the afternoon, British Colonel Dundas and Major Alexander Ross walked up the bluff to the Moore House. Waiting for them was Colonel Laurens and Count de Noailles. During the meeting, Ross and Laurens did most of the talking.

It was also reported, although probably not true, that Ross told Colonel Laurens, "Withdraw your Continentals and we will hold the place if it rains Frenchmen a year."[17] If it was said, it was probably meant as a light approach toward humor.

Because the main issues had pretty much been decided, both sides felt that the talks would go smoothly and would be over in a couple of hours. Washington had placed special American and French detachments, of 200 men on notice, to be ready to take over British defensive positions on the main roads into Yorktown.

An argument broke out over one particular article that Lafayette had insisted on being included. After looking over the articles that were written Colonel Ross said, "This is a harsh article [article three]." Colonel Laurens asked, "Which one?" Ross replied, "The troops shall march out with colors cased, and drums beating a British or a German march." Colonel Laurens agreed saying, "Yes, Sir, it is a harsh article."[18]

The Moore House behind American lines, facing the York River---Library of Congress

When Charleston fell to the British in 1780, General Benjamin Lincoln asked that he be allowed to surrender his army with the customary honors of war. This meant that his army would march from their works with flags flying, drums beating, and their band playing a tune of the conquering army. This signified that the beaten army was equal in bravery to the conquering army.

The British commander, Sir Henry Clinton, refused the request and he said that the flags were not to be flown and the drummers could not beat a British march. This was a humiliation to General Lincoln and a slur cast on the bravery of his troops.

Colonel Ross then asked why the article was there. Colonel Laurens quickly replied, "You seem to forget, Sir, that I was a capitulate at Charleston, where Gen. Lincoln, after a brave defence of six weeks' open trenches, by a very inconsiderable garrison, against the British army and fleet, under Sir Henry Clinton and Admiral Arbuthnot, and when your lines of approach were within pistol-shot of our field works, was refused any other terms for the gallant garrison, than marching out with colors cased, and drums not beating a British or a German march."[19]

Colonel Ross interrupted and declared that Cornwallis did not command at Charleston. Colonel Laurens pointed out that it was not the individual that was considered, rather it is the nation. He added that the article stand, or he would cease being a commissioner. Colonel Ross, realizing that he had no bargaining chip, was forced to allow the offending article to remain.

Ross then demanded that the honors of war be granted to the garrison at Gloucester. He argued that they were not even attacked or under siege. Laurens tried to convince Ross that Yorktown and Gloucester was one garrison. The two men compromised, so that the Gloucester garrison would be able to surrender with swords drawn and trumpets blowing, but their colors could not fly.

Another point of disagreement was the question over captured money. The British had little money, and Noailles insisted that Cornwallis, on his honor, state the amount in his military chest. Since it amounted to only 1,800 pounds sterling, Noailles was willing to not have it included it in the terms. Laurens, on the other hand, insisted that Cornwallis must turn over his military chest. Laurens felt that the new American government needed all the money it could get, regardless of the amount.

Cornwallis had also hoped to obtain favorable terms for the American Loyalists at Yorktown [article 10]. Washington said that their fate must be decided by civil authorities. Some of the Loyalist, or Tories, in Yorktown must have felt that their situation was dangerous. Washington also had said that American army deserters would be hung.

According to the pension application [S30455] of nineteen year old Henry Hayes in the Virginia militia at Yorktown, "Many of the Tories who fought under him [Cornwallis] were said to have escaped on the water, under cover of darkness, the night preceding the surrender." An undetermined number of Tories also escaped aboard the *Bonetta,* which was allowed to sail without being searched.

Since the personal property of Americans was to be returned to them, this would mean that any black slaves in Yorktown would be returned to their owners.

The British officers argued over nearly every point, which caused the discussion of terms to drag throughout the day requiring an extension of the truce until nine the next morning. Washington wrote in his diary, "The Commissioners met accordingly; but the business was so procrastinated by those on their side (a Colo. Dundas & a Majr. Ross) that Colo. Laurens & the Viscount De Noailles who were appointed on our part could do no more than make the rough draft of the Articles which were to be submitted for Lord Cornwallis's consideration."[20]

The negotiations ended before midnight, and a very tired Colonel Laurens carried a rough draft of the articles to General Washington. However, Washington was not completely happy with the results and made a few minor changes. One change was the article about the disposition of the Loyalists, which was revised and redrafted. Washington also changed the part in article IX that said medicine from American hospitals should be given to the British sick and wounded. He changed it to read that the medicine would come from the British supplies, and if more medicine was needed, then it should come from the British in New York. A copy of the completed articles was sent to Cornwallis in Yorktown for his signature.

The draft stated that the British would not be allowed to have music playing, when they marched out to surrender. The next morning Washington agreed that they could play a marching tune, but it must be one of their own tunes, and definitely not a mocking rendition of "Yankee Doodle."

The original song to the tune of Yankee Doodle was sung by British officers to make fun of the colonial "Yankees" that served with them in the French and Indian War. Their stereotype of an American was that of a simpleton or backwoods bumpkin, who believed he could put a feather in his hat and be stylish, thus the lyric, "stuck a feather in his hat and called it macaroni".

Macaroni refers to a flamboyant fashion trend of the time for European men who were members of the aristocrat. Doodle was a derogatory term that meant a fool or simpleton. The lyrics were meant to disgrace Americans, who thought they were more sophisticated than they really were.

As the war progressed Americans began to sing the song as a symbol of patriotism. It became a song of pride and defiance, when they added verses that mocked British troops and praised General Washington.

With the copy of the articles, a note was sent to Cornwallis saying that he [Washington] expected the copy to be signed by eleven' o'clock on the 19th, and the garrison to be ready to march out of the town within three hours. Cornwallis knew that he either accepted the articles as written or the siege would continue.

David Humphreys, the aide-de-camp to General Washington, reported,

> The commissioners met at the house of Mrs. Moore in the rear of the first parallel. They met on the 18th but were unable to come to a perfect understanding. Finally Washington prepared a rough draft of the terms he would accept, which were similar to those granted by Cornwallis to Gen. Lincoln at the surrender of Charlestown the year before. A fair copy was made of them and after some remonstrance at their harshness by Col. Ross they were agreed to by the British commissioners and signed by Cornwallis, Capt. Symonds, British commander on the York River, Washington, Rochambeau, de Barras and de Grasse.[21]

Even with peace at hand, some troops were taking no chances. Lieutenant John Bell Tilden wrote in his journal that at night the troops, "Lay on their arms all night." According to the diary of an unknown American soldier, "We had Eighty Pieces of Ordinance very heavy ready to fire at them in Case we should not agree."[22]

Chapter 13

Surrender Ceremony

"The British officers behaved like boys who had been whipped at school, some bit their lips, some pouted, others cried." --- The *New Jersey Gazette,* November 7, 1781

Friday October 19, 1781

(A warm, clear day)

After a peaceful night, the armies around Yorktown awoke to a bright sunny day. It would become the most important day since the war began on April 19, 1775. St. George Tucker of the Virginia Militia wrote in the margins of his journal, "At retreat last night the British played the tune of Welcome Brother Debtor to their conquerors. The tune was by no means disagreeabler."[1]

This Scottish tune was used in the military to announce the end of the day's activities and a time for rest. The first stanza goes,

> *Welcome, welcome, brother debtor,*
> *To this poor but merry place;*
> *Where no bailiff, dun, or fetter,*
> *Dare to shew a frightful face.*
> *But, kind Sir, as you're a stranger,*
> *Down your garnish you must lay;*
> *Or your coat will be in danger:*
> *You must either strip or pay.*[2]

George Washington sent an important letter to Claude Gabriel, Marquis de Choisy, at Gloucester, "Late this Evening I was honored with your favor of this date—without delay, & in much haste I inclose you a copy of such articles of the Capitulation as are immediately & essentially necessary for your Government. With much esteem and Respect I am Sir Yr Most Obt Ser.[3]

General Knox sat at his desk in his tent, and at eight o'clock that morning he wrote to his wife about the events,

> I have detained William [his brother] until this moment that I might be the first to communicate good news to the charmer of my soul. A glorious moment for American! This day Lord Cornwallis and his army march out and pile their arms in the face of our victorious army. The day before yesterday he desired commissioners might be named to treat of the surrender of his troops, the ships, and everything they possess. He at first requested that the Britons might be sent to Britain, and the Germans to Germany; but this the General refused,

155

and they have now agreed to surrender prisoners of war, to be kept in America until exchanged or released. They will have the same honors as the garrison of Charleston; that is, they will not be permitted to unfurl their colors, or play Yankee Doodle. We know not yet how many they are. The General has just requested me to be at head-quarters instantly, therefore I cannot be more particular.[4]

Early in the morning the articles of surrender were given to Cornwallis, along with a note that it needed to be signed by eleven o'clock, and that his troops must march out to surrender by two in the afternoon. As Cornwallis mulled over the articles, General Washington ate breakfast and then rode out to wait for the reply at the recently captured redoubt 10.

After Cornwallis signed the surrender articles, they were delivered by a messenger to General Washington at redoubt 10. There, he, the French General Rochambeau, and Admiral de Barras signed the articles. Under the signatures Washington added, "Done in the trenches before Yorktown Virginia, October 19, 1781." In the British lines the troops were very thankful that the siege was over and their lives had been spared.

News had been spreading of the surrender, and by late morning large crowds of people from the surrounding areas had arrived to see history made. Some were there hoping to reclaim their slaves, that had joined the British in hopes of gaining their freedom. It was a great day for the Virginians, because the British had been defeated on their soil and it was due to their own commander, George Washington.

Swedish Count Axel Fersen later wrote an interesting prediction he had about these people of Virginia,

> It really seems as if the Virginians were another race of men; instead of occupying themselves with their farms and making them profitable, each land owner wants to be a lord. All the work is done by negro slaves, who are ordered by the whites, and overseers under them.
>
> These Virginians have all the aristocratic instincts, and when one sees them it is hard to understand how they came to enter a general confederation and to accept a government founded on perfect equality of condition. But the same spirit which has led them to shake off the English yoke may lead them to other action of the same kind, and I should not be surprised to see Virginia detach herself, after the peace, from the other States.[5]

Doctor James Thacher wrote, "The concourse of spectators from the country was prodigious, in point of numbers probably equal to the military, but universal silence and order prevailed."[6] There was silence as the British slowly marched out between the two victorious armies. After the cold night, the soldiers standing and watching the British must have enjoyed the warm sun on their backs.

While the surrender was starting to take place, 500 hundred miles to the north General Clinton and the British fleet sailed from New York, and they would be at Yorktown in five days to save Lord Cornwallis.

The British march out and Allies take possession of their works:

The surrender was signed at noon, and at one o'clock the British flags were removed from their works, and the first American units began to move in to take possession. Soon there occurred the only hostility of the day, not between the allies and the British, but between an American officer and General von Steuben.

As the American troops reached a British fortification, Colonel Richard Butler, a fiery Irishman of the 5th Pennsylvania Regiment, ordered Lieutenant Ebenezer Denny, who had been carrying the American flag, to plant it at the top of the British fortification. The Baron Von Steuben, who was close to Denny, grabbed the flag from Denny's hand and planted it himself. He then stood on the parapet smiling, as he waved to the troops.

In the background Colonel Butler was livid, cursed the baron, and called him "an arrogant, ignorant knavish [a knave] foreigner."[7] Later, Butler sent Von Steuben an insulting letter that nearly caused a duel between the two men, until Washington and Rochambeau defused the situation.

Lieutenant Ebenezer Denny wisely played down the event in his journal, "Our division man the lines again. All is quiet. Articles of capitulation signed; detachments of French and Americans take possession of British forts. Major Hamilton commanded a battalion which took possession of a fort immediately opposite our right and on the bank of York River. I carried the standard of our regiment on this occasion. On entering the fort, Baron Steuben, who accompanied us, took the standard from me and planted it himself."[8]

As the British marched to surrender, at first glance, it looked like they were marching out on a holiday. Drums were beating, and the men were in bright fresh uniforms. But then you would notice that the army's colors were cased and not flying. Looking closer you would see some of the men crying as they marched, and others biting their lips to hold back the sorrow. Some of the men even appeared drunk. The British numbers also looked small, because they had left over 2,000 sick and wounded men back at Yorktown.

The *New Jersey Gazette* reported a few weeks later, "The British officers behaved like boys who had been whipped at school, some bit their lips, some pouted, others cried; their round, broad-brimmed hats were well adapted to the occasion, hiding those faces they were ashamed to show."[9]

Johann Conrad Dohla, like many of the troops on the British side, had never seen this many allied troops at one time during the war, and he exaggerated the number of allied soldiers,

> We, now captives, looked with wonder and astonishment at all these troops, which formed a line three men deep and extending for more than an English mile, because such a force had besieged us and could have eaten us up, and by comparison we appeared to be no more than a guard mount. The line from both armies was stretched out for nearly two miles. It is understandable how much space an army of forty thousand men requires, even when standing in two lines of men, three ranks deep. As we marched through, the enemy was amazed at our small force, as they had considered us to be more numerous.[10]

Von Closen disclosed in his diary a humorous event that occurred while the British were marching out. Admiral de Barras attended the ceremony on horseback. The admiral was a sailor, who was at home on the swaying and rolling of his ship on the ocean, but he was not so comfortable on horseback. The rest of the French officers were concerned for the admiral's lack of horsemanship. De Barras insisted that he be on a horse and remarked he would, if necessary, stay in the saddle all day to see the surrender.

The admiral was on his horse stationed among the rest of the French officers, when suddenly the horse began to relieve himself. The loud noise of the rushing water unnerved de Barras, who excitedly remarked to the others that he thought his horse was sinking. Laughter among the officers was probably delayed until a more appropriate time.

Later, historical accounts claimed that as the British marched, they played a tune called "The World Turn'd Upside Down." If true, it would have been a very fitting piece to play and would certainly have fit the American narrative. This song was first claimed to be played at the surrender in the 1828 book *Anecdotes of the Revolution* by Alexander Garden.[11] The tune was one version of an old folk tune that might have been played.

None of the eyewitness accounts in the journals or diaries said what tune was played. St. George Tucker said the drums beat a slow march, Johann Dolha said fifes and drums were playing, and Stephen Popp wrote that the bands were playing and drums beating, Ebenezer Denny wrote that the drums beat as if they did not care, and Sara Osborn said that the British played a melancholy tune. We may never know for sure what tune was played.

Cornwallis was either overcome with embarrassment, or fatigue because he did not appear at the surrender in person. Since Cornwallis claimed that he was "ill" the British were marched to the surrender site by Adjutant-General Dumas and General O'Hara. Many of the people that came to witness Cornwallis being humiliated were probably very disappointed that he was not present in person.

Surrender of the sword:

Earlier Lafayette suggested to Washington that General Lincoln should receive the sword of Lord Cornwallis, because he had to surrender to Cornwallis at Charlestown. Since Cornwallis did not attend the ceremony, he sent his sword by the hand of General O'Hara, his next in command.

As the British officers rode toward the allied generals, Dumas was at the left of O'Hara. When they were near the allies, O'Hara asked Dumas where Rochambeau was stationed. Dumas said, "On our left, at the head of the French line." Hearing that, O'Hara quickened the pace of his horse, so that he could surrender his sword to the French general. O'Hara did not want to surrender to an American. However, as O'Hara approached Rochambeau, the French general pointed out General Washington, and he led the British general to him. As General O'Hara raised his sword to give it up, Washington stopped him saying, "Never from so good a hand."[12]

General O'Hara apologized to Washington for General Cornwallis not coming out and said his commander was sick. Washington knew that if a second in command was sent to surrender, then it was proper for his own second in command to receive the sword. Washington then directed O'Hara to present the sword to General Lincoln, who accepted the sword and pointed O'Hara in the direction where his men should go to surrender their weapons.

In his memoirs General Rochambeau wrote about the surrender of the sword of Cornwallis,

Lord Cornwallis being sick, General O'Hara filed off the head of the garrison. As he came up to where I was standing, he presented his sword to me; I pointed to General Washington, who stood opposite to me at the head of the American army, and told him that the French army being only a auxiliary on this continent, it devolved on the American General to tender him his orders.[13]

Most of the men in the Virginia militia, that were present at the surrender, had never seen General Cornwallis. So any British officer with a decorative uniform and riding in the lead was assumed to be Cornwallis. Many years after this event, numerous militiamen claimed in their pension applications that they actually saw Cornwallis surrender his sword. Here are some examples:

John McMahan first joined the Virginia militia in 1777, and he stated in his pension application [S2808], "... after they joined the Army at Yorktown he was taken from the ranks by the commissary General, to take care of and drive 18, the former driver having been bitten by a spider, which rendered him unable to take care of his team. On the day of the Surrender declarant was but a few paces from where Washington stood – saw Cornwallis march out and surrender his sword to the American General. The British prisoners after the surrender were marched to Winchester Virginia." [This author finds it hard to believe that this wagon driver was this close to the actual surrender.]

Surrender of the British Army.---Library of Congress

Boston Ollis was ninety years old when he gave this pension statement [R7796] in 1834, "Was in the seige of York and was an artillaryman during the seige. Applicant saw Lord Cornwallace surrender himself to General Washington. Saw Lord Cornwallace take his sword by the point and hand the hilt to General Washington. Received it in his hand. Some short time handed the sword back to Lord Corn Wallace in the same manner that he had received it from him in. applicant does not now recollect the date of the day or year on which Lord Cornwallace surrender but it was in the fall season of the year applicant was marched as a guard over the prisioners from York to Winchester where he was honorably but verbally discharged by Col Rose."

George Painter served several tours in the Virginia militia starting in 1776. He said in his pension application [W8507], "Soon after I was drafted and served a Tower [tour] of 3 months under the same Captain we was in the taking of Corn Wallis at little York. I was in the whole of that Battle. We was under the command of General Stevens there I saw General Washington for the first time. I was in the lines not far off when Cornwallis surrendered his Sword. I was one of the Guard that took charge of the prisoners that was marched to Winchester in Virginia where I was Discharged and returned home."

Benjamin Cheatham first enlisted in the Virginia militia in 1776 and served several tours. The last tour was for nine months, and he stated in his pension application [S2429], "…he marched through Virginia as far as Jamestown, where they had an engagement with the enemy [this would be the Battle of Green Springs on July 6, 1781] in which applicant was engaged, he thinks Gen. Wayne Commanded part of the troops on the American side in this engagment, he himself was under the command of Gen. Lawson the Americans there drove the British from the ground & forced them to take shiping, & pursued them some distance down the River & the British thence went on to Little York where Lord Cornwallis was captured in October 1781. they then returned home, at the end of the said nine months & applicant was discharged by Gen. Lawson from the said last tour, he reached home on Wednesday, & on the following Sunday he volunteered & went directly to Yorktown & he was present at the Capture of Lord Cornwallis, and saw him surrender his sword to General Washington an American officer being about thirty steps from them when Cornwallis delivered him his sword & heard him tell Cornwallis to put on his hat." [Again, this author doubts that this private was close enough to hear what was being said.]

Archibald Armstrong was thirteen when he enlisted with his two brothers in the 1st New York Regiment. He served as a drummer, and his two brothers were fifers in the army. Archibald drummed the death march, when Major John Andre, the spy, was executed a year earlier. At Yorktown he sounded the salute when Cornwallis surrendered."[14]

William Dye served in the Virginia militia, and years after the war his widow, Sarah, filed for his pension [R8719]. She stated that her husband told her the following, "Her husband was present at the surrender of Cornwallis and saw that officer came out and surrender his sword to Washington. He said Cornwallis walked up to where Washington stood and struck his sword in the ground near Washington. Washington took the sword and turned it about and looked at it and then handed it back to Cornwallis again."

Surrendering the standards:

Surrender of British standards at Yorktown from *The Pictorial Field-book of the Revolution Vol. 1* by Benson John Lossing, 1850, page 525.

It had been arranged by Colonel Hamilton, the officer of the day, that the British and German regimental standards should be received by twenty-eight American sergeants, who were drawn up in line under the command of Ensign Robert Wilson, the youngest commissioned officer in the army. Wilson was eighteen years old at the time of the surrender and had entered the army at the age of twelve.

When the American sergeants approached the British captains to accept the standards, the British refused to present their flags to non-commissioned officers. Hamilton, sitting upon a horse at a distance, observed the hesitation by the British. He rode up and, when informed of the problem, he ordered Ensign Wilson to receive the flags and then hand them to the American sergeants.

Robert Wilson's wife applied for his pension [W7746] in 1853 and gave the following statement,

> He was the Ensign who was appointed by Colonel Hamilton the officer of the day to conduct the ceremony of receiving the Brittish Flags at the surrender of Lord Cornwallis at Yorktown; he (Wilson) being then the youngest Ensign in the army and that he performed that service as such Ensign & received the colours of twenty eight Regiments from twenty eight Brittish Captains & handed them over to twenty eight American Sergeants under the directions of Col. Hamilton. I had often talked over with said Wilson the __?__ & hardships he had passed through while a soldier & officer in the army of the Revolution & well remembers the accounts given by him of the same & which said accounts have been often repeated to others by him in her presence the truth of which I never doubted.

All but one of the regiments turned their standards or colors over to the Americans. Two members of the Royal Welsh Fusiliers wrapped their regimental flags around their bodies and under their clothes. They were paroled with other troops and sent back to England.

Description and conduct of the troops:

Washington told his men not to insult the enemy by huzzaing or shouting at them. "Posterity," he said, "will huzza for us."[15]

Seventeen year old Robert Whiteley of the Virginia militia and his two brothers were at the surrender. Robert said in his pension application [R11459], "That after the surrender of the American troops were formed into lines. That the soldiers were ordered not to laugh, talk or make any noise while the British troops passed between the American lines. That he saw the British troops passed between the lines carrying their muskets by the brick [butt of the gun?] and dragging the Bayonets on the ground."

The conduct of the two victorious armies was very different. By the French, the English were received with every mark of civility, and it was observed that salutes were universally exchanged between them, while such marks of courtesy were almost totally omitted by the Americans.[16]

The difference in conduct of the Americans toward the British should not have been a surprise. The Americans had been fighting the war for a long six years. Before the fighting they had suffered at the hands of the British for many years and a large number of the troops had lost friends or property in the war and were glad to be rid of the British. Most of the American troops did not share or understand the European code of military conduct as did the French.

Claude Blanchard, the Commissary-in-Chief under General Rochambeau, wrote in his journal about the attitude of the British troops, "The English displayed much arrogance and ill humor during this melancholy ceremony; they particularly affected great contempt for the Americans."[17]

Stephen Popp was a Hessian soldier, and in his diary he gave an interesting description of the French and American troops at the surrender,

> At 3-4 P.M. all of Lord Cornwallis' troops with all our personal effects and our side arms, colors covered, marched out of our lines on the Williamsburg road, between the Regiments of the enemy, which were all drawn up, with colors flying and bands playing, our drums beating, the French were on our right in parade, their General at the head, fine looking young fellows the soldiers were, on our left the Americans, mostly regular, but the Virginia militia too, but to look on them and on the others was like day and night. We were astonished at the great force and we were only a Corporal's Guard compared to their overwhelming numbers. They were well supplied and equipped in every way. We were marched to a level plain, where the French Hussars formed a circle around us, and there we lay down our arms etc. After depositing our arms, we marched back to our camps and had leave to go where we pleased. No one was allowed to go into our camp. The French mounted guard and patrol over it. Lt. Hayder of our's returned and told us how he and some English and German troops had been taken prisoners.[18]

Johann Conrad Dohla wrote how impressed he was with the appearance of the French troops,

> On the whole, the French troops made an excellent appearance. They were smart, tall, and well-built men, all wearing white gaiters, and some regiments wearing red uniforms, but most in white and a few in green. The German Alsace Regiment, however, wore blue uniforms. On our march, the Americans were on our left, or on the left wing, and lined up with Generals Washington, Gates, Greene, and Wayne. They stood in three ranks. First, the regulars, who also had hautboists and musicians making beautiful music and who presented a decent appearance. Next came the militia of Virginia and Maryland, who however, made a poor appearance, ragged and tattered.[19]

The French troops were in white uniforms, with plumed and decorated officers at their head. They were trimmed with gorgeous standards of white silk and embroidered with golden flour-de-lis floating along the line. The Americans were not such an attraction in outward appearances but were still eagerly eyed by their antagonists. Among the war-worn Continentals there was a variety of dress, poor at the best, distinguishing the men of different lines. But, to compensate for lack of show, there was a soldierly bearing about them which commanded attention. The militia formed in their rear, presented a less martial sight, so far as clothing and order were concerned.[20]

General Washington rode his favorite charger, named Nelson, which was a light sorrel, sixteen hands high, with white face and legs.[21]

Doctor James Thacher said it was "a glorious day," as he rode out to view the surrender. In his journal he made a comparison between the French and American troops,

> The French troops, in complete uniform, displayed a martial and noble appearance, their band of music, of which the timbrel formed a part, is a delightful novelty, and produced while marching to the ground, a most enchanting effect. The Americans though not all in uniform nor their dress so neat, yet exhibited an erect soldierly air, and every countenance beamed with satisfaction and joy.
>
> The Royal troops, while marching through the line formed by the allied army, exhibited a decent and neat appearance, as respects arms and clothing, for their commander opened his store and directed every soldier to be furnished with a new suit complete, prior to capitulation. But in their line of march we remarked a disorderly and unsoldierly conduct, their step was irregular, and their ranks frequently broken. Some of the platoon officers appeared to be exceedingly chagrined when given the word "ground arms," and I am witness that they performed this duty in a very unofficer like manner, and that many of the soldiers manifested a sullen temper, throwing their arms on the pile with violence, as if determined to render them useless.[22]

The Abbé Robin, Chaplain to the French Army, wrote his observations of the difference in the troops, "Cornwallis opened all the stores to the soldiers before the capitulation took place. Each had a new suit, but all their finery seemed to humble them the more, when contrasted with the miserable appearance of the Americans."[23]

Baron Von Closen, a German in the French service, paid the American soldiers a compliment, even though their appearance was dirty and ragged, "In passing between the two armies, they showed the greatest scorn for the Americans, who, to tell the truth, were eclipsed by our army in splendor of appearance and dress, for most of these unfortunate persons were clad in small jackets of white cloth, dirty and ragged, and a number of them were almost barefoot. The English had given them the nickname of Yankee Doodle. What does it matter! An intelligent man would say. These people are much more praise-worthy and brave to fight as they do, when they are so poorly supplied with everything."

Laying down of arms:

At two o'clock the British troops marched between the American and French troops in a field to the left of the French lines to lay down their weapons. The army that had been invaders of the south for the past fourteen months were now prisoners of war.

Many of the British soldiers were not happy about having to surrender their weapons to the Americans, who they considered rebels and traitors. They turned to face the French as their way of letting it be known that they thought them as the conquerors.

Lafayette, as a way of retaliation, had the band of the light infantry play "Yankee Doodle." "Then", said Lafayette, "they did look at us, my dear sir, but were not very well pleased."[24] This was a song that the British used to ridicule the Americans at the beginning of the war, and which they sung to all their prisoners. This insult to the British troops caused them to throw their weapons down so hard that some were broken. A word from General Lincoln put a stop to this.

British General Dumas observed that Colonel Abercromby, of the English guards, at the moment when his troops laid down their arms, went away quickly, covering his face and biting his sword.[25]

In the field French Hussars [light cavalry] had formed a closed circle. One regiment after another marched into this circle, stacked arms, and laid down all weapons. Colonel von Seybothen led his men into the circle and gave the commands, "Present arms!" Then, "Ground your weapons and lay down cartridge boxes and sabers!" His cheeks wet with tears.[26]

General Knox and his brother William watched as the British soldiers surrendered their weapons. At the end, Knox rounded up more than 7,320 muskets from the defeated soldiers. He was pleased with the events of the day, because during the war the British had displayed an arrogant attitude and showed little respect for the American army.

Johann Conrad Dohla wrote in his diary,

> All officers of Cornwallis's army, English as well as German, were allowed to keep their swords, as an honor from the French, which is a custom of war with them. All of the high enemy generals were present in the circle and showed their goodwill and best wishes toward the captured troops. Our two regiments were especially well received by them.[27]

Lieutenant William Feltman of the 1st Pennsylvania wrote in his journal, "The British army marched out and grounded their arms in front of our line. Our whole army drew up for them to march through, the French army on their right and the American army on their left. The British prisoners all appeared to be much in liquor. After they grounded their arms they returned to town again."[28]

The long march back to British lines and treatment by allied forces:

Major St. George Tucker of the Virginia Militia wrote in his journal about the surrender and the British beating a march,

> At two OClock to day a Detachmt. of American Light Infantry and French Grenadiers took possession of the horn-work on the East End of Yorktown—Our Army was drawn up in a Line on each side of the road extending from our front parallel to the Forks of the Road at Hudson Allen's the Americans on the right, the French on the left. Thro' these Lines the whole British Army march'd their Drums in Front beating a slow March. Their Colours furl'd and Cased. I am told they were restricted by the capitulation from beating a French or American march. General Lincoln with his Aids conducted them—Having passed thro' our whole Army they grounded their Arms & march'd back again thro' the Army a second Time into the Town—The sight was too pleasing to an American to admit of Description.[29]

As the British troops marched back to Yorktown, some Americans began to taunt and shout threats at them. The American officers ordered their men to stop, which allowed the British soldiers to march back in silence.

Later, the English and French officers were friendly to each other. The French even sent food into Yorktown for them and lent them money. But the Americans and the English shared bitter feelings and they had as little to do with each other as possible.

The Germans of the two armies, the Hessians of Cornwallis' command and the Chasseurs of Lauzun's Regiment, fell into each other's arms, embracing each other; so strong was the feeling of language and race.[30]

Hessian soldier Johann Conrad Dohla described the treatment by the victors,

> When all this was over, we marched back between both armies, but in silence, into our lines and camo, with nothing more than a bit of our remaining equipment in the knapsacks on our backs. All courage and bravery that animates soldiers at times had left us. As we marched back through the armies, the Americans, as victors, made sport of us. We reentered our lines and tents and had complete freedom to go into the city, or the lines, or wherever we wished.
>
> Mostly the French behaved well toward us, but of the Americans, no one except the officers was permitted in the city or in our lines, because the French Grenadiers had formed a ring entirely around our positions and occupied Yorktown with a strong force, and they allowed no one to enter for fear that the American militia, which is always ready to steal, might also steal or plunder or otherwise abuse us as is their practice.[31]

Hessian Captain Johann Ewald said that after the surrender every officer was treated by the French with courtesy and respect. He felt that General Washington was not pleased with the overly friendly actions of the French toward the British officers. Ewald wrote in his diary, "…a cool conduct began to prevail among the two diverse nations [U.S. and French] which, in good fortune, had formed only one."[32]

Chevalier de Chastellux, a general in the French Army, described the behavior of the surrendering troops, "After the surrender, the English behaved with the same over-bearing insolence as if they had been conquerors; the Scots wept bitterly, while the German only conducted themselves decently, and in a manner becoming prisoners.[33]

The British marched back to their tents through the same lines and were given a few days of rest, before they were sent off as prisoners of war.

Surrender at Gloucester:

Caleb Jenkins joined the Virginia militia at the age of sixteen. Five years later he was at Yorktown and he stated in his pension application [S8757], "At the time of the surrender the Company to which he was attached was on the Eastern side of Sarah's Creek, a short distance from Gloucester town, watching the movements of the British forces at that place."

The surrender of Gloucester was not as well documented as the surrender of Yorktown. There were 153 sick soldiers out of the over 1,000 troops that surrendered there.

Washington wrote to General George Weedon of the Virginia Militia at Gloucester,

> I am extremely apprehensive that if great care is not taken, the Arms and Accoutrements which the British are to lay down this day at Gloucester will be embezzeled or exchanged. I shall therefore expect that the strictest Guard may be placed over them from a Corps on which you can depend, the Officer commanding it to be answerable for the number surrendered, untill a Commissary of Stores shall take regular possession of them—In the mean time, let them be put in as secure a place as possible.[34]

Colonel Tarleton communicated to General Cloise that he was concerned about his personal safety, if he surrendered to the Virginia Militia. There were many in the militia that had a deep hatred for Tarleton, which the British Colonel had earned. General Cloise told the colonel that he would surrender to the Legion of Lauzun and the Corps of Mercer, and the rest of the allied troops would be held back in camp.

At three o'clock Tarleton and his cavalry rode out with sabers drawn. They were followed by Simcoe's Queens' Rangers. The French then took possession of the British redoubts and stationed protection for the British from any hostility.

Henry Cook served several tours in the Virginia militia. In 1781 he joined the militia again as a substitute for his father, and he served under General Muhlenberg as they marched to Williamsburg. He stated in his pension application [S3181],

> I then marched to Hog Island and crossed James River, then to Old Williamsburg and there fell in with the main army commanded by General Washington. Then marched to Yorktown and after remaining on the York side for some time crossed the Little York River and was stationed on the Gloucester side under the command of General Weeden and remained there until the surrender of Cornwallis. After he had surrendered two companies were detached to take all the property belonging to the Americans which the British had taken from them, in one of which companies he served and took upward of six hundred Negroes from the British and put them under guard in the fort on the Gloucester side. Then the company which fell under my command by the sickness of Captain Night and Lieutenant Nance were ordered to convey the prisoners to the barracks at Albemarle Court House, but before we reached that place his brother John Cook was taken sick and by the

permission of Col. Baytop (I think), we were both permitted to return home some time in November same year 1781 with orders to hold himself in readiness to go into service again if needed but was never called upon anymore.

Losses during the siege:

Reported losses on both sides vary from source to source. One of the official British reports had 156 killed, 326 wounded, and 70 missing from Yorktown. Other reports ranged from 142 to 309 killed and 326 to 595 wounded. Total captured ranged from 7,416 to 7,685. This does not include the soldiers that escaped aboard the *Bonetta*.

Gaspard de Gallatin, of the French Army, reported in his journal that the losses at Gloucester were, "…a total of 1,850 troops. Killed, 389, wounded, 679, and taken prisoner or deserted, 135."[35]

Washington reported that American losses from the start of the siege to the capture of redoubts 9 and 10, were 234 killed and sixty-five wounded. After the taking of the two redoubts, losses were small. The French reported sixty killed and 193 wounded. The number killed did not include the number of men that later died from their wounds. Militia numbers were not always included in the total. Some sources had up to 300 Americans and 52 Frenchmen killed.

In addition to the over 7,000 men prisoners, the Americans received 400 horses, 174 cannons, and 40 vessels, of which most were sinking or damaged. One source reported over 8,000 prisoners and 214 guns.

St. George Tucker wrote,

> Three thousand two hundred & seventy three Men march'd out & grounded their Arms on the York side of the River—Including the non commissioned Officers the Garrison in York amounted to five thousand five hundred and sixty four Men, and two hundred & fifty four commission'd Officers, including thirty two Surgeons with their Mates—Lord Cornwallis and General [Charles] O Hara are not included—I have not yet heard the strength of the post at Gloucester—It is about a thousand Men I believe—At York there were taken sixty five pieces of Brass Ordnance, and twenty two Standards.[36]

There was no report of the number of civilians that were killed or wounded. Most of their property was destroyed or plundered.

The end of the day:

That night General Washington gave a dinner for the general officers of all three armies. Cornwallis, still feeling "ill" respectfully declined and again sent General O'Hara in his place. The only British high officer not invited to the social event was the hated Colonel Tarleton. It was a very sociable evening, however, but as the evening wore on the atmosphere began to change. The Americans became noticeably annoyed at the friendship that began to show between the British and French officers.

It appeared to the Americans that the French and British felt themselves social equals that were above the Americans. After all, most of the American officers came from a common background. Alexander Hamilton, born out of wedlock, started out as a clerk, both Lincoln and Washington were former farmers, and Anthony Wayne was a tanner.

The French artillery officer, Jean-Francois de Clermont Crevecoeur, felt that the French and English officers shared a good upbringing that bonded them together and the Americans should not be surprised they chose to be together. It did not help matters when the French General Rochambeau loaned Cornwallis a large sum of money to pay his troops. The money was later repaid by General Clinton in New York, and as a token of his appreciation he also sent 100 bottles of wine.

In the American camp there was one man that suffered from sadness while all the rest were shouting and dancing with joy. When General Washington left his home at Mount Vernon the previous September, he allowed his beloved twenty-seven year old step-son, John Parke Custis (Jacky), to accompany him to Yorktown. The young man had begged his step-father, the day before he left, to allow him to take part in the war, that up until now he had not seen. Reluctantly Washington had agreed to let him come.

Jacky had come down with the "bilious fever", which had ravaged both allied and British soldiers during the siege. The young man was suffering from nausea, vomiting, high fever, and strong diarrhea, and he should have been in bed. But he convinced Doctor James Craik, George Washington's personal physician, to allow him to attend the surrender ceremony. A carriage was summoned and Jacky was set in it, and he watched the surrender at a short distance away. After it was over, Doctor Craik thought it wise to have Jacky taken to the home of Colonel Bassett, the husband of Mrs. Washington's sister, at Eltham. Washington knew that his step-son was seriously ill, but because of all the pressing matters before him, he could only send a short note to his wife about her son.

Portrait of John "Jacky" Parke Custis---New York Public Library

Washington's wife and Jacky's young wife hurried to the sick man's bedside. Days later Washington was finally able to visit the boy, and he rode all night to the Bassett house. He arrived just in time to see his step-son take his last breath. The young man that wanted to take part in the siege became one of its last causalities. Jacky Custis died on November 5, 1781, and he left behind a widow and two children.

Later Washington, while at Mount Vernon, wrote to Lafayette, "I arrived at Eltham, the seat of Colonel Bassett, in time to see poor Custis breathe his last. This unexpected and affecting event threw Mrs. Washington and Mrs. Custis, who were both present, into such deep distress that the circumstances of it, and a duty I owed to the deceased in assisting at his funeral, prevented my reaching this place [Mount Vernon] till the 13th." Later Washington told the grieving widow, "Your two children I adopt as my own."[37]

The night of the surrender Washington took great pleasure in writing to Congress about the surrender of Cornwallis. The letter was sent to Thomas McKean the President of Congress,

> I have the Honor to inform Congress, that a Reduction of the British Army under the Command of Lord Cornwallis, is most happily effected—The unremitting Ardor which actuated every Officer & Soldier in the combined Army on this Occasion, has principally led to this Important Event, at an earlier period than my most sanguine Hopes had induced me to expect.
>
> The singular Spirit of Emulation, which animated the whole Army from the first Commencement of our Operations, has filled my Mind with the highest pleasure & Satisfaction—and had given me the happiest presages of Success.
>
> On the 17th instant, a Letter was received from Lord Cornwallis, proposing a Meeting of Commissioners, to consult on Terms for the Surrender of the Posts of York & Gloucester—This Letter (the first which had passed between us) opened a correspondence, a copy of which I do myself the Honor to inclose that Correspondence was followed by the Definitive Capitulation, which was agreed to, & Signed on the 19th Copy of which is also herewith transmitted—and which, I hope, will meet the Approbation of Congress.
>
> I should be wanting in the feelings of Gratitude, did I not mention on this Occasion, with the warmest Sense of Acknowlegments, the very chearfull & able Assistance, which I have received in the Course of our Operations, from his Excellency the Count de Rochambeau, and all his Officers of every Rank, in their respective Capacities. Nothing could equal this Zeal of our Allies, but the emulating Spirit of the American Officers, whose ardor would not suffer their Exertions to be exceeded.
>
> The very uncommon Degree of Duty & Fatigue which the Nature of the Service required from the officers of Engineers & Artillery of both Armies, obliges me particularly to mention the Obligations I am under to the Commanding & other Officers of those Corps.

I wish it was in my Power to express to Congress, how much I feel myself indebted to The Count de Grasse and the Officers of the Fleet under his Command, for the distinguished Aid and Support which has been afforded by them; between whom, & the Army, the most happy Concurrence of Sentiments & Views have subsisted, and from whom, every possible Co-operation has been experienced, which the most harmonious Intercourse could afford.

Returns of the Prisoners, Military Stores, Ordnance, Shipping & other Matters, I shall do myself the Honor to transmit to Congress, as soon as they can be collected by the Heads of Departments, to which they belong.

Colo. Laurens & the Viscount de Noailles, on the Part of the combined Army, were the Gentlemen who acted as Commissioners for formg & settg the Terms of Capitulation & Surrender herewith transmitted—to whom I am particularly obliged for their Readiness & Attention exhibited on the Occasion.

Your Excellency & Congress will be pleased to accept my Congratulations on this happy Event, & believe me to be with the highest Respect & Esteem Sir Your Excellencys Most Obedient and most humble Servant.[38]

Colonel Tench Tilghman---Library of Congress

After the surrender terms were signed, Washington asked Colonel Tench Tilghman to carry his letter to the President of Congress in Philadelphia to inform them of the good news. Also, included was a note relating to the bearer of the letter,

> Sir, Col. Tilghman, one of my aide-de-camp, will have the honor to deliver these dispatches to your excellency. He will be able to inform you of every minute circumstance which is not particularly mentioned in my letter. His merits, which are too well known to need my observations at this time, have gained my particular attention, and I could wish that they may be honored by the notice of your excellency and congress.[39]

David Forman wrote to Washington at nine o'clock on the 19th to give him news of the British fleet from New York,

> I am this day Informed from good Authority that Agreeable to my Opinion offered your Excly in my letter of the 18th The Troops did come down in the Transports.
>
> I am also Informed that no Transports will go to Sea with the Men of War, and the Reason of employing Transports and Store Ships was nearly for the purpose of Making the Ships of War so light as to insure them a Quick passage over the Barr—these 80 & 90 Gun Ships not being able to pass it at any Time with there Compliment of Stores on Board and only at Spring Tides when They are ligtned—I am also well informed that the Reason of these failing to get out Yesterday was for want of Water—The Tide not haveing been so high by more than a foot as usual allthough at the Time of Spring Tides.
>
> Last Evening Genl Clinton and his Family went on Board the princessa of 74 Guns of the Troops were all Taken on board the Ships of War out of the Transports.
>
> This Morning Some of these Ships of War got over the Barr and it was Expected the Whole Fleete would have got out—wheather it did or not I have not heard and I may add that being well informd they would sail as Soon as they got out I desired my Horsemen not to Return again untill the Fleet Saild unless some entire New Matter Turned up—I was allso Informed this Morning that Twelve of the fleet was in the offing under the Convoy of some Frigates—Mr Rivington publishes the arrival of an Express boat from Lord Cornwallace that says His Lordships Garrison was in high Spirits the 12th Inst.

I have wrote thus for in order to save every minute of Time that I may only have to add the Sailing of the Fleete and dispatch the Express Immediately.

Ten OClock. I have This Minute Accts That all The Ships of War Sailed between Sun down and Dark and the Transports after delivering the Baggage Stores were returning to New York.⁴⁰

With the surrender, the marines and seamen of the British navy were prisoners of the French and the land forces of the United States. All military equipment was to be delivered to the Americans unimpaired. The army prisoners were to be sent into the interior of Virginia, Maryland, and Pennsylvania and be given the same amount of rations as the American soldiers. Lord Cornwallis would travel to New York on the sloop *Bonetta,* which would not be searched. The sloop would be returned to the French with all hands on board.

Lieutenant Ebenezer Wild, of the 1ˢᵗ Massachusetts Regiment, wrote about the surrender in his journal and finished by writing, "The prisoners are to remain in York and Gloucester till conveniences will permit of their marching to the places of their destination which is the back parts of Virginia and Maryland."⁴¹

Chapter 14

Personal Accounts of the Surrender

"We were heartily glad the siege was over, for we all thought there would be another attack, if Gen Cornwallis had delayed the surrender." ---Hessian soldier Stephen Popp

British and Hessian accounts:

Johann Conrad Dohla, a Hessian soldier, thanked God that his life had been spared during the siege. He gave a detailed description of the surrender in his diary,

> The unfortunate day for England when the otherwise so famous and brave General Lord Cornwallis, with all his troops and the ships in the harbor, had to surrender to the united French and American troops under the command of General Washington, and the Marquis de Lafayette.
>
> On this day, in the morning, I went for the last time on the engineer watch. At twelve o'clock noon all watches and posts were cancelled. Only a regimental watch of one sergeant with twelve men remained on duty a few hours more. During the cancellation of the watches, Private Riedel, of Beust's Company of our regiment, deserted. He had a wife and child at New York. Now the Capitulation was final. The French and Americans immediately occupied our works and the line and all magazines and storehouses.
>
> Nothing of our equipment and uniform items was taken or even touched; instead we were treated according to law and fairness and the customs of war. We were, on one side, happy that finally this siege was ended, and that it was done with a reasonable accord, because we always believed we would be taken by storm. If it had continued only a few more days, it would really have resulted in a major attack, because the French Grenadiers already had such orders.
>
> For my part, I also had good reason to thank God that He was my Protector, Powerful Helper, and Savior, who during the siege had so graciously saved my life and protected my body and all my limbs from illness, wounds, and all enemy shots. Oh! How many thousand bullets and deathly situations have I encountered face to face!
>
> During the afternoon, between three and four o'clock, all troops, with all their belongings, weapons, and side arms, with covered colors but with drums and fifes marched out of our lines and the camp. Brigadier General O'Hara led us out and surrendered us.
>
> We marched along Williams Street, or on the road that leads to Williamsburg, in columns, with shouldered arms, through the entire enemy army, while our drummers beat a march. The entire army of the combined powers, France and America, stood under arms, by regiment, with dressed ranks. In front of each regiment stood the generals and staff officers, who in part, among the French had splendidly dressed orderlies by their sides. All the French generals wore large stars and French military decorations. On the right of each French regiment a white silk flag, decorated with three silver embroidered lilies, was paraded. Behind the flag stood drummers and fifers, and before the flag, the hautboists, who played splendid music.[1]

Captain Samuel Graham of the 76th British Regiment wrote in his memoir about the surrender and his visit to the French lines,

> On the 19th the garrison marched out betwixt the two lines of American and French troops reluctantly enough, and laid down their arms. A corporal next to me shed tears, and, embracing his firelock, threw it down, saying, "May you never get so good a master." This over, the regiments set about fixing upon the officers who were to remain on parole of honour with the troops.
>
> In the 76th this was done by casting lots, which was also the mode followed by the field officers of the British army; and it having fallen upon Colonel Lake, that officer expressed himself in such a manner on the occasion, as induced Major Gordon to say that he would take the duty for him, an offer which was joyfully accepted. It fell to my lot to be one of the captains of the 76th detailed to remain with the soldiers in America. Our departure was fixed at the following morning, so that little time was given for preparation, but having a great desire to visit the enemy's works, which we had so long contemplated with feelings understood by human nature, but which language can ill describe, accompanied by a friend I visited the French lines, and met with much courtesy from the French.
>
> On top of the Parapet where the guns were placed which had been spiked in the "sortie," they showed me a grave, saying, "Voila un de vos brave gens" [Here lies one of your brave people]. It was that of a serjeant in the Foot Guards who had fallen there. [2]

British Naval officer Bartholomew James described the events of the 19th in his journal,

> Seeing that the enemy was determined to confine us to such terms as they alone chose to grant, and that we had not as yet experienced the fire of the flanking redoubts with a number of pieces of heavy artillery then ready to open on us, and finding that the garrison was reduced to about three thousand effective men in want of both provision and ammunition, his lordship thought it, as he himself expresses, necessary to save the lives of the few brave men then left in the garrison, and accordingly at noon we surrendered prisoners of war to the United States of America, the navy only excepted, who became prisoners to the Comte de Grasse. At one o'clock a regiment of American troops, followed by another of French, took possession of the works with drums beating and colours flying: the British flag was struck, and the American one displayed on our works. At three o'clock the garrison marched out with drums beating and colours cased to the enemy's lines, where, having grounded their arms, they returned again into the town; the enemy at the same time marched in and took possession of the garrison.[3]

For the Hessian soldier Stephen Popp it was a day of happiness, because the siege was over and he had survived. He also was promoted to Lieutenant. He wrote in his diary,

> The terms of surrender finally agreed on. At 12 M. our lines were withdrawn and the French and Americans marched in and took possession of our works, lines, magazines, and storehouses, nothing was disturbed, and our arms and equipments were left to us. Everything was done in regular military way. We were heartily glad the siege was over, for we all thought there would be another attack, if Gen Cornwallis had delayed the surrender, the French Grenadiers were to lead it, during the siege the enemy had fired more than 8000 great bombs, of from 100 to 100 and 200 pounds.[4]

American and French Accounts:

Colonel Jonathan Trumbull, friend and adviser to General Washington, wrote about the day in his journal,

All matters being settled the articles are this day signed, and the troops march out, etc. This day Earl Cornwallis is invited to dine, but excuses himself on account of health. Keeps his Quarters. General O'Hara conducts the troops and is attended by General Lincoln. Our army ranged in two lines through which the prisoners pass. The Americans on the right, the Allies on the left. The two Generals with their suits at the head of their lines on horseback. A Grand Spectacle! A useful lesson to the pride and ambition of man. General O'Hara dines at Head Quarters, very social and easy.[5]

Sergeant Joseph Plumb Martin described the surrender in his book,

The next day we were ordered to put ourselves in as good order as our circumstances would admit, to see (what was the completion of our present wishes) the British army march out and stack their arms. The trenches, where they crossed the road leading to the town, were leveled and all things put in order for this grand exhibition. After breakfast, on the nineteenth, we were marched onto the ground and paraded on the right-hand side of the road, and the French forces on the left. We waited two or three hours before the British made their appearance. They were not always so dilatory, but they were compelled at last, by necessity, to appear, all armed, with bayonets fixed, drums beating, and faces lengthening. They were led by General O'Hara, with the American General Lincoln on his right, the Americans and French beating a march as they passed out between them. It was a noble sight to us, and the more so, as it seemed to promise a speedy conclusion to the contest. The British did not make so good an appearance as the German forces, but there was certainly some allowance to be made in their favor. The English felt their honor wounded, the Germans did not greatly care whose hands they were in. The British paid the Americans, seemingly, but little attention as they passed them, but they eyed the French with considerable malice depicted in their countenances. They marched to the place appointed and stacked their arms; they then returned to the town in the same manner they had marched out, except being divested of their arms.[6]

Lieutenant John Bell Tilden showed no emotions, as he wrote in his journal about the surrender and the end of the siege, "At 1 o'clock the terms for surrendering the garrisons of York and Gloucester were agreed on, when Major Hamilton with a detachment marched into town and took possession of their works. I attended the Baron [Steuben] in town; nothing worthy of notice in it, except the earth much torn up by our shells."[7]

Major St. George Tucker of the Virginia Militia wrote in his journal about the surrender and the British beating a march,

At two OClock to day a Detachmt. Of American Light Infantry and French Grenadiers took possession of the horn-work on the East End of Yorktown. Our Army was drawn up in a Line on each side of the road extending from our front parallel to the Forks of the Road at Hudson Allen's the American on the right, the French on the Left. Thro' these Lines the whole British Army march'd their Drums in Front beating a slow march. Their Colours furl'd and Cased. I am told they were restricted by the capitulation from beating a French or American march. General Lincoln with his Aids conducted them. Having passed thro' our whole Army they grounded their arms & march'd back again thro' the Army a second Time into the Town. The sight was too pleasing to an American to admit of Description.[8]

Sarah Matthews Reed Osborn was twenty-six at the time of the siege of Yorktown. Her first husband, William Reed, died of a wound he received while serving in Virginia. She married Aaron Osborn in January of 1780. Aaron had joined the army without Sarah's knowledge but when he did tell her, he asked her to go with him. Sarah refused, until she was promised transportation either on horseback or in a supply wagon.

On November 20, 1837, in order to obtain a window's pension [pension application W4558] and land bounty of 160 acres, Sarah gave the following deposition about her experiences in the war. Her grandson filed the pension application for her. Sarah was referred to as the deponent in the transcript, as she described the surrender,

> They dug entrenchments nearer and nearer to Yorktown every night or two till the last. While digging that, the enemy fired very heavy till about nine o'clock next morning, then stopped, and the drums from the enemy beat excessively. Deponent was a little way off in Col. Von Schaick, or the officers, marque and a number of officers were present among whom was Captain Gregg, who, on account of infirmities did not go out much to do duty, the drums continued beating, and all at once the officers hurrahed and swung their hats, and deponent asked, "what is the matter now?" One of them replied "are not you soldier enough to know what it means?" Deponent replied "no", they then replied, "the British have surrendered." Deponent having provisions ready, carried the same down to the entrenchments that morning and four of the soldiers whom she was in the habit of cooking for ate their breakfast. Deponent stood on one side of the road and the officers upon the other side, when the British officers came out of the town and rode up to the American officers and delivered up their swords which the deponent thinks were returned again, and the British officers rode right on before the army who marched out beating and playing a melancholy tune, their drums covered with black hankf's and their fifes with black ribbons toed around them—into old field and there grounded their arms and then returned into town again to await their destiny.
>
> Deponent recollects seeing a great many American officers some on horse back and some on foot but can not call them by names. Washington, Lafayette, and Clinton were among the number. The British General at the head of the army was a large portly man, full face, and the tears rolled down his cheeks as he passed along. But it was not Cornwallis. She saw the latter afterwards and his being a man of diminutive appearance and having crossed eyes [probably General O'Hara].
>
> On going into town she noticed two dead negroes lying by the musket house. She had the curiosity to go into a large building that stood nearby and there she noticed the cupboards smashed to piece and china dishes and other ware strewed around upon the floors and among the rest a pewter cover to a hot basin that had a handle on it. She picked it up supposing it belonged to the British, but the governor came in and claimed it as his said he would have the __?__ of giving it away as it was the last one out of 12 that he could see and accordingly presented it to the deponent and she afterwards brought it home with them to Orange Country sold it for old pewter which she has a hundred times regretted.

About three months after the birth of Sarah's last child, Aaron Osborn, Jr., she last saw her husband who left her at New Windsor and never returned. Sarah married her third husband John Benjamin in April 1787. He also served in the Revolutionary War. When John died in 1827, Sarah never remarried. She died at the age of 114 on April 20, 1859 in Mount Pleasant, Pennsylvania. She was granted a pension of $88 a year *"because of her own personal service"* during the war.[9]

Twenty-seven year old Colonel William Fontaine of the Virginia Militia stood with his men and the rest of the army that lined the road near Yorktown. He wrote to a friend on October 26, 1781, about the surrender of Cornwallis,

> I had the happiness to see that British army which so lately spread dismay and desolation through all our country, march forth on the 20th inst. [19th] at 3 o'clock through our whole army, drawn up in two lines about 20 yards distance and return disrobed of all their terrors, so humbled and so struck at the appearance

of our troops, that their knees seemed to tremble, and you could not see a platoon that marched in any order. Such a noble figure did our array make, that I scarce know which drew my attention most. You could not have heard a whisper or seen the least motion throughout our whole line, but every countenance was erect, and expressed a serene cheerfulness. Cornwallis pretended to be ill, and imposed the mortifying duty of leading forth the captives on Gen. O'Hara. Their own officers acknowledge them to be the flower of the British troops, but I do not think they at all exceeded in appearance our own or the French. The latter, you may be assured, are very different from the ideas formerly inculcated in us of a people living on frogs and coarse vegetables. Finer troops I never saw. His Lordship's defence I think was rather feeble. His surrender was eight or ten days sooner than the most sanguine expected, though his force and resources were much greater than we conceived.[10]

Colonel Henry Lee was at the ceremony and wrote in his memoirs,

Valiant troops yielding up their arms after fighting in defence of a cause dear to them (because the cause of their country), under a leader who, throughout the war, in every grade and in every situation to which he had been called, appeared the Hector of his host. Battle after battle had he fought; climate after climate had he endured; towns had yielded to his mandate, posts were abandoned at his approach; armies were conquered by his prowess; one nearly exterminated, another chased from the confines of South Carolina beyond the Dan into Virginia, and a third severely chastised in that State on the shores of James River. But here even he, in the midst of his splendid career, found his conqueror.

The road through which they marched was lined with spectators, French and American. On one side the commander-in-chief, surrounded by his suite and the American staff, took his station; on the other side, opposite to him, was the Count de Rochambeau, in like manner attended. The captive army approached, moving slowly in column with grace and precision. Universal silence was observed amid the vast concourse, and the utmost decency prevailed: exhibiting in demeanor an awful sense of the vicissitudes of human life, mingled with commiseration for the unhappy. The head of the column approached the commander-in-chief; O'Hara, mistaking the circle, turned to that on his left, for the purpose of paying his respects to the commander-in-chief, and requesting further orders; when, quickly discovering his error, with much embarrassment in his countenance he flew across the road, and, advancing up to Washington, asked pardon for his mistake, apologized for the absence of Lord Cornwallis, and begged to know his further pleasure. The General, feeling his embarrassment, relieved it by referring him with much politeness to General Lincoln for his government. Returning to the head of the column, it moved under the guidance of Lincoln to the field selected for the conclusion of the ceremony.

Every eye was turned, searching for the British commander-in-chief, anxious to look at that man, heretofore so much the object of their dread. All were disappointed. Cornwallis held himself back from the humiliating scene; obeying sensations which his great character ought to have stifled. He had been unfortunate, not from any false step or deficiency of exertion on his part, but from the infatuated policy of his superior [General Henry Clinton], and the united power of his enemy, brought to bear upon him alone. There was nothing with which he could reproach himself; there was nothing with which he could reproach his brave and faithful army: why not, then, appear at its head in the day of misfortune, as he had always done in the day of triumph? The British general in this instance deviated from his usual line of conduct, dimming the splendor of his long and brilliant career.[11]

Daniel Trabue, a former officer in the Virginia Militia, was present for the surrender of Cornwallis. He and his brothers probably made a lot of money selling "spirits" to the troops on both sides. He wrote in his journal,

The news [of the surrender] went far and near, and a vast number of people from Different towns and the country came forward to see the great and mighty sight.

The British had a very large gate in the South side of their fort, and on that side was a level old field. Our army was placed in a solid square column about half a mile or more around the fort gate; it was a great sight. Part of our line was Continental Troops, part was Militia, and part was French. On the out-side of this column of soldiery was a vast number of spectators, mostly in carriages such as chariots, Fayatons, chairs, and gigs, also some common wagons. The carriages were full of gentlemen, ladies and children, besides a number on horse-back, and some on foot. Some had come as far as the city of Richmond, which was upwards of 70 miles. There were many thousands of these spectators. General Washington and some of the officers with their aids were about the center of this vast column, immediately before the gate, and about 1/2 or 3/4 of a mile Distant. About the middle of the Day the big gate opened, and the red Coats marched out by Platoons in a solid column with some of their Officers. Our Officers, soldiers and spectators said "Did you ever see the like," and many words were spoken but not loud.

It was the most Tremendous and most admirable Sight that I ever saw. The countenances of our Officers, and soldiers all seemed to claim some credit for the great prize; and the countenances of the spectators seemed to say, also, that they deserved credit. It was truly a wonderful sight to see so many British coming out in their red coats to ground their arms. They marched straight up to General Washington, and gave up their swords and ground their arms or stacked them, and then returned to the Fort.

Our officers and soldiers mostly went to their tents while a few advanced near the Fort to guard the Prisoners. That night I noticed that the officers and soldiers could scarcely talk for laughing, and they could scarcely walk for jumping and Dancing and singing as they went about. There was a Colonel Smith from our County who was on parole. He said to his country men, "Boys, retaliate, remember Sutbery's Old Field, these are the very men that plundered our men, and used them so badly, plunder them; but do not be caught at it, as your Officers would not sanction it." And there was a number of them plundered sure enough.

The Continental Officers and soldiers guarded the Gates of the Fort, and none of the militia were allowed to go in the Fort; one reason was the small-pox was bad there. I had a relative who was a Continental Officer. He was Lieutenant John Trabue; the very next day I went with him all over the Fort. It seemed to be nearly one mile in length by 1/4 mile in width. It was truly a Dreadfully shocking sight to see the damage our bomb-shells had Done. When a shell fell on the ground it would sink under the ground so Deep that when it burst it would throw up a wagon load, or even more of Dirt; and when it fell on a house it Tore it to pieces. The British had a number of holes and Pits Dug all over the Fort, some large and some small with timber in the top edge; when the soldiers would see a shell coming near them they could jump in one of the pits and squat Down until it had burst.

They had some large holes under ground [i.e., caves] where Lord Cornwallis, and some of the nobles staid. They called them bomb-proof, but with all their caution a vast number of them were killed.

I have been told by some of the soldiers since, that there was always some one on the watch. They could see a shell coming, and at times there was Dreadful scampering, and sometimes they would come so often, they were much beset. Mr. Jacob Phillip told me a while before they surrendered they lost 40 men every hour. They threw a number of their arms and cannon in the Deep water.

When a shell would fall on any hard place, so that it would not go under the ground, a soldier would go to it and knock off the fiz, or neck, and then it would not burst. The soldier then received a shilling for that act. They said they did not care much about their life, but that the shilling would buy spirits! There were a number of negroes in the Fort engaged in filling up these holes in the ground, and making all things look as smooth as possible.

The British Officers and Tories looked much dejected, and they had sad countenances, as I saw them passing I hardly heard them say a word. I thought the English soldiers, and Hessians Did not seem to Care much about it.

Everything in the Fort looked gloomy and sad. Lord Cornwallis and his other Officers looked not only sad, but ashamed. They had lived under the ground like ground Hogs. The negroes looked condemned, for the British had promised them their freedom, but instead of freedom they made them haul wagons, by hand, with timber to build their works, and made them work very hard with spades.

> I left their Fort and went to our army, and what a Great Contrast our men presented. They were pert and lively, and still rejoicing. We sold our spirits very fast; the British, and French had plenty of hard money.[12]

Lieutenant Ebenezer Denny of the 4th Pennsylvania Regiment wrote in his journal about the terrible condition of the British lines,

> The British army parade and march out with their colors furled; drums beat as if they did not care how. Grounded their arms and returned to town. Much confusion and riot among the British through the day; many of the soldiers were intoxicated; several attempts in course of the night to break open stores; an American sentinel killed by a British soldier with a bayonet; our patrols kept busy. Glad to be relieved from this disagreeable station. Negroes lie about, sick and dying, in every stage of the small pox. Never was in so filthy a place-some handsome houses, but prodigiously shattered. Vast heaps of shot and shells lying about in every quarter, which came from our works. The shells did not burst, as was expected. Returns of British soldiers, prisoners six thousand, and seamen about one thousand. Lord Cornwallis excused himself from marching out with the troops; they were conducted by General O'Hara. Our loss said to be about three hundred; that of the enemy said not more than five hundred and fifty. Fine supply of stores and merchandise had; articles suitable for clothing were taken for the use of the army. A portion furnished each officer to the amount of sixty dollars.[13]

Washington wrote in his diary,

> 19th. In the Morning early I had them copied and sent word to Lord Cornwallis that I expected to have them signed at 11 Oclock and that the Garrison would March out at two O'clock—both of which were accordingly done. Two redoubts on the Enemys left being possessed (the one by a detachment of French Grenadiers, & the other by American Infantry) with orders to prevent all intercourse between the army & Country and the Town—while Officers in the several departments were employed in taking acct. of the public Stores &ca.[14]

A large number of the soldiers at Yorktown filed for pensions many years later. Here are some of their statements,

John Charlton joined the militia in 1781 at the age of twenty. He stated in his pension application [S2425],

> He had not been at home not more than a month when he was drafted a third time. He went to Cumberland Courthouse where the militia were directed to assemble, and after they had assembled marched off to Little York under Capt. Rich'd. Allen. After he got there & had joined the Regular Continental Army under Gen'l. Washington, they were employed for several days in the works which afterwards compelled the British General, Cornwallis, to surrender himself a prisoner. Here he join Gen'l. Washington, Gen'l. Lafayette &c. He also saw the English General after he became a prisoner in our hands. He particularly remembers a little Frenchman, (who by the legs was much of a gentleman) who acted as major over us after we got to the Regular Army at Little York – his name was Looman (in English)]. he used frequently to declare that his soldiers did not care anything about him, but always said that he loved them – but he was mistaken, for his soldiers were sincerely attached to him. He had many oddities in his conduct & language – such for instance as in attempting to say battalion, he would with much difficulty get out battalia. all of which were sources of amusement to his soldiers. After Cornwallis surrendered, his applicant's Company under Capt. Allen was dispatched with the prisoners to Winchester in Virginia – here we were dismissed.

James Broyhill first enlisted in the Virginia Militia to fight Indians. On his last enlistment the twenty year old was sent to Yorktown. In his pension application [S32136] he stated,

This Declarant, the third time entered the service, about the first of August immediately preceding the surrender of Cornwallis. He volunteered under one Captain Fleming Bates of Halifax County Virginia, Captain Roberts & Faulkner commanded companies from the same County. We went to Yorktown under the Command of Colonel Rodgers, & there found the Army collecting under General Washington. This declarant was then taken from Bates' Company & placed under Captain Faulkner of the Artillery. This declarant was present when the Army of Cornwallis grounded their arms. The British troops marched out of Yorktown, in solid column, between the lines of the American Army, into an old field, where they deposited first their drums, with the fifes on the heads of the drums; struck their colors into the soil, laid their guns on the ground, faced about & marched back into Yorktown. This declarant, with his company & others was engaged in working upon the Breast works & the fortifications during the most of the time that they were there up to about the period of the surrender of Cornwallis. Previous to the surrender, this Declarant was ordered out, to gather corn for the horses in Camp under one Stephen Rand Forage master. After the Surrender he was again placed under the command of Captain Bates, where he was taken sick and discharged.

John Clements was drafted into the militia at the age of seventeen and served several tours in Virginia. He said in his pension application [S12511],

He was present again on James River when the British fired on and blew up a magazine ship, in the river. He was on a pacquett guard and saw the ship blow up. That this service was performed, during and after Arnold's invasion he supposes. [The invasion of New London on September 6, 1781.]

That in the begining of September in the year of the surrender of York and very soon after the army passed through Goochland he was again drafted and marched as private in the company of militia from that county under Captain Duke – Joined the army at WmsBurg marched with the army to York and Bates was made capt. He worked in the trenches, and was often exposed to the fire of the enemy. Once a fascine that he and another were carrying was cut in two by a ball. That he saw many Continental and militia troops, and also the French – was present at the capitulation and having been put to cut down the entrenchments he saw the whole British army march out of their works. He was then detached to guard the prisoners of war to Winchester. Major Welsh commanded. Marched quite to Winchester and was discharged. That he reached home just before Christmas and that in this tour he served three and a half months.

Christian Rasor was twenty-two when he served a second tour in the Virginia Militia. He described the surrender and the hardship in getting back home in his pension application [R8599],

The applicant actively engaged in strengthening the American lines at Yorktown until the surrender of Cornwallis, this applicant says he was stationed near the park of the American Artillery where the British grounded their guns, drums, fifes, swords & flags in regular lines and marched without them back again into Yorktown. the applicant says the British looked fine and marched well and upon the whole the scene was very impressive. this applicant or the company to which he was attached was detailed with other Militia to conduct a portion of the prisoners taken at Yorktown to within four miles of Winchester here the applicant and the troops or American force he served with verbally discharged without rations or the means of obtaining them. the applicant was eighty miles distant from his home in Culpepper and he as well as others suffered greatly from hunger, no one being willing to sell us food, for the paper money we had received for our services.

Twenty year old William Neel stated in his pension application [S15945],

Siege of Lord Cornwallis, the siege had commenced before the troops with whom I served had marched down, the firing of Cannon I heard many miles before we arrived. The British Army was surrounded and pent up by the American and french forces, with batteries and breastworks on both sides of the river Gloster as well as York Town, in the river between the two Towns lay the ships belonging to the British army it was said, I saw their masts standing up, but dont recollect to have seen any part of their hulls above water, here I remained to the end of the siege attending to such duties as was assigned to me by my superiors. It was fine clear day when the prisoners marched out, their form was by plattoons, with muffled colours and Drums. Their Drums beating a low tone, this I saw and witnessed and was the grandest sight I ever looked at, as the long dreaded Enemy marched so tamely with their arms glittering in the Sun, the place where they were stacked was in an old field in the direction of Williamsburg, and marched back to the town. To the above statement of all those scenes, I was an Eye witness, and bore an humble part in all its toils and dangers. about this time I was taken with the Bloody flux [diarrhea in which blood is mixed with the intestinal discharge], and was reported and certified by the Surgeon unfit for duty, was discharged and started for home, how long I was on the road I dont remember, indeed I have often thought few ever escaped from the jaws of death more narrowly than I did, to get home being reduced to such extreme weakness, was unable to walk but a short distance without resting.

William Hill was thirty-one when he was at Yorktown, and probably many of the troops would have considered him an old man. He was in the militia from North Carolina, and he stated in his pension application [R5016],

We was ordered to march for little York and was there at the Surrender of Cornwallis he said he saw the British troops march out to lay down their arms through an avenue made by a line of the American troops on one side and the French troops on the other side he said he saw General O'Hara offer General Washington Cornwallis' sword but Washington refused to take it because O'Hara was not the Commander in chief Washington directed him to one of his Brigadier Generals to Direct O'Hara what to do.

Asa Redington was born in Boxford, Massachusetts on December 22, 1761. He first enlisted in June of 1778 and reenlisted twice after his discharges. He served for a total of five years and also spent time as a member of General Washington's special guard. In his pension application [S15962] he described his trip to Yorktown,

I sailed up the river [James], and landed on the north bank, some 6 or 8 miles from Yorktown—remained here several days, dragging heavy cannon from the landing up a steep bank of the River—about this time our Col. Scammell received a mortal wound and soon after died—he was succeeded in the command by Lt. Colo. Huntington of Conn.. This I continued during the siege, employed in severe and dangerous duty, until the army under Lord Cornwallis capitulated, & I had the pleasure of seeing them march out, prisoners of war & ground their arms.

Chapter 15

Prisoners Begin to Leave

"I pity Lord Cornwallis, for whom I have a high respect." --- Lafayette in a letter to his wife after meeting Cornwallis.

Saturday October 20, 1781

(Pleasant during the day and very cool at night)

Since the surrender the day before, some of the Americans on guard duty were faced with the lack of discipline by some of the British soldiers in York. The British had found amounts of rum that they filled their canteens with, and they began to drink through the night. The soldiers were seen crawling around, shouting, singing, and at times cursing. On several occasions they tried to break into public stores in town and were stopped by the guards. During one of these times, a drunken British soldier grabbed a bayonet and killed an American guard with it.

There was sporadic looting and stealing by both sides from stores in town. The merchants were left with only one choice, which was to close their doors to protect their property. This action enabled speculators to move in and sell goods at inflated prices.

Soon after the British were marched out on the 21st, the shops would reopened. This led to the exchange of harsh words between the French and American officers. The French had ample money and were able to buy as much as they wanted. It was ordered that the French were forbidden to purchase some goods that were in York, while the Americans were at liberty to purchase them. The reason for this was the Americans were in need of everything, and since they were badly paid, they wanted to be allowed to buy the merchandise cheaply.

During the morning, in his General Orders, Washington issued congratulations to the combined armies on their success and bravery. Also to celebrate the capture of Cornwallis, General Washington ordered that all of those men under arrest should be pardoned and set free. He said that, "Divine service shall be performed tomorrow in the different brigades and divisions." He recommended that all troops not on duty to attend.[1]

It was now time for General Cornwallis to write to his superior officer Sir Henry Clinton, a person he did not like, and give him the bad news. His letter began, "I have the mortification to inform your Excellency that I have been forced to give up the posts of York and Gloucester, and to surrender the troops under my command, by capitulation, on the 19th instant, as prisoners of war to the combined forces of America and France."[2]

He continued in the letter telling Clinton that he "never saw this post in a favorable light." He also stated that he would have attempted to escape through Gloucester immediately when Washington arrived at Williamsburg, or he would have attacked them in the open field. The reason he did not do these things was due to his Excellency's letters that, "…every possible means would be tried by the navy and army to relieve us."[3]

In the lengthy letter Cornwallis gave an account of all the events that led up to the surrender on the 19th. He praised the courage of his men and singled out General O'Hara and Colonel Abercrombie for their leadership.

This was the beginning of the blame game that Cornwallis and Clinton played with each other for years to come. As soon as the letter was received by Clinton, he wrote to Lord George Germain, the Secretary of State for America in the British government, and told him that he blamed the Royal Navy and Germain himself for this defeat.

Naval Captain Thomas Symonds, who was the other British officer that signed the Articles of Capitulation, sent the bad news to Rear Admiral Graces, "I am very Sorry to inform you that the Garrison of York, and the Vessels that remained in the River, surrendered to the Enemy by Capitulation yesterday afternoon, after a siege of seventeen days."[4] Also, included in the letter was information about the events of the last week that led to the surrender.

During the day the British prisoners were gathered to be marched to Winchester, Virginia and Fredericktown, Maryland. General Washington wrote in his diary, "Winchester & Fort Frederick in Maryland, being the places destined for the reception of the Prisoners they were to have commenced their March accordingly this day, but were prevented by the Commissary of Prisoners not having completed his Accounts of them & taken the Paroles of the Officers."[5]

In the afternoon, Lafayette called on Cornwallis and visited him in his quarters. It was the first meeting between the "boy" who had escaped and the man who was now his prisoner. Cornwallis thanked Lafayette for the humane treatment of the British prisoners. The British general also showed Lafayette, on a map of Virginia, how he had planned to escape the night the storm struck.

Lafayette later wrote to his wife, "I pity Lord Cornwallis, for whom I have a high respect; he is kind enough to express some esteem for me, and after having allowed myself the pleasure, in the capitulation, of repaying the incivilities at Charlestown, I do not intend to carry my vengeance any further."[6]

Before Cornwallis left for New York the first week in November, he repaid Lafayette's visit and was in for a surprise, when he saw a spy he had hired in the Frenchman's camp. James Armistead, a slave that was given permission to serve in the Continental Army by his master in 1781, was employed by Lafayette as a spy. In the spring of 1781, Lafayette sent James to spy on Cornwallis, who was near Portsmouth, Virginia. He used the cover of an escaped slave from the

Americans. James met Cornwallis, who later recruited James to return to the American lines to spy on them.

Armistead, acting as a double agent, supplied Cornwallis with false information. Once James delivered a fake document to Cornwallis that was in a soiled and crumpled condition. He said he found the information it on the side of the road, and it contained information about a large number of replacement American troops on the way to Virginia. Cornwallis believed the fake report and kept his troops in a defensive position.

James later sent a report to Lafayette that sixty British ships were anchored in the York River, and that the British were fortifying downstream at Yorktown. This information led General Washington to send a French fleet to the mouth of the York River and blockade the British.[7]

After the surrender, the following observation by Lord Cornwallis showed the high esteem he had for two of the American officers, "There could be no more formidable antagonist in a charge, at the head of his cavalry, than Colonel William Washington; and that he had never taken a position in the vicinity of General Green's army, that Colonel H. Lee did not find out his weak point, and strike at it before morning."[8]

Hessian soldier Johann Conrad Dohla was recovering from the many sleepless nights that occurred during the siege. He wrote in his diary about the allies taking over the British lines, "The French officers and sailors today visited the captured English ships, raided the French flags and pennants on them. The Americans also raised a large flag on the water battery at Yorktown. It had thirteen stripes."[9]

Hessian Captain Johann Ewald felt that General Washington was not very pleased with the friendly relations between the French officers and the enemy's officers. Washington had French guards relieved by Americans at both posts. Ewald described the treatment of the ill soldiers in his journal, "Our poor sick and wounded lay without medicine and provisions in such pitiable circumstances that the hardest heart had to be moved. Their food consisted of stinking salted meat and some flour or worm-eaten biscuit. These unfortunates died like flies from want, and the amputated arms and legs lay around in every corner and were eaten by the dogs."[10]

Ewald went on and described the temperament of Cornwallis at this time, "Lord Cornwallis, who had constantly overwhelmed me with special favors, was in ill humor and not disposed to speak for anything for his friends."[11]

On November 3rd, Admiral de Grasse provided three ships to carry 213 British officers to New York. With the officers was a strange assortment of shipmates that Ewald described as, "…officers' servants and camp followers, among whom twenty-two had their wives and children, or their stinking amazons with them. There were some fifty various white and black two-footed creatures of both sexes, I could not see their faces because they hid them; they probably were contraband. There were also thirty-one dogs and pigs."[12]

The evening of the 20th, General Rochambeau had a dinner for several of the British officers, including General O'Hara, who was the only member of Cornwallis' staff that spoke perfect French. The Frenchman was quite surprised with how gaily the captured officers accepted their defeat. Since Cornwallis did not attend due to "sickness", the group decided to call upon the British General. Surprisingly, Cornwallis received them with dignity and cordiality.

Baron Cromot de Bourg, an aid to Rochambeau, wrote in his diary about the dinner that night,

> M. de Rochambeau gave a dinner to General O'Hara and several English prisoners. I confess that they sang froid, and gayety even, of these gentlemen amazed me. I could not imagine that the day after such a catastrophe as had happen to them they could forget it. Moreover, General O'Hara talked a great deal and very intelligently. He has traveled a great deal, and has an extensive acquaintance. When we rose from the table we paid a visit to Lord Cornwallis, who had declared himself to be ill the evening before. He received us well and in a very proper manner.[13]

For many days after the surrender, the superior officers of the allied army competed with each other in showing acts of civility and attention to the defeated English. Entertainments were given in succession by all the major generals, with the exception of Baron Von Steuben.

Baron Von Steuben was embarrassed, because he did not have the funds to throw a party. The Baron remarked, "We are, God knows, miserably poor! We are constantly feasted by the French without giving them even a bit of wurst. I can stand it do longer. I will give one grand dinner to our allies, should I eat soup with a wooden spoon forever after."[14] To raise the money, the Baron sold his favorite horse to Colonel Stewart and borrowed money from his aid Major North.

When Von Steuben left for Philadelphia around the first of November, the only money he had for the 300 mile journey was one gold coin. George Washington insisted that the Baron take twenty guineas as a loan. Washington knew that it was a small amount to give compared to the contribution von Steuben made to the cause of liberty.

Hospitalities were cordially exchanged between the leaders of the armies. Toast were given, jokes were cracked, and laughter was heard as stories were told, as if they had always been friends and companions.

At one dinner General O'Hara remarked in a complimentary tone, that he considered himself fortunate to have not having surrendered to the American Army alone. "Probably," replied Lafayette, "General O'Hara does not like repetitions." This alluded to the fact that he was an officer in the army of General Burgoyne that surrendered years earlier to the Americans.[15]

It was not until November 3rd that Cornwallis finally joined in the dinners given for the officers. At one of the grand dinners given for them, Washington gave a toast to the British army and then made a speech in which he paid Cornwallis and his men a compliment. Cornwallis replied that the war was at an end, and the two parties would soon embrace as friends.

Colonel Tarleton was the only major officer not invited to any of the social events. Tarleton asked Lafayette if the neglect was perhaps accidental. Lafayette knew that it was not the case, and he referred Tarleton to Colonel Laurens for an explanation. Laurens told Tarleton, "No, Colonel Tarleton, no accident at all; intentional, I can assure you, and meant as a reproof for certain cruelties practiced by the troops under your command in the campaigns of the Carolinas."[16]

Tarleton quickly replied, "What, sir, and it is for severities inseparable from war, which you are pleased to term cruelties, that I am to be disgraced before junior officers? Is it, sir, for a faithful discharge of my duty to my king and my country, that I am thus humiliated in the eyes of three armies?"[17]

Colonel Laurens interrupted him and said, "Pardon me, there are modes, sir, of discharging a soldier's duty, and where mercy has a share in the mode, it renders the duty more acceptable to both friends and foes."[18] Tarleton then walked away to his headquarters and mostly stayed there, until he left Virginia.

On October 20th, Lafayette wrote to Jean-Frédéric Phélypeaux, first minister of state under King Louis XVI of France. He described the surrender of Cornwallis by writing, "The play, sir, is over---and the fifth act has just been closed; I was in a somewhat awkward situation during the first acts; my heart experienced great delight at the final one."[19]

After the siege had ended, Joseph Plumb Martin wrote about the sad plight of the slaves that were with Cornwallis,

> During the siege, we saw in the woods herds of Negroes which lord Cornwallis, (after he had inveigled them from their proprietors,) in love and pity to them, had turned adrift, with no other recompense for their confidence in his humanity, than the small pox for their bounty and starvation and death for their wages. They might be seen scattered about in every direction, dead and dying, with prices of ears of burnt Indian corn in the hands and mouths, even of those that were dead.
>
> After the siege was ended many of the owners of these deluded creatures, came to our camp and engaged some of our men to take them up, generally offering a guinea a head for them. Some of our Snappers and Miners took up several of them that belonged to a Col. Banister; when he applied for them, they refused to deliver them to him unless he would promise not to punish them. He said he had no intention of punishing them, that he did not blame them at all, the blame lay on Cornwallis. I saw several of those miserable wretches delivered to their master; they came before them for free choice, either go with him or remain where they were; that he would not injure a hair of their heads if they returned with him to their duty. Had the poor souls received a reprieve at the gallows, they could not have been more overjoyed than they appeared to be at what he promised them; their ague fit soon left them. I had a share in one of them by assisting in taking him up; the fortune I acquired was small, only one dollar; I received what was then called its equivalent, in paper money, if money it might be called, it amounted to twelve hundred dollars, all of which I afterwards paid for one single quart of rum to such a miserable state had all paper stuff, called money depreciated.[20]

Sunday October 21, 1781

(Pleasant during the day and very cool at night)

Claude Blanchard wrote the following in his journal about the first dinner Cornwallis accepted after his surrender,

> I visited our works and those of the English; I perceived the effect of our bombs and balls. I made this visit with M. de Viomenil, who had been to see Cornwallis, who had not yet appeared; he had even sent a refusal to Mr. Washington, who had invited him to dinner. M. de Viomenil invited him to dinner, and the English general accepted. I regretted that I could not be present at this first meeting of Cornwallis with the French and American generals. He behaved well there and praised our troops, especially the artillery, which he said was the first in Europe.[21]

Rochambeau went on board the *Ville de Paris* to see de Grasse, to thank him, and to confer with him. De Grasse spoke of leaving now that the siege was over. Rochambeau also sent de Lauzun to France to carry the news of the capture of York. De Lauzun left the next day aboard the frigate *Surveillante*.

On Sunday morning Chaplain Evans, preached a victory sermon from the text, I Samuel 7:12 "Then Samuel took a stone, and set it between Mizpeh and Shen, and called the name of it Ebenezer, saying, thus far the Lord has helped us."[22]

At Yorktown all the armies had their own chaplains. The Hessians were mainly Lutheran and Reformed Church, the French were mainly Roman Catholic, and the British were Church of England and Church of Scotland.

On the 20th, at least a dozen men, most were deserters, from the Maryland regiments were discovered hiding among the British troops. They were turned over to the American Commissary of Prisoners and court-martialed. A few proved that they never joined the American army, so they were not deserters and were treated as prisoners of war. The ones that did desert the American army were tried, convicted, and hanged.

On the 21st, General Washington gave his general orders for the day. He was concerned about finding American deserters among the British prisoners,

> General Wayne's Brigade for duty tomorrow to parade at ten ô clock on their own parade.
>
> Major General the Marquis de la Fayette's division to furnish a corporal and four privates daily as a guard for the Hospital.
>
> Major Graham is appointed a Member of the Court martial of which Colonel Cortlandt is President vice Major Rice.
>
> The Troops are to be in readiness to move at the shortest notice. The regiment under the command of Colonel Craig is to join Wayne's Brigade and Gaskins is to join that of Gist. As it has been represented that there are a number of Deserters from the American Army among the Prisoners taken at the surrender of York and Gloucester it is directed that an Officer from every Corps or State line with a number of noncommissioned officers who know their deserters may attend when the Prisoners are assembled to march· then to point out and apprehend those of their respective corp.[23]

General Lincoln sent a message to George Washington voicing his concern about what was going on in the town of York,

> My dear General, I find from the Report of Colo. Barber, who is on Duty in York, that there are many Irregularities—the Enemy are yet issuing Stores, and a great Number of the Men are seen with two new Hats each—From the Appearance of the Baggage of the Officers he thinks all is not right. There are so many people crowding into Town that it is impossible to preserve it from Confusion. This cannot be prevented while the guards are kept at the Distance they now are—I think they should be carried up to the Enemy's Lines, & All from the American Corps, as the French do not understand the Language—No person should be permitted to pass without Leave in Writing from Head Quarters. Every Person, excepting the Guards, should be ordered out of Town until every Matter is properly arranged, and our stores secured—Some Mode should be adopted by your Excellency with Respect to the Goods in the Hands of private Merchants. Unless something is immediately done neither the publick nor the Army will have any Benefit from the Purchase of them. I have the honor to be My dear general Your Excellencys most obedient servant. B. Lincoln.[24]

British prisoners are marched to Williamsburg that afternoon:

The British troops were gathered together, and in the early afternoon they began their march as prisoners out of Yorktown. More than 6,000 men would be divided and marched to prison camps to either Winchester, Virginia or Frederick, Maryland. The two Hessian regiments marched slowly to Williamsburg, and then to Fredericksburg, Virginia, and passed many homes of German settlers. From there they went on to Frederick, Maryland, where they remained.

Most officers were on parole and were free to leave for England or any British port in America. The only exception to this was 180 officers that were ordered to stay with the prisoners to keep order and discipline. Many of the prisoners escaped during the march. Some headed toward British held areas with hopes of returning to England. Many others blended into the countryside and began a new life in America.

Ebenezer Denny wrote, "Joined by a new raised regiment from Pennsylvania. Officers hastened to partake of the siege, but were too late. British troops march into the interior to Winchester and other places. Some of our officers return to Pennsylvania, others take their place. Militia employed leveling the lines. Our brigade prepare for a long march."[25]

Many of the militiamen that guarded the prisoners on their march, wrote about it years later in their pension applications: William Burnett said he was a bound boy, and at the age of fifteen he ran away and joined the militia. After serving several tours he returned home. He said in his pension application [R540] using his own backwoods English,

> ...after he Arived at home and had stayed thare he thinks three or four Days thare was a call for men to guard some prisners he agane volenteerd under James Arnold Captain other officers not Recolected and went in to the neighbourhood of Prince Edward Cort house and while garding the Prisners an officer Road up on a panting horse with a cockt hat on and orderd the guards to form a squar with the prisners in the inside and then the news of the Sorender of Lord Corn Walles was Read and Remembers that the officer threw his cockt hat up in the are and allmos Every American present Don the same and the words America is ours

seamd to allmost Rende the are such was the joy at that time the prisners war orderd to Prence Edward Cort house and thare he was Dechareg.

Conrad Kymes served in the militia at the age of 17 and stated in his pension application [R5928],

> I resided in Louden County above mentioned, and was marched from there to join the American troops at Little York, and remained there, until the place was surrendered by Lord Cornwallis, to the combined force of French and Americans commanded by the Count Rochambeau & General Washington himself – that said surrendered took place before my Tour had expired, the exact time when I was drafted, I do not recollect nor remember precisely the time when I was discharged but after the surrender of Cornwallis, as above, this applicant states that I was one of the detachment, that was sent a guard to conduct 1100 British & 400 prisoners taken at York to the American Garrison at Winchester, that I went with said prisoners as a guard to the Virginia State line, at which place I was relieved by other American troops from Maryland, and was then permitted to return to my home in Louden County Virginia.

John Bradshaw first entered the service in 1776 at the age of eighteen as an Indian spy. He stated in his application [S6738],

> That he was at the Siege of Yorkand at the taking of Lord Cornwallis and his army; that the British Army was marched out between two lines of the American Army to the place where they laid down their arms and then they returned through the same lines to their encampment in York Town, and on the next day they were marched out with their knapsacks on, and then took up their line of march under a strong escort or guard of the American Soldiers to the Barracks at Winchester Virginia; that he was one of the guard who escorted the prisoners to Winchester where he was discharged on the next day.

Hessian Johann Conrad Dohla began his march to a prison camp at three in the afternoon. He wrote in his journal,

> The officers received horses to ride, and the regiment, two wagons for the officers' baggage, wives, and artillerymen. All of the sick and wounded remained behind in Gloucester, with one of our medics. All of us walked with canes, and with knapsacks, camp kettles, and canteens hanging on us. Our first march was five or six Virginia miles, of which makes one German hour. We camped overnight under the open sky in a meadow and had very little food to divide and eat.[26]

Claude Blanchard rode into the camp of some of the prisoners, and he wrote in his journal his impressions of the captive troops that were being marched away,

> The English and Hessian troops, prisoners of war, also left the camp; they were very fine-looking men. The Germans preserved order and a certain discipline; on the contrary, there was very little order among the English, who were proud and arrogant. There was no call for this; they had not even made a handsome defense, and, at this very moment, were beaten and disarmed by peasants who were almost naked, whom pretended to despise and who, nevertheless, were their conquerors.[27]

Colonel Daniel Trabue, who was peddling goods to American soldiers during the siege, wrote in his journal about traveling with some of the British prisoners on the first day,

> The next morning [October 21th] preparations were made to start off with our prisoners to Winchester, Va. All our soldiers, and the French were not needed to go with the prisoners, so only a part of the Militia went with them. A number of backwoods Riflemen wanted to sell their guns; one young man applied to me and

said, "I live in Rockbridge County, am sick, and want to go home, I will sell my gin for 20s. [about $4.00] I saw tears in his eyes so gave him $10.00 for it…After I got home I sold it for $15.00.

This morning we started off with the prisoners. I was told that when all were together at Yorktown, namely the French fleet, the French Infantry, and spectators and Tories, they exceeded 1,000,000…We went 12 miles and got to Williamsburg, and encamped near the town on the east. The British encamped near a small stream; their tents were on the big road within 200 yards of the town. The sentries were about 50 yards Distant.

The British General, and Field Officers were mounted, but the subalterns and soldiers were s foot. They had baggage wagons to carry their baggage; the Officers still wore their swords, and went about as they pleased. Our wagon and tent were on the big road within 200 yards of the town.[28]

Lieutenant William McDowell later wrote in his journal, "This afternoon the prisoners marched out of town, under the care of three divisions of Militia. We had orders to hold ourselves in readiness to march at the shortest notice."[29] McDowell would not leave Yorktown until November 5.

Captain Samuel Graham, of the British 76th Foot Regiment, was with one of the groups of British prisoners that marched out. He recorded the march in his journal,

The British prisoner moved out of Yorktown in two divisions, escorted by regiments of militia or state troops; one took the direction of Maryland, the other, to which I belonged, moved to the westward of Virginia. Our guards were all from the upper part of the state, called backwoodsmen, between whom and the inhabitants of the lower parts there existed no cordiality; and at night when we halted they not only allowed, but even encouraged our men to pull down and make fires of the fence rails, as we had been accustomed to do when we had arms in our hands; and when a proprietor complained, they only laughed at him. They did not scruple also to let us make free with a turnip field.[30]

A problem between the Americans and the French began to surface after the surrender. The French insisted on keeping the slaves that they had captured. The French officers were happy to gain servants so cheaply. Virginia officials appealed to Rochambeau, who said that without proof of ownership he would not take them away from his officers. Besides, he said that the blacks said they were free, and some of them were brought to Yorktown by the French. Without proof of ownership, the Americans were out of luck and went home empty-handed.

Chapter 16

Final Days

"Before, we ran off and hid from you, but now we are thankful to see you in the condition you are in!" ---- American women to British Colonel Tarleton, now a prisoner of war.

Monday October 22, 1781

(Pleasant during the day and very cool at night)

Colonel Richard Butler visited the town of York, and what he observed led to harsh words toward the British in his journal,

> I observed the greatest villainy practiced by the British; they don't appear to have any idea of honor in any of their actions. They have completely plundered everything in their power, and do not pay the least regard to any treaty. I also find the greatest abuses committed by persons who pass into the town, and instead of the army being benefitted by any sale of goods or privilege to purchase, the stores are kept shut, such answers an excellent purpose for all speculations by the rascals who take advantage of such times.[1]

Washington sent a pleasant note to Cornwallis reminding him that he should send his military chest as required in the surrender articles. "My Lord, The Pay Master General of my Army not being at present with me—I have to desire that your Lordship will cause the Military Chest of your Army to be delivered into the Care of my Q. Master General, who has my Orders to take charge of it."[2]

Doctor James Thacher attended the religious service held by Pastor Evans the day before and on this day he wrote in his journal about the British march through Virginia,

> In the progress of the royal army through the state of Virginia the preceding summer, they practiced the most abominable enormities, plundering negroes and horses from almost every plantation, and reducing the country to ruin. Among the prodigious assemblage of spectators at the time of surrender, were a number of planter searching for the property which had been thus purloined from the estates.[3]

The doctor continued in his journal with the story, which had circulated among the American troops, of the horse taken from Colonel Tarleton by the owner of the animal. He then described the destruction of the town of York, "Rich furniture and books were scattered over the ground, and the carcasses of men and horses half covered with earth."

He also wrote of the losses on both sides and the amount of military stores the allied army had obtained. He said they received from the military chest of Cornwallis, "…two thousand one hundred and thirteen pounds six shillings sterling."[4]

Colonel Daniel Trabue, who was traveling with a group of the British prisoners, wrote of British Colonel Tarleton having his horse taken from him. The American civilians were told that if the British had taken any of their property from them, they could now reclaim what was theirs,

The next morning a Mr. Day came to our tent and said he was steward to Sir Paton Skipeth, and that the horse that Colonel Tarleton was riding belonged to his master; that moreover the horse was worth 500 pounds, and he had come all the way from Dan River determined to get it. Mr. Day went into a marshy place, nearby and cut him a sweet gum stick as thick as a man's wrist. It was not long before the might Colonel Tarleton with his servant came riding along in high style.

Mr. Day was in the road and said "Good morning Colonel Tarleton, this is my horse, Dismount;" holding the horse, he Drew his cudgel as if to strike. Colonel Tarleton jumped off quicker than ever I saw a man in my life. Mr. Day went off in a very long trot through Williamsburg.

As we passed through Town, after a breakfast about 8 o'clock, we saw the windows and doors full of people, and often heard the remark, "the British Officers do not look as saucy as they did." Even the Ladies remarked, and Col. Tarleton, with their soldiers pass by, "Before, we ran off and hid from you, but now we are thankful to see you in the condition you are in.!"[5]

Irvine Hyde, a nineteen year old Virginia militiaman, was present at this event and wrote about it in his pension application [R5464], "I remember to have seen Col. Talton on the day of the surrender riding a fine imported Stallion called black and all Black. I knew this horse well for he had belonged to one Sir Peyton Skipwell of Virginia."

Tarleton was on his way to have dinner with Baron de Viomenil, when his horse was taken away. The embarrassed officer suddenly found himself on foot and more than a mile from his destination. A passing French officer was riding by with his orderly and witnessed what had happened. The Frenchman had his orderly loan the British Colonel his horse, so he could finish his journey.

The Americans took special delight in seeing Colonel Tarleton be made a fool of. The only other person that was hated more than him was Benedict Arnold, the traitor. An example of the hatred for Arnold can be found in the following story about him.

General Benedict Arnold had been one of George Washington's favorite Generals and a hero at the Battle of Saratoga. During the battle Arnold was rallying his men, when his horse was hit in one of the final volleys in the battle. Arnold's leg was broken by both a musket ball and the horse falling on it. It was the same leg that was shot in an earlier battle. This left him crippled for a long period of time.

After Benedict Arnold turned traitor in 1780, he went from hero to one of the most hated men in America. He joined the British army, and during one expedition he asked a patriot captain, who had been taken prisoner, what he thought the Americans would do with him [Arnold] if he should fall into their hands. The officer replied, "They will cut off the leg, which was wounded when you were fighting for the cause of liberty, and bury it with honors of war, and hang the rest of your body on a gibbet."[6]

Days later when the prisoners reached Winchester, the British officers invited General Daniel Morgan to dine with them. Morgan in a conversation with the British Captain Samuel Graham jokingly remarked, "The British still owned him one lash."[7]

When asked for an explanation, Morgan told the captain that during the French and Indian War he drove a wagon for the British. For some grave offence he was sentenced to receive 500 lashes. Morgan remarked that he counted every lash as it fell, and he only received 499.

Toward the end of the afternoon, Johann Conrad Dohla and the rest of the Hessian prisoners arrived at Williamsburg. After marching through the city, they set up camp one mile away. They received food, and surprisingly they were given some freedom, "We also had much freedom, which allowed us to go into the city for food and water. Here, for the first time, we receive American rations. For good hard cash, which we had, and which was rare here, we could get all kinds of foodstuffs, but everything was rather high-priced."[8]

Captain Samuel Graham, of the British 76th Foot Regiment, was in front of the column of prisoners as they marched by a farm. Graham and several men encountered Mrs. Ashley. Graham asked her for some food for himself and a couple of the men with him. She looked at his uniform and asked if he was militia. Graham told her no, so she said, "Continental, mayhap?" He again replied no, and Mrs. Ashley realized who he was with.

She said, "Oh! I see you are one of the sarpints, [snake, serpent] one of old Wallace's men; well now, I have two sons, one was at the catching of Johnny Burgoyne, [Battle of Saratoga] and the other at that of you; and next year they are both going to catch Clinton at New York; but you shall be treated kindly, my mother came from the old country."[9]

Graham did not record in his journal if she gave them any food or not. [This author suspects that she probably did with another ear full of boasting.]

Rumors of the surrender hit Philadelphia:

Word from a messenger with news of the surrender had reached Philadelphia. Governor Lee of Maryland had received news from Admiral de Grasse that Cornwallis had requested a truce. The news spread around town, but it was still not official that the surrender had taken place.

Anna Rawle Clifford was a twenty-four year old Quaker living in Philadelphia. She was a Loyalist who was outraged over the persecution of the Loyalists in Philadelphia, after news of a possible surrender of Cornwallis reached the city. She expressed her thoughts in letters sent to her mother Rebecca and her step-father Samuel.

> The first thing I heard this morning was that Lord Cornwallis had surrendered to the French and American— intelligence as surprising as vexatious. People who are so stupidly regardless of their own interest are undeserving of compassion, but one cannot help lamenting that the fate of so many worthy persons should be connected with the failure or success of the British army.
>
> "Uncle Howell" [Joshua Howell who had married Anna's step-fathers sister Catharine] came in soon after Breakfast, and tho' he is neither Whig or Tory, looked as if he had set up all night; he was glad to see all here so cheerful, he said. When he was gone Ben Shoemaker arrived; he was told it as he came along, and was astonished. However, as there is no letter from Washington, we flatter ourselves that it is not true. [10]

Baron Cromot de Bourg wrote in his diary about the news reaching Philadelphia, "This even gave occasion to the Gazetteers to distinguish themselves, a matter the Americans neglect no more than the English, too happy when their public papers are not filled with falsehoods."[11]

Tuesday October 23, 1781

(Pleasant during the day and very cool at night)

Sailing of the Bonetta:

The British sloop *Bonetta* was allowed to sail without being inspected. It was believed that nearly 250 deserters and loyalists were aboard. In a little over a week they reached New York, and some of the passengers were so riotous that the ship's captain risked the safety of his ship to put them ashore during a storm.

As the ship sailed from Yorktown it was observed by Colonel Richard Butler, who was not happy with the ship's cargo, "The Sloop of war Bonnetta fell down the river, with her iniquitous cargo of deserters, stolen negroes, and public stores that the British officers had secreted, in violation of treaty and in breach of honor."[12]

Butler mentioned that the British had stolen goods aboard the *Bonetta*. Colonel Timothy Pickering, who was the Quartermaster General of the Continental Army, had been sent by Washington on the 23rd to take possession of the enemy's public stores that were now the property of the Americans. Pickering reported, "Colonel Dearborn informs me that a large proportion of the public stores thus lost (tents particularly) were taken away by the soldiers and women in the British hospitals."[13]

Not only were the British guilty of not turning over the stores, Pickering also complained that the French were as guilty. Pickering sent a party of men to take charge of the British cavalry horses, but the French refused to give them up unless there was a written order from Washington. The Americans also tried to take possession of some tents and Pickering later wrote "…the officer of the French guards refused to let him take a tent unless he could produce an order from your Excellency, Count Rochambeau, or General Choisi. Night came on, and the tents were chiefly stolen. In two hours the persons I had assigned for that service would have had them in store." Some French were found loading two boats with tents."[14]

Colonel John Simcoe, who sailed upon the only British ship that left Yorktown without being searched by the Americans, recorded in his journal,

> Earl Cornwallis, on account of Lieut. Col. Simcoe's dangerous state of health, permitted him to sail for New York in the *Bonetta*, which by an article in the Capitulation was to be left at his disposal, a sea-voyage being the only chance, in the opinion of the physicians, by which he could save his life. On board of this vessel sailed as many of the Rangers, and of other corps, deserters from the enemy, as she could possibly hold; they were to be exchanged as prisoners of war, and the remainder of Early Cornwallis's army were marched prisoners into the country.[15]

Before he departed, Cornwallis visited the general officers in return for their visits. He also visited the headquarters of General Washington to pay his respects and await his orders. The British general was received with all the courtesy due his rank. The two generals soon formed a friendship and they would sometimes ride together to inspect the leveling of the works.

After spending the past three day relaxing and visiting other soldiers, Lieutenant William Feltman and his brigade were sent to Gloucester. He wrote in his journal that he found it "full of sick British."[16] For the next several days he had light duty and spent his time walking around the area, and at times, he drank a little too much wine. On November 5th, William and his regiment marched out of Yorktown toward the north.

Wednesday October 24, 1781

(Pleasant during the day and very cool at night)

Johann Conrad Dohla wrote in his journal that some of the prisoners on their march to the prison camp resisted the Americans guards, "On the march some English soldiers resisted the command of the escorting Americans, and it went so far, since they would not give in, that the militia had to fire on them, which resulted in one English prisoner being killed and three men wounded."[17]

A week later the prisoners were divided, and most of the Scots and English were taken to Fort Frederick in Maryland. On November 5th, Dohla and his group reached Winchester, which was their winter quarters.

Hessian soldier Stephen Popp arrived in Williamsburg with the rest of the prisoners. He described in his journal his one day stay at Williamsburg,

> We got our first supply of provisions from the Americans, fresh meat, meal etc., we got wood and water in the town. A good many of our deserters came to see us, but we gave them a rough welcome to show our contempt. Much provision was brought for sale by the farmers, who were glad to get our silver for it. Williamsburg is an attractive place, with good buildings, church with steeples, town hall and prison all built of brick. The French and Americans had hospitals here for their sick and wounded and kept them well guarded.[18]

Colonel Richard Butler observed many of the French nobles leaving for France with their attendants on board the *Hermione* frigate. The nobles carried with them duplicates of the surrender of the British army.

British fleet finally arrives:

Twenty-five British ships of the line, two fifty gunships, several frigates, and 7,000 reinforcements under Clinton had arrived on the 24th at the Chesapeake Bay to save Cornwallis. Sir Henry Clinton received news that Cornwallis had surrendered. Had he not surrendered, Clinton had planned to land his troops on the James River and move toward the enemy lines.

French Admiral de Grasse made no attempt to come out of the Chesapeake Bay to face the British. His job had been completed, and he was anxious to sail to the West Indies. Clinton found that the French fleet outnumbered his own, so after lingering for a few days off the Capes, he returned to New York on the 29th. Graves sent the *Rattlesnake* to London with the news of the surrender.

British Admiral Graves, having already received orders to report for duty in the West Indies, left for Jamaica on November 10th. Shortly after arriving in the West Indies, Graves, concerned for his reputation following the debacle at Yorktown, requested and received permission to return to England to defend himself.

An interesting story about British Admiral Graves appeared in the papers on October 24, 1781,

> About four o'clock this morning a Schooner Boat came alongside with three Men in it, who upon being taken on board and examined, gave the following account,
>
> Jonas Rider a Black Man, says he left York Town on Thursday the 18th in a four Oard Boat in Company with a Captain and People belonging to the Sloop Tarleton, the property of a Mr. Yound of New York, to which Place they were going.
>
> That they left York Town to make Escape, as it was said the Troops were going to give it up; There had been no firing for a Day and a half before he left it, and it was reported that Lord Cornwallis was making terms to be sent to England and also respecting private property.
>
> He gives an Account of his being taken twice, and of his escaping to a Dispatch Boat that had been sent from the Fleet the Day before Yesterday.
>
> James Robinson (a black) Pilot to the Charon Man of War, left York Town with Rider because he heard there was a treaty to surrender the Place.
>
> Robert Moyse left York Town with the above, he was told the Army had surrendered Prisoners of War, according to the Terms granted at Pensacola. That all the People that could were making their escape. He is very positive they have capitulated, and that the Place was to be given up on Friday at One O'clock; there has been no firing since; He understood that our People wanted Ammunition.[19]

Washington wrote in his diary about the British fleet approaching, "Received advice, by Express from General Forman, of the British Fleet in the Harbour of New York consisting of 26 Sail of the line, some 50s. & 44s.—Many frigates—fire Ships & Transports mounting in the whole to 99 Sail had passed the Narrows for the hook, & were as he supposd, upon the point of Sailing for Chesapeak. Notice was immediately communicated to the Count de grasse."[20]

Anna Rawle Clifford, the loyalist living in Philadelphia, wrote to her parents that the news of the surrender of Cornwallis was true. "I feel in a most unsettled honor. I can neither read, work, or give my attention one moment to anything. It is too true that Cornwallis is taken. Thighman is just arrived with dispatches from Washington which confirm it."[21]

John Charles Philip von Kraft was a Hessian soldier on duty in New York City when he got the word of the surrender of Cornwallis. He wrote in his journal,

All day and night we heard loud and continuous gun and musket firing of the rebels, the origin of which of which we at first did not know. But shortly afterwards we heard with sorrow, that the otherwise so celebrated Gen Lord Cornwallis had been taken prisoner by the French and Rebels in the South, where, besides the English, also the Hessian Bose and Erb Prinz regiments were captured, and it was not wrong to conjecture that Savanna would soon follow in this pitiful run of ill-fate. It afterwards was deserted by our troops. Lord Cornwallis soon after came on parole to New York and from there to England.[22]

Congress receives the news:

Colonel Tilghman had ridden express and traveled 300 miles non-stop to carry the message to Congress. During the night he rode up, cold and wet, to the house of Thomas McKean and arrived in the early morning hours. The ride had taken two extra days, because he lost a day when the boat carrying him up the Chesapeake ran aground. The next day with the boat freed, the wind died down and they traveled only twenty miles.

Tilghman feared that if the news of the surrender reached Philadelphia before he did, then Congress would be alarmed that they had not heard the news from Washington. So Tilghman, who by this time was ill with a fever, rode the remainder of the way, and several times he stopped to borrow a fresh mount.

At last after midnight, he reached the house of Thomas McKean, dismounted, and began banging on McKean's door shouting at the top of his voice the good news. McKean opened his upstairs bedroom window and shouted down below, "What is the matter with you my friend?"[23]

A nearby night watchman nearly arrested Tilghman until he heard the news of the surrender. Then the watchman, an old German man, called out, "Basht dree o'glock, and Gornwal—lis isht da—ken." [Past three o'clock and Cornwallis is taken.][24]

Cornwallis is taken! Lieut. Col. Tilghman of Washington's staff announcing the surrender of Cornwallis, from the steps of the State House, (Independence Hall) at midnight, October 23, 1781. Lithograph by Currier & Ives, 1876. Library of Congress.

At once the news began to spread around the city from one night watchman to another. Soon thousands of people were awakened on this cold frosty night with the good news. Houses around the city began to light up, and people went out into the streets to find out more information and to celebrate. At daybreak cannons began to fire, and church bells rang in celebration.

It was a joyful occasion for the Patriots, but the Loyalists in the city stayed in their homes and did not light candles. For them it would be a long and frightful few days.

Congress met at an early hour, and Charles Thomson read the letter sent by General Washington. Edmund Randolph made a motion that was passed, which was for Congress to go in procession at two that afternoon to the Dutch Lutheran Church and give thanks to God for this victory.

Colonel Tilghman, like most of the American troops, was out of money, so he asked the members of Congress for a draft to cover the expenses of his trip. The Congressmen said they could not, because there was no money in the national treasury. Finally, some members of Congress each gave him a dollar from their own money. With the money the ill soldier could now afford a place to sleep and some food to eat. It was the least they could do for a man that had risked all he had for the past five years fighting the British.

Thursday October 25, 1781

(Pleasant during the day and very cool at night)

As the news of the surrender of Cornwallis spread throughout Philadelphia, mobs of people celebrating began to take out pent up anger on local Loyalists. Anna Rawle Clifford wrote to her mother about the mob attacking her house and other Quaker homes,

> I suppose dear Manny, thee would not have imagined this house to be illuminated last night, but it was. A mob surrounded it, broke the shutters and the glass of the windows, and were coming in, none but forlorn women here. We for a time listen for their attacks in fear and trembling till, finding them grow more loud and violent, not know what to do, we ran into the yard. Warm Whigs of one side, and Hartley's of the other (who were treated even worse than we), rendered it impossible for us to escape that way. We had not been there many minutes before we were drove back by the sight of two men climbing the fence. We thought the mob coming in thro' there, but it proved to be Coburn and Bob Shewell, who called to us not to be frightened, and fixed lights up at the window, which pacified the mob, and after three huzzas they moved off. A number of men came afterwards to see us. French and J.B. nailed boards up at the broken panels, or it would not have been safe to have gone to bed. Coburn and Shewell were really very kind; had it not been for them I really believe the house would have been pulled down.[25]

Anna continued in her letter about hearing glass breaking in the neighborhood during the night. She said that large mobs roamed throughout the area going house to house threating the owners and damaging the property. She described the attack on Mr. and Mrs. Gibbs, "Mr. Gibbs was obliged to make his escape over a fence, and while his wife was endeavoring to shield him from the rage of one of the men, she received a violent bruise in the breast, and a blow in the face which made her nose bleed."[26]

Anna went on to write that one of her neighbors, that was with the mob, destroyed the property of others in the neighborhood, and then he felt bad for what he had done. He told Mrs. Galloway that he "was sorry for her furniture, but not for a windows." Many of the people in the mob later felt the same way.

One of Anna's neighbors was another Quaker Loyalist, forty-six year old Elizabeth Drinker. Elizabeth's husband owned a shop, and that night half of his goods were stolen. She described in her diary what happened at her home on the corner of Front Street and Drinker's Alley,

> Gen. Cornwallis was taken, for which we grievously suffered, by way of rejoicing. A mob assembled about 7 o'clock or before, and continued their insults until near 10, to those whose Houses were not illuminated. Scarcely one Friend's [Quaker] House escape. We had nearly 70 panes of glass broken; ye sash lights and two panels of the front Parlor broke in pieces---ye Door cracked and violently burst open; when they threw stones into ye House for some time, but did not enter. Some fared better and some worse. Some Houses, after breaking ye door, they entered, and destroyed the Furniture &c. Many women and children were frightened into fits, and 'tis a mercy no lives were lost.[27]

The jubilation of the news in Congress was matched by words of revenge toward Cornwallis. Revenge was wanted for the perceived atrocities committed by him in the south. There was a resolution proposed that the British General be hung at once by Washington. Fortunately, the motion failed by a narrow margin, or Washington would have been placed in a very difficult position.

Friday October 26, 1781

(Rainy and cool)

A special committee of Congress proposed a draft of a proclamation which recommended that December 13th be kept as a day of thanksgiving throughout the United States for this victory. It was later unanimously adopted.

There was much left to be done at Yorktown, as the allied army prepared to leave and retire to winter quarters. John Hudson from New York had joined had joined the army at the age of twelve, and much of the time he was used for guard duty. A funny story told how earlier John was tricked into enlisting for an extended period of time. He said in his pension application [S41665],

> The levies mounted guard with the regular troops, and one morning just after being relieved at the usual hour, I had gone into our quarters and was sitting on the ground with my gun between my knees, when it went off accidentally and apparently without cause, the ball passing out of the hovel, but injuring no one. However, it was an offence punishable with one hundred lashes, and the corporal of the quarter guard immediately came in with a file of men and took me to the guard house. Here a conversation took place between the sergeant major and quarter-master sergeant, and one of them remarked with an oath, that it was a shame to give a boy like this an hundred lashes for what was notoriously an accident. This was said, purposely loud enough for me to hear. Then turning to me he added…"come my lad, the best way for you to get out of this,

will be to enlist—come along with us". I jumped up immediately, and had my name entered on the muster roll of the company, which was that of Captain Austin, and now I was fairly entered for the campaign.

He goes on in the application describing his final days at Yorktown,

Our army staid at Yorktown until cold weather set in, for the purpose of leveling the works. We found hundreds of shells which had not exploded, from the circumstance of the fuse falling undermost in which case they do not go off. These we gathered up in wagons, and put them on board vessels to take to Gen. Greene, who was still carrying on the war in South Carolina. There was a party of French prisoners who had gathered up a four house wagon load of these shells. By some _____ not easily explained, an explosion took place, which tore the wagon to fragments; killed the horses, and twelve of the Frenchmen employed in the service. I saw these twelve men neatly laid out in a marquee all in a row with white linen burial clothes. This would not have been for them, or any one else, during the progress of the siege.

Conclusion

"O God! It is all over! It is all over!" ----Prime Minister Lord North on hearing of the surrender.

The final days for the troops:

Joseph Plumb Martin wrote about his last days at Yorktown and the troops leaving,

> Our corps of Snappers and Miners were now put on board vessels to be transported up the bay; I was on board a small schooner, the Captain of our company and twenty others of our men were in the same vessel. There was more than twenty tons of beef on board, salted in bulk in the hold; we were obliged to remain behind to deal out this beef in small quantities to the troops that remained here. I remained part of the time on board, and part on shore, for eighteen days after all the Americans troops were gone to the northwest, and none remaining but the French. We according left Yorktown and set our faces toward the Highlands of New York. It was now the month of November.[1]

Henry Dearborn, a member of General Washington's staff, was starting to prepare to leave Yorktown. He came down with a fever and was experiencing difficulty finding teams to pull the wagons transporting their baggage. Most of the oxen were dead with some type of disease. He left Yorktown around the 6th of November.

Lieutenant Ebenezer Wild of the 1st Massachusetts Regiment had spent most of the week relaxing and visiting with others. He left by schooner from Yorktown on November 2nd and eventually arrived at West Point.

The French ship *Andromaque* left Yorktown on the 27th with Count Guillaume de Deux-Ponts aboard. He was sent to the court of the King of France with the mission of asking favors, and he was carrying a duplicate of the news sent earlier about the surrender. The Count wrote in his journal, "We found ourselves off Cape Henry, we saw the frigate *Concorde* making signals to us, repeating those of the frigate *Hermione*, to inform that a squadron of forty-four sails. There was no reason to doubt they were the enemy."[2]

After spotting the British ships, the *Andromaque* returned to Yorktown and left again on the 1st of November. This time they escaped detection from the British fleet. The Count wrote, "The Count de Grasse sent an ensign on board of the *Andromaque*, to wish us a pleasant voyage, and to permit our captain, M. de Ravanel, to set sail."[3]

On November 5th Cornwallis and O'Hara sailed from Yorktown aboard the *Cochrane* to meet with Clinton in New York. Cornwallis was given this parole,

> I, Charles Earl Cornwallis, Lieutenant-General and Commander of His Britanick Majesty's forces, do acknowledge myself a prisoner of war to the United States of America, and having permission from his Excellency General George Washington, agreeable to capitulation, to proceed to New York and Charlestown, or either, and to Europe, do pledge my faith and word of honor, that I will not do or say anything injurious

to the said United States, or armies thereof, or their allies, until duly exchanged; I do further promise that whatever required by the Commander-in-Chief of the American army, or the Commissary of prisoners for the same, I will repair to such place as they or either of them may require. Given under my hand at Yorktown, 28th day of October, 1781.[4]

By the first week in November most of the troops around Yorktown had departed. The militia had left either with the prisoners, or they had returned home. The regular army was divided and went either with Washington to the north, or marched to join General Greene in the south. The British prisoners were in prison camps, and the officers left behind went to England or New York. The French went into winter quarters in Virginia. The French fleet had already left for the West Indies.

De Grasse departed for the West Indies on November 4th. Before he left, Washington presented him with two handsome horses, which was a gift of appreciation for all he had done at Yorktown. Washington tried to get him to remain in the area to coordinate actions to free Charlestown and Savannah from British rule. But de Grasse felt his job was done, and there was need of his fleet in the West Indies. De Grasse did agree to leave four ships in the Chesapeake Bay to guard the entrance to the James and York Rivers.

Toward the end of October, rumors about the defeat of Cornwallis began to circulate around New York City. British troops could hear bells ringing in celebration and sporadic firing of muskets and cannons. On October 27th the rumors were finally verified, that Cornwallis had surrendered and the surrender agreement was read at British headquarters.

The British fleet returned to New York on the 7th of November, and Sir Henry Clinton immediately returned to his headquarters. Some on his staff were under the delusion that the fleet could return and save the British army. Those hopes soon faded, and the general feeling at headquarters was gloom and pointing blame for the horrific loss.

The blaming began:

Cornwallis began to complain that Clinton did not adequately support him, and that Clinton had withheld reinforcements that he had promised by the 5th of Oct. In reply, Clinton said that the invasion of Virginia was undertaken in a rash and unadvised manner.

Clinton was blamed for letting the Allied Army go across the Hudson River, march through Jersey, and cross the Delaware without opposition. The commander of the fleet was blamed for letting himself be fooled by Admiral de Grasse, when he entered the Chesapeake. The blaming went on for years to come.

The news reached England:

News of the surrender finally reached England on the 25th of November, and the dispatch was brought to Lord Germain at his residence at noon. He and three other men traveled to see Lord North to give him the bad news.

When they gave the Prime Minister the news, he threw his arms about and shouted, "O God! It is all over! It is all over!"[5] Later when someone asked Lord George Germain how Lord North felt when he got the news, he said, "As he would have taken a ball to the breast."[6]

A dispatch was sent to King George with the news. The King's reply back was returned with "calmness, dignity and self-command." Lord George did note, however, that the King "has omitted to mark the hour and the minute with his usual precision."[7]

King George met with parliament and said he intended to continue the fight in America. This started debates and arguments that lasted for months. It would finally lead to a change in the King's government and a change in policy. A peace commission would be established and peace talks would begin.

News reaches France:

On the 27th of November the news reached France. The French were elated, for they felt they had avenged their loss of Canada to the British. However, like England, the war proved to be a drain on the government's finances. Years later, Lafayette told Napoleon, when the Emperor sneered at the smallness of the armies engaged in the American Revolution, "It was the grandest of causes, won by the skirmishes of sentinels and outposts."[8]

Conclusion:

The American victory at Yorktown resulted in the end of any further major operations between England and the United States. The surrender of Cornwallis did not end the war. England continued fighting the French and Spanish elsewhere around the world. The British war effort was critically wounded but not defeated. King George wanted to continue the war in America, and he felt that the surrender of Cornwallis was just a setback. However, there was no support for the war in the House of Commons, so negotiations for peace were started at once. The House of Commons went on record to say that any Englishman who advised continuing the war would be considered an enemy to his country.

The surrender at Yorktown turned the British public against the war, but the British military in America continued to fight. It would be another two years before American Independence was completed. At the end of 1781, there were still 30,000 British soldiers in America. They occupied New York City, Savannah, Charleston, Canada, and parts of Florida. There were also pockets of Tory resistance particularly in New York, and the Indians would continue to be a problem as the Americans moved westward. General Washington now struggled to keep his army intact to face the remaining British in New York. Many of the French troops had returned home, and the American militiamen returned to their farms and shops.

Instead of continuing the war in America, the British chose to put its dwindling resources toward fighting the French and Spanish for control of Europe, and to keep the remainder of the British Empire intact. The final peace treaty was signed in Paris in September 1783, and the last of the British army left New York City in November. What most people thought was impossible eight years earlier had now become a reality. Washington was then able to return to Mount Vernon and be relieved of his burden, or so he thought.

The war with the colonies was a war that England should have won. They had a professional army, the largest navy at that time, ample supplies, and a strong economy. The defeat came down to poor leadership and arrogance toward the treatment of the American colonies. King George, Henry Clinton, Lord Cornwallis, Lord Germain, and the others in leadership lost America, and the Americans outlasted them.

One cannot over emphasize the role of George Washington in the war. He was a leader so loved and respected by his men that they would stay and fight for him even without pay, while achieving only a few victories the first few years of the war. Benjamin Franklin summed up Washington's importance at a dinner with diplomats years after the Revolution. Attending were the French and English Ambassadors along with Benjamin Franklin of the United States.

The English Ambassador rose and gave a toast to his homeland, "To England, the sun whose bright beams enlighten and fructify the remotest corners of the earth." Not to be outdone, the French Ambassador rose and politely said, "To France, the moon whose mild steady, and cheering rays are the delight of all nations, consoling them in darkness and making their dreariness beautiful."

Ben Franklin slowly rose and in a very dignified way he said, "To George Washington, the Joshua who commanded the sun and the moon to stand still, and they obeyed him."[9]

Another factor in the American victory was the Americans showed a fighting spirit that could not be duplicated among the British troops. Men such as Samuel Whittemore nearly eighty years old and crippled, who on April 19, 1775 as the British were marching back from Lexington and Concord, was waiting for them near his home. With his musket, sword, and a pair of dueling pistols, he killed three of the British before they shot and bayonetted him and left him for dead. He survived for another eighteen years.

There was Richard Knight who served in a Pennsylvania regiment for four years and fought in four major battles. He left the army as a veteran at the age of thirteen. Or, there was Bishop Tyler who went off to war with a warning from his mother, to never let her hear that he died of a wound in his back.

There were women like Margaret Cochran Corbin who helped her husband and his cannon crew, when the British attacked Fort Washington in 1776. When her husband was killed, she took over the firing of the cannon. During the fight she was hit by three grape shots, which nearly severed her left arm, wounded her in the jaw, and wounded her left breast. She recovered, and when she died in 1800 she was buried at West Point.

Oliver Cromwell was the son of a slave, who served in a New Jersey Regiment from 1777 until 1783. He fought in seven major battles including Yorktown. General Washington had such great affection for him, that after the war he personally wrote and signed Cromwell's discharge papers.

There was Nicholas Cusick, also known as Kaghnatsho, a Tuscarora Indian Chief. He formed a band of Indian Rangers that fought with Washington and was credited with saving the life of General Lafayette.

These are just a few of the thousands of Americans that believed in a dream and were willing to face countless personal hardships in the name of freedom. Most of their names will never be known, but what they accomplished will live on.

End Notes

Introduction

1. From George Washington to John Laurens, 15 January 1781, *Founders Online,* National Archives.
2. ____, *New York Continental Line, Magazine of American History, Vol. VII, December 1881, No. 6.* New York: A, S. Barnes.
3. From George Washington to John Laurens, April 9, 1781. Founders Online, National Archives.
4. ___, *The Letters of Horace Walpole Earl of Oxford, Vol. IV.* Philadelphia, Pennsylvania: Lea and Blanchard, 1842, 230 and 231.
5. Popp, Stephan, *Popp's Journal, 1777-1783.* Philadelphia, Pennsylvania, 1902, 17.

Chapter 1 Yorktown

1. Graham, Colonel James J., *Memoir of General Graham with Notices of the Campaigns in which he was engaged from 1779 to 1801.* Edinburgh, Scotland: R. & R. Clark, 1862, 56-57.
2. Miller, John Chester, *The World by the Ears: Thomas Jefferson and Slavery.* New York: Free Press, 1877, 24.

Chapter 2 The Siege Begins

1. Laughton, John Knox, editor, *Journal of Rear-Admiral Bartholomew James 1752-1828.* London: Printed for the Navy Records Society, 1896, 118. The Americans had marched that morning from Williamsburg. James inflated the number of American and French forces by several thousand. Fifteen thousand men may had seemed like twenty-six thousand at the time.
2. Graham, Colonel James J., *Memoir of General Graham with Notices of the Campaigns in which he was engaged from 1779 to 1801.* Edinburgh, Scotland: R. & R. Clark, 1862, 58-58.
3. Rosengarten, J.G., *The German Allied Troops in the North American War of Independence 1776-1783.* Albany, New York: Joel Munsell's Sons, 1893, 208.
4. Dohla, Johann Conrad, translated and edited by Bruce E. Burgoyne, *A Hessian Diary of the American Revolution, 1913 Edition.* Norman, Oklahoma: University of Oklahoma Press, 1993, 161.
5. Duane, William, Translated from a French Manuscript and Thomas Balch, editor, *The Journal of Claude Blanchard, Commissary of the French Auxiliary Army Sent to the United States during the American Revolution, 1780-1783.* Albany, New York: J. Munsell, 1876, 145.
6. Johnston, Henry P., *The Yorktown Campaign and the Surrender of Cornwallis 1781.* New York, New York: Harper & Brothers, 1881, 105.
7. Martin, Joseph Plumb, *Narrative of Some of the Adventures, Dangers and Sufferings of a Revolutionary Soldier.* Hallowell, Maine: Glazier, Masters & Co., 1830, 131.
8. ____, *The Historical Magazine and Notes and Queries concerning the Antiquities, History and Biography of America, Vol VII.* New York, New York: John G. Shea, 1864, 106.
9. Meras, E. Jules, *Memoirs of the Duc De Lauzun.* New York, New York: Sturgis & Walton, 1912, 324.
10. Diary entry: September 1781, *Founders Online,* National Archives.
11. From George Weedon to George Washington, 29 September 1781, *Founders Online,* National Archives.
12. Wright, M.W.E., *Memoirs of the Marshal Count De Rochambeau Relative to the War of Independence of the United States.* Paris: 1838, 65-66.
13. Riley, Edward M., *St George Tucker's Journal of the Siege of Yorktown, 1781.* The William and Mary Quarterly Vol. 5 No. 3, July, 1948, 375-395.
14. Feltman, Lieut. William, *The Journal of Lieut. William Feltman of the First Pennsylvania Regiment 1781-1782.* Philadelphia, Pennsylvania: Henry Carey Baird, 1853, 15.

15. Denny, Major Ebenezer, *Military Journal of Major Ebenezer Denny, an Officer in the Revolutionary and Indian Wars.* Philadelphia, Pennsylvania: J.B. Lippincott, 1859, 40-41.
16. Martin, *Narrative of Some of the Adventures, Dangers and Sufferings of a Revolutionary Soldier,* 129.
17. Washington's General order 28 September 1781, *Founders Online,* National Archives.
18. From George Weedon to George Washington, 29 September 1781, *Founders Online,* National Archives.
19. Meras, E. Jules, *Memoirs of the Duc De Lauzun.* New York, New York: Sturgis & Walton, 1912, 324-325. The French had contempt for the American militia. At the battle of Camden the British attacked a larger force of militia, which broke and ran. French General Johann Kalb was wounded and later died at the battle.
20. Tarleton, Colonel, *A History of the Campaigns of 1780 and 1781, in the Southern Provinces of North America,* London: T. Cadell, 1787, 383.
21. Feltman, *The Journal of Lieut. William Feltman of the First Pennsylvania Regiment 1781-1782,* 15.
22. Unknown person, *War Diary, May 26, 1781-July 4, 1782.* Connecticut Society of the Sons of the American Revolution.
23. Laughton, *Journal of Rear-Admiral Bartholomew James 1752-1828,* 119.
24. Ross, Charles, editor, *Correspondence of Charles, First Marquis Cornwallis.* London: John Murray, 1859, 122.
25. Popp, Stephan, *Popp's Journal, 1777-1783.* Philadelphia, Pennsylvania, 1902, 18.
26. Dohla, *A Hessian Diary of the American Revolution, 1913 Edition,* 164.
27. Johnston, *The Yorktown Campaign and the Surrender of Cornwallis 1781,* 122.
28. Diary entry: 29 September 1781, *Founders Online,* National Archives.
29. Riley, *St George Tucker's Journal of the Siege of Yorktown, 1781,* 375-395.
30. Brooks, Noah, *Henry Knox A Soldier of the Revolution.* New York: G.P. Putnam's Sons, 1900, 157.

Chapter 3 British Leave a Gift and a Hero Falls

1. Cornwallis, Earl, *Answer to Sir Henry Clinton's Narrative of the Campaign in 1781 in North America.* Philadelphia, Pennsylvania: John Campbell, 1866, 202-203.
2. Tarleton, Colonel, *A History of the Campaigns of 1780 and 1781, in the Southern Provinces of North America,* London: T. Cadell, 1787, 385.
3. Laughton, John Knox, editor, *Journal of Rear-Admiral Bartholomew James 1752-1828.* London: Printed for the Navy Records Society, 1896, 119.
4. Popp, Stephan, *Popp's Journal, 1777-1783.* Philadelphia, Pennsylvania, 1902, 18.
5. Dohla, Johann Conrad, translated and edited by Bruce E. Burgoyne, *A Hessian Diary of the American Revolution, 1913 Edition.* Norman, Oklahoma: University of Oklahoma Press, 1993, 164.
6. Thacher, James M.D., *A Military Journal during the American Revolutionary War, from 1775 to 1783.* Boston, Massachusetts: Richardson and Lord, 1827, 335.
7. Wormeley, Katharine Prescott, translator, *Diary and Correspondence of Count Axel Fersen.* London: William Heinemann, 1902, 50.
8. Wright, M.W.E., *Memoirs of the Marshal Count De Rochambeau Relative to the War of Independence of the United States.* Paris: 1838, 66-67.
9. Green, Samuel Abbott, *My Campaigns in America, a Journal Kept by Count William De Deux-Ponts.* Boston, Massachusetts: J.K. Wiggin and Wm. Parsons Lunt, 1868, 136.
10. Diary entry: 30 September 1781, *Founders Online,* National Archives.
11. Bugbee, James M., *The Journal of Ebenezer Wild 1776-1781, Who Served as an Corporal, Sergeant, Ensign, and Lieutenant in the War of the Revolution.* Cambridge, Massachusetts: John Wilson & Son, 1891, 77.
12. ____, *The Historical Magazine and Notes and Queries concerning the Antiquities, History and Biography of America, Vol VII.* New York, New York: John G. Shea, 1864, 107.
13. Egle, William Henry, *Journals and Diaries of the War of the Revolution with Lists of Officers and Soldiers, 1775-1783, Journal of Lieut. William McDowell.* Harrisburg, Pennsylvania, 1893, 300.

14. George Washington General Orders, 30 September 1781, *Founders Online,* National Archives.
15. From George Washington to George Weedon, 30 September 1781, *Founders Online,* National Archives.
16. Wright, M.W.E., *Memoirs of the Marshal Count De Rochambeau Relative to the War of Independence of the United States.* Paris: 1838, 67-68. Prince William Henry arrived in New York on September 26, 1781, and was the first of royal lineage to visit America. With the capture of Cornwallis, Virginia remained in American hands leaving the Prince with no state to govern. In March of 1782 Washington approved a plan to kidnap the Prince in British occupied New York City. The purpose may have been able to exchange him for Americans kept in prisons in the city. He later disapproved of the plan.
17. Feltman, Lieut. William, *The Journal of Lieut. William Feltman of the First Pennsylvania Regiment 1781-1782.* Philadelphia, Pennsylvania: Henry Carey Baird, 1853, 16.
18. Judd, Jacob, *The Revolutionary War Memoir and Selected Correspondence of Philip Van Cortlandt.* Tarrytown, New York: Sleepy Hollow Restorations, 1976.
19. Letter of October 4, 1781 published in *Freeman's Journal Philadelphia for October 24, 1781, Issue XXVII,* 2-3. Colonel Stephen Moylan was the commander of the 4th Regiment Continental light Dragoons.
20. Judd, *The Revolutionary War Memoir and Selected Correspondence of Philip Van Cortlandt,* 61-62. His burial site is unknown.
21. Johnston, Henry P., *The Yorktown Campaign and the Surrender of Cornwallis 1781.* New York, New York: Harper & Brothers, 1881, 123. Pickering, Octavius, *The Life of Timothy Pickering, Vol. I.* Boston, Massachusetts: Little, Brown, and Company, 1867, 302.
22. _____, *Extracts from the Journal of Lieutenant John Bell Tilden, Second Pennsylvania Line, 1781-1782, The Pennsylvania Magazine of History and Biography, Vol. XIX.* Philadelphia, Pennsylvania: Historical Society of Pennsylvania, 1895, 58-59. The tearing down of buildings Tilden heard was probably some of the buildings of the town of York. Most of the trees in the area had already been cut down earlier to make British fortifications. The British were probably running out of lumber.
23. Thacher, *A Military Journal during the American Revolutionary War, from 1775 to 1783,* 335.
24. Riley, Edward M., *St George Tucker's Journal of the Siege of Yorktown, 1781.* The William and Mary Quarterly Vol. 5 No. 3, July, 1948. 375-395. Colonel Scammel was taken prisoner by two officers who permitted a Dragoon to ride up & shoot him after he surrendered.
25. Lossing, Benson J., *Hours with the Living Men and Women of the Revolution.* New York, NY: Funk & Wagnalls, 1889, 196.
26. Lee, Henry, *Memoirs of the War in the Southern Department of the United States, Vol. II.* Philadelphia, Pennsylvania: Bradford and Inskeep, 1812, 496. Alexander Scammell was the highest ranking American officer killed during the battle.

Chapter 4 Preparations and the First Skirmish

1. Johnston, Henry P., *The Yorktown Campaign and the Surrender of Cornwallis 1781.* New York, NY: Harper & Brothers, 1881, 166.
2. Laughton, John Knox, editor, *Journal of Rear-Admiral Bartholomew James 1752-1828.* London: Printed for the Navy Records Society, 1896, 119-120.
3. Pickering, Octavius, *The Life of Timothy Pickering, Vol. I.* Boston, MA: Little, Brown, and Company, 1867, 303.
4. Green, Samuel Abbott, *My Campaigns in America, a Journal Kept by Count William De Deux-Ponts.* Boston, MA: J.K. Wiggin and Wm. Parsons Lunt, 1868, 137.
5. Egle, William Henry, *Journals and Diaries of the War of the Revolution with Lists of Officers and Soldiers, 1775-1783, Journal of Captain James Duncan.* Harrisburg, PA, 1893, 747-748.
6. _____, *The Historical Magazine and Notes and Queries concerning the Antiquities, History and Biography of America, Vol VII.* New York, NY: John G. Shea, 1864, 107.
7. Crowder, Jack Darrell, *Underage Warriors.* Berwyn Heights, MD: Heritage, 2017, 355-365.

8. Johnston, *The Yorktown Campaign and the Surrender of Cornwallis 1781*. 126.
9. Linn, John Blair and William H. Egle, editors, *Pennsylvania in the War of the Revolution Battalions and Line 1175-178, Vol. II.* Harrisburg, PAQ: Lane & Hart, 1880, 662.
10. _____, *Diary of Capt. John Davis, of the Pennsylvania Line, The Virginia Magazine of History and Biography, Vol. I, No.1.* July 1893, 303.
11. Sparks, Jared, *The Writings of George Washington being His Correspondence, Addresses, Messages, and other Papers, Official and Private.* Boston, MA: Russell, Odiorne, and Metcalf, 1835, 171-172.
12. Dohla, Johann Conrad, translated and edited by Bruce E. Burgoyne, *A Hessian Diary of the American Revolution, 1913 Edition.* Norman, OK: University of Oklahoma Press, 1993, 164-165.
13. Tustin, Joseph P., editor, *Diary of the American War A Hessian Journal of Captain Johann Ewald.* New Haven, CT, 1979, 329.
14. Johnston, *The Yorktown Campaign and the Surrender of Cornwallis 1781*, 125.
15. _____, *The Historical Magazine and Notes and Queries concerning the Antiquities, History and Biography of America, Vol VII,* 107.
16. Linn and Egle, *Pennsylvania in the War of the Revolution Battalions and Line 1175-178, Vol. II.* 748.
17. Ibid, 662.
18. Riley, Edward M., *St George Tucker's Journal of the Siege of Yorktown, 1781.* The William and Mary Quarterly Vol. 5 No. 3, July, 1948, 375-395.
19. Tarleton, Colonel, *A History of the Campaigns of 1780 and 1781, in the Southern Provinces of North America,* London: T. Cadell, 1787, 378-388.
20. Simcoe, Lieut. Col. J.G., *Simcoe's Military Journal, a History of the Operations of a Partisan Corps, called The Queen's Rangers.* New York, NY: Bartlett & Welford, 1844, 251-252.
21. Meras, E. Jules, *Memoirs of the Duc De Lauzun.* New York, NY: Sturgis & Walton, 1912, 327. Lauzun was not aware that Washington had ordered the American Weedon to keep his poorly trained Virginia troops away from the British dragoons.
22. Balch, Thomas, translator, *The French in America during the War of Independence of the United States.* Philadelphia, Pennsylvania: Porter & Coates, 1891, 191.
23. Carrington, Henry B., *Battles of the American Revolution.* New York, NY: A.S. Barnes, 1876, 633.
24. _____, *The Historical Magazine and Notes and Queries concerning the Antiquities, History and Biography of America, Vol VII,* 107.
25. Egle, *Journals and Diaries of the War of the Revolution with Lists of Officers and Soldiers, 1775-1783, Journal of Captain James Duncan,* 748.
26. Johnston, *The Yorktown Campaign and the Surrender of Cornwallis 1781,* 127.
27. Thorne, John Calvin, *Rev. Israel Evans, Chaplain of the American Army.* Concord, NH, 1902.
28. Laughton, *Journal of Rear-Admiral Bartholomew James 1752-1828,* 120.
29. Riley, *St George Tucker's Journal of the Siege of Yorktown, 1781,* 375-395.
30. _____, *The Pennsylvania Magazine of History and Biography Vol. XIX.* Philadelphia, PA: Historical Society of Pennsylvania, 1895, 60.
31. Duane, William, Translated from a French Manuscript and Thomas Balch, editor, *The Journal of Claude Blanchard, Commissary of the French Auxiliary Army Sent to the United States during the American Revolution, 1780-1783.* Albany, NY: J. Munsell, 1876, 146.
32. Linn and Egle, *Pennsylvania in the War of the Revolution Battalions and Line 1175-178, Vol. II,* 662.
33. Bugbee, James M., *The Journal of Ebenezer Wild 1776-1781, Who Served as an Corporal, Sergeant, Ensign, and Lieutenant in the War of the Revolution.* Cambridge, MA: John Wilson & Son, 1891, 77.
34. Martin, Joseph Plumb, *Narrative of Some of the Adventures, Dangers and Sufferings of a Revolutionary Soldier.* Hallowell, Maine: Glazier, Masters & Co., 1830, 172.
35. Dohla, *A Hessian Diary of the American Revolution, 1913 Edition,* 165.
36. Laughton, *Journal of Rear-Admiral Bartholomew James 1752-1828,* 120.
37. Linn and Egle, editors, *Pennsylvania in the War of the Revolution Battalions and Line 1175-178, Vol. II.* 663.

38. ____, *Proceedings of the Massachusetts Historical Society 1875-1876*. Boston, MA: Published by the Society, 1876, 335.
39. Martin, *Narrative of Some of the Adventures, Dangers and Sufferings of a Revolutionary Soldier*. 166-167.
40. ____, *The Historical Magazine and Notes and Queries concerning the Antiquities, History and Biography of America, Vol VII,* 107.
41. Riley, *St George Tucker's Journal of the Siege of Yorktown, 1781,* 375-395.
42. Denny, Major Ebenezer, *Military Journal of Major Ebenezer Denny, an Officer in the Revolutionary and Indian Wars.* Philadelphia, PA: J.B. Lippincott, 1859, 41.

Chapter 5 Quiet Before the Storm

1. Harper, Lillie De Puy Van Culin, *Colonial Men and Times, containing the Journal of Col. Daniel Trabue.* Philadelphia, PA: Innes & Sons, 1915, 111-112.
2. Martin, Joseph Plumb, *Narrative of Some of the Adventures, Dangers and Sufferings of a Revolutionary Soldier.* Hallowell, Maine: Glazier, Masters & Co., 1830, 167-168.
3. Crowder, Jack Darrell, *Underage Warriors.* Berwyn Heights, MD: Heritage, 2017, 355-365.
4. Riley, Edward M., *St George Tucker's Journal of the Siege of Yorktown, 1781.* The William and Mary Quarterly Vol. 5 No. 3, July, 1948, 375-395.
5. ____, *The Pennsylvania Magazine of History and Biography Vol. XIX.* Philadelphia, PA: Historical Society of Pennsylvania, 1895, 337-338.
6. Johnston, Henry P., *The Yorktown Campaign and the Surrender of Cornwallis 1781.* New York, NY: Harper & Brothers, 1881, 132.
7. Tilghman, Tench, *Memoir of Lieut. Col. Tench Tilghman Secretary and Aid to Washington,* Albany, NY: J. Munsell, 1876, 104.
8. Laurens, John, *The Diary of Col. John Laurens, The Collector, A Magazine for Autograph and Historical Collectors, Vol XV, No. 10, August.* New York: 1902. 122, 167.
9. Johnston, *The Yorktown Campaign and the Surrender of Cornwallis 1781.*
10. Landers, Colonel H.L., *The Virginia Campaign and the Blockade and Siege of Yorktown 1781.* Washington D.C.: Government Printing Office, 1931, 190-191.
11. Thacher, James M.D., *A Military Journal during the American Revolutionary War, from 1775 to 1783.* Boston, MA: Richardson and Lord, 1827, 337.
12. Dohla, Johann Conrad, translated and edited by Bruce E. Burgoyne, *A Hessian Diary of the American Revolution, 1913 Edition.* Norman, OK: University of Oklahoma Press, 1993, 165-166.
13. Tarleton, Colonel, *A History of the Campaigns of 1780 and 1781, in the Southern Provinces of North America,* London: T. Cadell, 1787, 389.
14. Johnston, *The Yorktown Campaign and the Surrender of Cornwallis 1781,* 132.
15. Martin, *Narrative of Some of the Adventures, Dangers and Sufferings of a Revolutionary Soldier.* 168.
16. Crowder, *Underage Warriors,* 355-365.
17. Selig, Robert A., *Military History Magazine.* February 2003.
18. Egle, William Henry, *Journals and Diaries of the War of the Revolution with Lists of Officers and Soldiers, 1775-1783, Journal of Captain James Duncan.* Harrisburg, PA, 1893, 749.
19. Johnson, William J., *George Washington the Christian.* New York: The Abingdon Press, 1919, 42. For the letter to Governor Dinwiddie. ____, *Ladies Home Journal, Philadelphia December 1895 Vol. XIII, No. 1.* Page 4. for the quote to Bushrod.
20. Martin, *Narrative of Some of the Adventures, Dangers and Sufferings of a Revolutionary Soldier.* 172.
21. Laughton, John Knox, editor, *Journal of Rear-Admiral Bartholomew James 1752-1828.* London: Printed for the Navy Records Society, 1896, 120-121.
22. ____, *The Historical Magazine and Notes and Queries concerning the Antiquities, History and Biography of America, Vol VII.* New York, NY: John G. Shea, 1864, 103.

23. Egle, *Journals and Diaries of the War of the Revolution with Lists of Officers and Soldiers, 1775-1783, Journal of Captain James Duncan.* 750.
24. Riley, *St George Tucker's Journal of the Siege of Yorktown, 1781*, 375-395.
25. Bugbee, James M., *The Journal of Ebenezer Wild 1776-1781, Who Served as an Corporal, Sergeant, Ensign, and Lieutenant in the War of the Revolution.* Cambridge, MA: John Wilson & Son, 1891, 78.

Chapter 6 Artillery of Yorktown

1. Gallatin, Gaspard de, *Journal of the Siege of York-Town.* Washington D.C.: Government Printing Office, 1931, 27 & 31-32.
2. Brooks, Noah, *Henry Knox A Soldier of the Revolution.* New York: G.P. Putnam's Sons, 1900, 155-156.
3. Thacher, James M.D., *A Military Journal during the American Revolutionary War, from 1775 to 1783.* Boston, MA: Richardson and Lord, 1827, 340.
4. Ibid, 241.

Chapter 7 The Allies Roar Back

1. Landers, Colonel H.L., *The Virginia Campaign and the Blockade and Siege of Yorktown 1781.* Washington D.C.: Government Printing Office, 1931, 195.
2. Tarleton, Colonel, *A History of the Campaigns of 1780 and 1781, in the Southern Provinces of North America,* London: T. Cadell, 1787, 389-390.
3. Dohla, Johann Conrad, translated and edited by Bruce E. Burgoyne, *A Hessian Diary of the American Revolution, 1913 Edition.* Norman, OK: University of Oklahoma Press, 1993, 166. Dohla indicated that General Greene was at Yorktown, which he was not. There was only one German regiment at Yorktown not five.
4. Ibid, 167.
5. Popp, Stephen and Joseph G. Rosengarten, *The Pennsylvania Magazine of History and Biography, Vol. 26, No. 2.* Pennsylvania: University of Pennsylvania Press, 1902, 19.
6. Graham, Colonel James J., *Memoir of General Graham with Notices of the Campaigns in which he was engaged from 1779 to 1801.* Edinburgh, Scotland: R. & R. Clark, 1862, 60.
7. Laughton, John Knox, editor, *Journal of Rear-Admiral Bartholomew James 1752-1828.* London: Printed for the Navy Records Society, 1896, 121.
8. Johnston, Henry P., *The Yorktown Campaign and the Surrender of Cornwallis 1781.* New York, NY: Harper & Brothers, 1881, 167.
9. Gallatin, Gaspard de, *Journal of the Siege of York-Town.* Washington D.C.: Government Printing Office, 1931, 3-4.
10. Judd, Jacob, *The Revolutionary War Memoir and Selected Correspondence of Philip Van Cortlandt.* Tarrytown, NY: Sleepy Hollow Restorations, 1976, 62.
11. Crowder, Jack Darrell, *Underage Warriors.* Berwyn Heights, MD: Heritage, 2017, 355-365.
12. Bugbee, James M., *The Journal of Ebenezer Wild 1776-1781, Who Served as an Corporal, Sergeant, Ensign, and Lieutenant in the War of the Revolution.* Cambridge, MA: John Wilson & Son, 1891. 78.
13. Custis, George Washington Parke, *Recollections and Private Memoirs of Washington by His Adopted Son, George Washington Parke Custis.* New York, NY: Derby & Jackson, 1860, 243.
14. Thacher, James M.D., *A Military Journal during the American Revolutionary War, from 1775 to 1783.* Boston, MA: Richardson and Lord, 1827, 339.
15. Martin, Joseph Plumb, *Narrative of Some of the Adventures, Dangers and Sufferings of a Revolutionary Soldier.* Hallowell, Maine: Glazier, Masters & Co., 1830, 168-169. Martin used the words, "Star Spangled Banner." These words were first penned by Francis Scott Key in September of 1814 in a poem called the *Defence of Fort M'Henry.* Martin, it is believed, kept a journal during the war and years later added thoughts and detail to his work. His narrative was published in 1830, twenty years before his death.

16. Denny, Major Ebenezer, *Military Journal of Major Ebenezer Denny, an Officer in the Revolutionary and Indian Wars.* Philadelphia, PA: J.B. Lippincott, 1859, 41.
17. Stone, Edwin Martin, *Our French Allies Rochambeau and His Army, Lafayette and His Devotion, D'Estaing, DeTernay, Barras, DeGrasse and Their Fleets in the Great War of the American Revolution from 1778-1782.* Providence, RI: Providence Press Co., 1884, 432.
18. Feltman, Lieut. William, *The Journal of Lieut. William Feltman of the First Pennsylvania Regiment 1781-1782.* Philadelphia, PA: Henry Carey Baird, 1853, 693-694.
19. ____, *Orderly Book of the Siege of Yorktown from September 26th, 1781, to November 2nd, 1781.* Philadelphia, Pennsylvania, 1865, 31.
20. Dohla, *A Hessian Diary of the American Revolution, 1913 Edition,* 167-168.
21. Popp, *The Pennsylvania Magazine of History and Biography, Vol. 26, No. 2,* 19.
22. Laughton, *Journal of Rear-Admiral Bartholomew James 1752-1828,* 121-122.
23. Stone, Edwin Martin, *Our French Allies Rochambeau and His Army, Lafayette and His Devotion, D'Estaing, DeTernay, Barras, DeGrasse and Their Fleets in the Great War of the American Revolution from 1778-1782.* Providence, RI: Providence Press Co., 1884, 194.
24. Lee, Henry, *Memoirs of the War in the Southern Department of the United States.* New York, NY: University Publishing Co. 1869, 500.
25. Riley, Edward M., *St George Tucker's Journal of the Siege of Yorktown, 1781.* The William and Mary Quarterly Vol. 5 No. 3, July, 1948, 375-395.
26. Johnston, *The Yorktown Campaign and the Surrender of Cornwallis 1781,* 167.
27. Harper, Lillie De Puy Van Culin, *Colonial Men and Times, containing the Journal of Col. Daniel Trabue.* Philadelphia, PA: Innes & Sons, 1915, 312.
28. Johnston, *The Yorktown Campaign and the Surrender of Cornwallis 1781.* 139-140.
29. Crowder, *Underage Warriors,* 355-365.
30. ____, *Proceedings of the Massachusetts Historical Society 1875-1876.* Boston, MA: Published by the Society, 1876, 335.
31. Laurens, John, *The Diary of Col. John Laurens, The Collector, A Magazine for Autograph and Historical Collectors, Vol XV, No. 10, August.* New York: 1902, 122.
32. ____, *Proceedings of the Massachusetts Historical Society 1875-1876.* 336.
33. Thacher, *A Military Journal during the American Revolutionary War, from 1775 to 1783,* 339-340.
34. Wormeley, Katharine Prescott, translator, *Diary and Correspondence of Count Axel Fersen.* London: William Heinemann, 1902, 51.
35. Green, Samuel Abbott, *My Campaigns in America, a Journal Kept by Count William De Deux-Ponts.* Boston, MA: J.K. Wiggin and Wm. Parsons Lunt, 1868, 140-141.
36. Kapp, Friedrick, *The Life of Frederick William Von Steuben Major General in the Revolutionary Army.* New York, NY: Mason Brothers, 1859, 457-458.
37. Duane, William, Translated from a French Manuscript and Thomas Balch, editor, *The Journal of Claude Blanchard, Commissary of the French Auxiliary Army Sent to the United States during the American Revolution, 1780-1783.* Albany, NY: J. Munsell, 1876, 148.
38. Lee, *Memoirs of the War in the Southern Department of the United States,* 499.

Chapter 8 Closer to the British Lines

1. Ross, Charles, editor, *Correspondence of Charles, First Marquis Cornwallis.* London: John Murray, 1859. 125.
2. Dohla, Johann Conrad, translated and edited by Bruce E. Burgoyne, *A Hessian Diary of the American Revolution, 1913 Edition.* Norman, OK: University of Oklahoma Press, 1993, 168-169.
3. Tarleton, Colonel, *A History of the Campaigns of 1780 and 1781, in the Southern Provinces of North America,* London: T. Cadell, 1787, 396.

4. Laughton, John Knox, editor, *Journal of Rear-Admiral Bartholomew James 1752-1828*. London: Printed for the Navy Records Society, 1896, 122-123.
5. Egle, William Henry, *Journals and Diaries of the War of the Revolution with Lists of Officers and Soldiers, 1775-1783, Journal of Captain James Duncan*. Harrisburg, PA, 1893, 751.
6. Johnston, Henry P., *The Yorktown Campaign and the Surrender of Cornwallis 1781*. New York, NY: Harper & Brothers, 1881, 141.
7. Kapp, Friedrick, *The Life of Frederick William Von Steuben Major General in the Revolutionary Army*. New York, NY: Mason Brothers, 1859, 457.
8. Guild, *Yorktown, The Lesson That It Teaches*. The American Monthly Magazine, Vol. XXXVII, December, 1910, No. 6, 446.
9. Denny, Major Ebenezer, *Military Journal of Major Ebenezer Denny, an Officer in the Revolutionary and Indian Wars*. Philadelphia, PA: J.B. Lippincott, 1859, 42.
10. Laurens, John, *The Diary of Col. John Laurens, The Collector, A Magazine for Autograph and Historical Collectors, Vol XV, No. 10, August*. New York: 1902, 122.
11. Duane, William, Translated from a French Manuscript and Thomas Balch, editor, *The Journal of Claude Blanchard, Commissary of the French Auxiliary Army Sent to the United States during the American Revolution, 1780-1783*. Albany, NY: J. Munsell, 1876, 148.
12. Feltman, Lieut. William, *The Journal of Lieut. William Feltman of the First Pennsylvania Regiment 1781-1782*. Philadelphia, PA: Henry Carey Baird, 1853, 694.
13. Pickering, Octavius, *The Life of Timothy Pickering, Vol. I*. Boston, MA: Little, Brown, and Company, 1867, 304.
14. Ibid, 304-305.
15. Ibid, 306-307.
16. Riley, Edward M., *St George Tucker's Journal of the Siege of Yorktown, 1781*. The William and Mary Quarterly Vol. 5 No. 3, July, 1948, 375-395.
17. *Founders Online*, National Archives.
18. Chamberlain Mellen, *Memorial of Captain Charles Cochrane a British Officer in the Revolutionary War*. Cambridge, MA: John Wilson & Son, 1891, 12.
19. Dohla, *A Hessian Diary of the American Revolution, 1913 Edition*, 169-170.
20. Laughton, *Journal of Rear-Admiral Bartholomew James 1752-1828*. 123-124.
21. Feltman, *The Journal of Lieut. William Feltman of the First Pennsylvania Regiment 1781-1782*, 695.
22. Duane, *The Journal of Claude Blanchard, Commissary of the French Auxiliary Army Sent to the United States during the American Revolution, 1780-1783*, 149.
23. Johnston, *The Yorktown Campaign and the Surrender of Cornwallis 1781*, 167.
24. ____, *Proceedings of the Massachusetts Historical Society 1875-1876*. Boston, MA: Published by the Society, 1876, 335.
25. Anderson, Joseph, editor, *The Town and City of Waterbury Connecticut, From the Aboriginal Period to the year Eighteen Hundred and Ninety-five, Vol. I, A Journal of Josiah Atkins*. New Haven, CY: The Price & Lee Company, 1896, 479-481.
26. From Alexander Hamilton to Elizabeth Hamilton, [12 October 1781], *Founders Online*, National Archives.
27. Sparks, Jared, *The Writings of George Washington being His Correspondence, Addresses, Messages, and other Papers, Official and Private*. Boston, MA: Russell, Odiorne, and Metcalf, 1835, 178.
28. Laughton, *Journal of Rear-Admiral Bartholomew James 1752-1828*, 124.
29. Thacher, James M.D., *A Military Journal during the American Revolutionary War, from 1775 to 1783*. Boston, MA: Richardson and Lord, 1827, 340-341.
30. Egle, *Journals and Diaries of the War of the Revolution with Lists of Officers and Soldiers, 1775-1783, Journal of Captain James Duncan*, 751.

Chapter 9 The Noose Tightens

1. Green, Samuel Abbott, *My Campaigns in America, a Journal Kept by Count William* De Deux-Ponts. Boston, MA: J.K. Wiggin and Wm. Parsons Lunt, 1868, 142.
2. Feltman, Lieut. William, *The Journal of Lieut. William Feltman of the First Pennsylvania Regiment 1781-1782*. Philadelphia, PA: Henry Carey Baird, 1853, 20.
3. Balch, Thomas, translator, *The French in America during the War of Independence of the United States*. Philadelphia, Pennsylvania: Porter & Coates, 1891, 202.
4. Burgoyne, Bruce, translator, *A Hessian Diary of the American Revolution*. Norman, OK: University of Oklahoma Press, 1993, 170-171.
5. Popp, Stephen and Joseph G. Rosengarten, *The Pennsylvania Magazine of History and Biography, Vol. 26, No. 2*. Pennsylvania: University of Pennsylvania Press, 1902, 19-20.
6. Rice, Howard and Anne Brown, *American Campaigns of Rochambeau's Army, 1780-1783: The Journals of Clermont-Crevecoeur, Verger and Berthier*. Princeton, NJ: Princeton University Press, 1972, 146.
7. Laughton, John Knox, editor, *Journal of Rear-Admiral Bartholomew James 1752-1828*. London: Printed for the Navy Records Society, 1896, 125.
8. Graham, Colonel James J., *Memoir of General Graham with Notices of the Campaigns in Which He Was Engaged from 1779 to 1801*. Edinburgh, Scotland: R. & R. Clark, 1862, 61.
9. Tarleton, Colonel, *A History of the Campaigns of 1780 and 1781, in the Southern Provinces of North America,* London: T. Cadell, 1787, 396-397.
10. Tustin, Joseph P., editor, *Diary of the American War A Hessian Journal of Captain Johann Ewald*. New Haven, CT, 1979, 335-336.
11. Landers, Colonel H.L., *The Virginia Campaign and the Blockade and Siege of Yorktown 1781*. Washington D.C.: Government Printing Office, 1931, 199.
12. Levasseur, A. *Lafayette in American in 1824 and 182, Vol. 1*. Philadelphia, PA: Carey and Lea, 1829. 189.
13. Rousselet, Louis, *The Drummer Boy, A Story of the Days of Washington*. London: Sampson Low, Marston, Searle, & Rivington, 1883, 273-274.
14. Ibid, 274.
15. Johnston, Henry P., *The Yorktown Campaign and the Surrender of Cornwallis 1781*. New York, NY: Harper & Brothers, 1881, 142.
16. _____, *Diary of Captain James Duncan of Colonel Moses Hazen's Regiment in the Yorktown Campaign.* Ancestry.com, 752.
17. Stone, Edwin Martin, *Our French Allies Rochambeau and His Army, Lafayette and His Devotion, D'Estaing, DeTernay, Barras, DeGrasse and Their Fleets in the Great War of the American Revolution from 1778-1782*. Providence, RI: Providence Press Co., 1884, 441.
18. Ibid, 434.
19. Custis, George Washington Parke, *Recollections and Private Memoirs of Washington by His Adopted Son, George Washington Parke Custis*. New York, NY: Derby & Jackson, 1860, 241.
20. Ibid, 241.
21. Martin, Joseph Plumb, *Narrative of Some of the Adventures, Dangers and Sufferings of a Revolutionary Soldier*. Hallowell, Maine: Glazier, Masters & Co., 1830, 169-171.
22. Stone, *Our French Allies Rochambeau and His Army, Lafayette and His Devotion, D'Estaing, DeTernay, Barras, DeGrasse and Their Fleets in the Great War of the American Revolution from 1778-1782,* 441-442.
23. Seelye, Elizabeth Eggleston, *The Story of Washington*. New York, NY: D. Appleton, 1893, 302.
24. Balch, *The French in America during the War of Independence of the United States,* 201-202.
25. Selig, Robert A., *The William and Mary Quarterly Vol. 50, No. 3 (July, 1993), 575-590.*
26. Rice, Howard C., editor, *The American Campaigns of Rochambeau's Army: 1780, 1781, 1782, 1783, Vol. 2,* Princeton, NJ: Princeton University Press, 1972, 141-143.

27. Green, Samuel Abbott, *My Campaigns in America, a Journal Kept by Count William De Deux-Ponts*. Boston, MA: J.K. Wiggin and Wm. Parsons Lunt, 1868, 142-147.
28. Stone, *Our French Allies Rochambeau and His Army, Lafayette and His Devotion, D'Estaing, DeTernay, Barras, DeGrasse and Their Fleets in the Great War of the American Revolution from 1778-1782.*.439. Seelye, Elizabeth Eggleston, *The Story of Washington*. New York, NY: D. Appleton, 1893, 302-303. William "Billy" Lee was George Washington's enslaved manservant. Lee stayed with Washington throughout the war. When Washington died in 1799, Lee was the only slave mentioned by name in his will. He was given his freedom, $30.00 a year, and the option of remaining on Washington's estate. Lee chose to remain at Mount Vernon until his death in 1810.
29. Egle, William Henry, *Journals and Diaries of the War of the Revolution with Lists of Officers and Soldiers, 1775-1783, Journal of Captain James Duncan*. Harrisburg, PA, 1893, 751.
30. Riley, *St George Tucker's Journal of the Siege of Yorktown, 1781*, 375-395.
31. _____, *The Pennsylvania Magazine of History and Biography Vol. XIX*. Philadelphia, PA: Historical Society of Pennsylvania, 1895, 62.
32. *Founders Online,* National Archives.
33. Denny, Major Ebenezer, *Military Journal of Major Ebenezer Denny, an Officer in the Revolutionary and Indian Wars*. Philadelphia, PA: J.B. Lippincott, 1859, 42-43.
34. _____, *The Historical Magazine and Notes and Queries concerning the Antiquities, History and Biography of America, Vol VII*. New York, NY: John G. Shea, 1864, 109.
35. Green, *My Campaigns in America, a Journal Kept by Count William De Deux-Ponts*, 148.
36. Johnston, Henry P., *The Yorktown Campaign and the Surrender of Cornwallis 1781*. New York, NY: Harper & Brothers, 1881.
37. Thacher, James M.D., *A Military Journal during the American Revolutionary War, from 1775 to 1783*. Boston, MA: Richardson and Lord, 1827, 341.
38. Muhlenberg, Henry A., *The Life of Major-General Peter Muhlenberg of the Revolutionary Army*. Philadelphia, PA: Carey and Hart, 1849, 272.
39. Duane, William, Translated from a French Manuscript and Thomas Balch, editor, *The Journal of Claude Blanchard, Commissary of the French Auxiliary Army Sent to the United States during the American Revolution, 1780-1783*. Albany, NY: J. Munsell, 1876, 150.
40. Shepherd, William, *A History of the American Revolution, Published in London under the Superintendence of the Society for the Useful Knowledge*. Columbus, OH: Isaac N. Whiting, 1834, 242-243.
41. Cutter, William, *The Life of General Lafayette*. Cincinnati, OH: H.W. Derby, 1856, 135.

Chapter 10 A Desperate Attempt to Escape

1. Ross, Charles, editor, *Correspondence of Charles, First Marquis Cornwallis*. London: John Murray, 1859, 125.
2. Laughton, John Knox, editor, *Journal of Rear-Admiral Bartholomew James 1752-1828*. London: Printed for the Navy Records Society, 1896, 125.
3. Lengel, Edward G., *General George Washington: A Military Life*. New York: Random House, 2005, 341. There are various versions of skin the bastards. Some report he said, "skin the hounds," others "skin the beggars."
4. Tustin, Joseph P., editor, *Diary of the American War A Hessian Journal of Captain Johann Ewald*. New Haven, CT, 1979, 336-337.
5. Dohla, Johann Conrad, translated and edited by Bruce E. Burgoyne, *A Hessian Diary of the American Revolution*. Norman, OK: University of Oklahoma Press, 1993, 171.
6. Tarleton, Colonel, *A History of the Campaigns of 1780 and 1781, in the Southern Provinces of North America,* London: T. Cadell, 1787, 398-399.
7. Tustin, *Diary of the American War A Hessian Journal of Captain Johann Ewald*, 337.

8. Carrington, Henry B., *Battles of the American Revolution.* New York, NY: A.S. Barnes, 1876, 640.
9. Tarleton, *A History of the Campaigns of 1780 and 1781, in the Southern Provinces of North America,* 400.
10. ____, *Diary of a French Officer 1781, The Magazine of American History with Notes and Queries, Vol. VII, Oct., No. 4.* New York: A.S. Barnes, 1881, 287.
11. Green, Samuel Abbott, *My Campaigns in America, a Journal Kept by Count William De Deux-Ponts.* Boston, MA: J.K. Wiggin and Wm. Parsons Lunt, 1868, 149.
12. Wormeley, Katharine Prescott, translator, *Diary and Correspondence of Count Axel Fersen.* London: William Heinemann, 1902, 52.
13. Leake, Isaac Q., *Memoir of the Life and Times of General John Lamb an Officer of the Revolution.* Albany, NY: Joel Munsell, 1850, 279-280.
14. Denny, Major Ebenezer, *Military Journal of Major Ebenezer Denny, an Officer in the Revolutionary and Indian Wars.* Philadelphia, PA: J.B. Lippincott, 1859, 43.
15. Crowder, Jack Darrell, *Underage Warriors.* Berwyn Heights, MD: Heritage, 2017. 355-365.
16. ____, *The Historical Magazine and Notes and Queries concerning the Antiquities, History and Biography of America, Vol VII.* New York, NY: John G. Shea, 1864, 110.
17. Riley, Edward M., *St George Tucker's Journal of the Siege of Yorktown, 1781.* The William and Mary Quarterly Vol. 5 No. 3, July, 1948, 375-395.
18. *Founders Online,* National Archives.
19. Smith, Hermon Dunlap, *Revolutionary War Journals of Henry Dearborn 1775-1783.* Chicago: The Caxton Club, 1939, 220.
20. *Founders Online,* National Archives.
21. Martin, Joseph Plumb, *Narrative of Some of the Adventures, Dangers and Sufferings of a Revolutionary Soldier.* Hallowell, Maine: Glazier, Masters & Co., 1830, 171.
22. Alexander Hamilton to Marquis de Lafayette, [15 October 1781], *Founders Online,* National Archives.
23. Ford, Henry Jones, *Alexander Hamilton.* New York, NY: Charles Scribner's Sons, 1920, 124.
24. Williams, Catherine R., *Biography of Revolutionary Heroes: Contains the Life of Gen. William Barton and also, of Captain Stephen Olney.* Providence, RI: published by the author, 1839, 284-285. When Lafayette visited the United States, in 1824, Captain Olney was not forgotten. A play was given in New York City about the siege and Captain Olney was made to appear as a prominent character. When Lafayette came to Providence he met on the steps of the Statehouse by Olney and was instantly recognized. Lafayette embraced Olney with such affection that it brought tears to many of the people watching.
25. Levasseur, A. *Lafayette in American in 1824 and 182, Vol. 1.* Philadelphia, PA: Carey and Lea, 1829, 190.
26. Wormeley, *Diary and Correspondence of Count Axel Fersen,* 52.

Chapter 11 Capitulation

1. ____, *The American Revolution Writings from the War of Independence, Letter from James Robertson to Lord Amherst.* New York, New York: Literary Classics of the United States, 2001, 742.
2. Simcoe, Lieut. Col. J.G., *Simcoe's Military Journal, a History of the Operations of a Partisan Corps, called The Queen's Rangers.* New York, NY: Bartlett & Welford, 1844, 253-254.
3. Popp, Stephen and Joseph G. Rosengarten, *The Pennsylvania Magazine of History and Biography, Vol. 26, No. 2.* Pennsylvania: University of Pennsylvania Press, 1902, 246.
4. Ibid, 246.
5. Dohla, Johann Conrad, translated and edited by Bruce E. Burgoyne, *A Hessian Diary of the American Revolution, 1913 Edition.* Norman, OK: University of Oklahoma Press, 1993, 173.
6. Tustin, Joseph P., editor, *Diary of the American War A Hessian Journal of Captain Johann Ewald.* New Haven, CT, 1979, 338-339.
7. Green, Samuel Abbott, *My Campaigns in America, a Journal Kept by Count William De Deux-Ponts.* Boston, MA: J.K. Wiggin and Wm. Parsons Lunt, 1868, 150.

8. Landers, Colonel H.L., *The Virginia Campaign and the Blockade and Siege of Yorktown 1781.* Washington D.C.: Government Printing Office, 1931, 203.
9. Sparks, Jared, *The Writings of George Washington being His Correspondence, Addresses, Messages, and other Papers, Official and Private.* Boston, MA: Russell, Odiorne, and Metcalf, 1835, 181-182.
10. Marshall, John, *The Life of George Washington Written for the Use of Schools.* Philadelphia, PA: James Crissy, 1839, 219.
11. *Founders Online, National Archives.*
12. Lee, Henry, *Memoirs of the War in the Southern Department of the United States.* New York, NY: University Publishing Co. 1869, 507.
13. *Founders Online,* National Archives.
14. Thompson, Parker C., *From Its European Antecedents to 1791 The United States Army Chaplaincy Vol. 1.* Department of the Army Washington D.C., 1978, 200-201.
15. Duane, William, Translated from a French Manuscript and Thomas Balch, editor, *The Journal of Claude Blanchard, Commissary of the French Auxiliary Army Sent to the United States during the American Revolution, 1780-1783.* Albany, NY: J. Munsell, 1876, 151.
16. Harper, Lillie De Puy Van Culin, *Colonial Men and Times, containing the Journal of Col. Daniel Trabue.* Philadelphia, PA: Innes & Sons, 1915, 113.
17. Riley, Edward M., *St George Tucker's Journal of the Siege of Yorktown, 1781.* The William and Mary Quarterly Vol. 5 No. 3, July, 1948, 375-395.
18. _____, *Proceedings of the Massachusetts Historical Society 1875-1876.* Boston, MA: Published by the Society, 1876, 337.
19. Bugbee, James M., *The Journal of Ebenezer Wild 1776-1781, Who Served as an Corporal, Sergeant, Ensign, and Lieutenant in the War of the Revolution.* Cambridge, MA: John Wilson & Son, 1891, 80.
20. _____, *The Pennsylvania Magazine of History and Biography Vol. XIX.* Philadelphia, PA: Historical Society of Pennsylvania, 1895, 63.
21. Denny, Major Ebenezer, *Military Journal of Major Ebenezer Denny, an Officer in the Revolutionary and Indian Wars.* Philadelphia, PA: J.B. Lippincott, 1859, 44.
22. Thacher, James M.D., *A Military Journal during the American Revolutionary War, from 1775 to 1783.* Boston, MA: Richardson and Lord, 1827, 343-344.
23. Martin, Joseph Plumb, *Narrative of Some of the Adventures, Dangers and Sufferings of a Revolutionary Soldier.* Hallowell, Maine: Glazier, Masters & Co., 1830, 173.
24. Pickering, Octavius, *The Life of Timothy Pickering, Vol. I.* Boston, MA: Little, Brown, and Company, 1867, 307-308.
25. Smith, Hermon Dunlap, *Revolutionary War Journals of Henry Dearborn 1775-1783.* Chicago: The Caxton Club, 1939, 220-221.
26. *Founders Online,* National Archives.
27. *Founders Online,* National Archives.

Chapter 12 Agreeing to Terms of Surrender

1. Popp, Stephan, *Popp's Journal, 1777-1783.* Philadelphia, PA, 1902, 246.
2. Dohla, Johann Conrad, translated and edited by Bruce E. Burgoyne, *A Hessian Diary of the American Revolution.* Norman, OK: University of Oklahoma Press, 1993, 173.
3. Laughton, John Knox, editor, *Journal of Rear-Admiral Bartholomew James 1752-1828.* London: Printed for the Navy Records Society, 1896, 126.
4. Tarleton, Colonel, *A History of the Campaigns of 1780 and 1781, in the Southern Provinces of North America,* London: T. Cadell, 1787, 400-401.
5. Kapp, Friedrick, *The Life of Frederick William Von Steuben Major General in the Revolutionary Army.* New York, NY: Mason Brothers, 1859, 458.

6. ____, *The Historical Magazine and Notes and Queries concerning the Antiquities, History and Biography of America, Vol VII.* New York, NY: John G. Shea, 1864, 111.
7. Denny, Major Ebenezer, *Military Journal of Major Ebenezer Denny, an Officer in the Revolutionary and Indian Wars.* Philadelphia, PA: J.B. Lippincott, 1859, 44.
8. Riley, Edward M., *St George Tucker's Journal of the Siege of Yorktown, 1781.* The William and Mary Quarterly Vol. 5 No. 3, July 1948, 375-395.
9. *Founders Online,* National Archives.
10. Feltman, Lieut. William, *The Journal of Lieut. William Feltman of the First Pennsylvania Regiment 1781-1782.* Philadelphia, PA: Henry Carey Baird, 1853, 21.
11. Thacher, James M.D., *A Military Journal during the American Revolutionary War, from 1775 to 1783.* Boston, MA: Richardson and Lord, 1827. 344-345. Congress had proposed that Mr. Laurens be exchanged for British General Burgoyne, the proposal was rejected by the British Government. After Cornwallis was captured he was exchanged for Mr. Laurens on December 31, 1781.
12. Bugbee, James M., *The Journal of Ebenezer Wild 1776-1781, Who Served as an Corporal, Sergeant, Ensign, and Lieutenant in the War of the Revolution.* Cambridge, MA: John Wilson & Son, 1891, 80.
13. From Alexander Hamilton to Elizabeth Hamilton, [18 October 1781], *Founders Online,* National Archives.
14. *Founders Online,* National Archives.
15. Ross, Charles, editor, *Correspondence of Charles, First Marquis Cornwallis.* London: John Murray, 1859, 525-526.
16. Wrong, George, Chester Martin, and Walter Sage, *The Story of Canada.* Toronto: The Ryerson Press, 1931, 100.
17. Leslie, Frank, *Popular Monthly Vol. XII, July to December, 1881.* New York, NY: Frank Leslie's Publishing House, 1881, 655.
18. Garden, Alexander, *Anecdotes of the American Revolution, Illustrative of the Talents and Virtues of the Heroes and Patriots.* Charleston, South Carolina: A.E. Miller, 1828, 18. ____, *Letters and Papers Relating Chiefly to the Provincial History of Pennsylvania with some Notices of the Writers.* Philadelphia, PA: Crissy & Markley, 1855, 284-285.
19. Garden, *Anecdotes of the American Revolution, Illustrative of the Talents and Virtues of the Heroes and Patriots.* 18-19. ____, *Letters and Papers Relating Chiefly to the Provincial History of Pennsylvania with some Notices of the Writers.* 284-285.
20. *Founders Online,* National Archives.
21. Humphreys, Frank Landon, *Life and Times of David Humphreys, Soldier—Statesman—Poet.* New York, NY: G.P. Putnam's Sons, 1917, 228.
22. Unknown person, *War Diary, May 26, 1781-July 4, 1782.* Connecticut Society of the Sons of the American Revolution.

Chapter 13 Surrender Ceremony

1. Riley, Edward M., *St George Tucker's Journal of the Siege of Yorktown, 1781.* The William and Mary Quarterly Vol. 5 No. 3, July, 1948, 375-395.
2. ____, *The Primitive Methodist Magazine for the year 1883.* London: Ralph Fenwick, 1883, 31.
3. *Founders Online,* National Archives.
4. Drake, Francis S., *Life and Correspondence of Henry Knox.* Boston, MA: Samuel G. Drake, 1873. 70.
5. Wormeley, Katharine Prescott, translator, *Diary and Correspondence of Count Axel Fersen.* London: William Heinemann, 1902, 55.
6. Thacher, James M.D., *A Military Journal during the American Revolutionary War, from 1775 to 1783.* Boston, MA: Richardson and Lord, 1827, 346.
7. Philips, Donald T., *On the Wing of Speed, George Washington and the Battle of Yorktown.* Lincoln, NE: iUniverse Star, 2006.

8. Denny, Major Ebenezer, *Military Journal of Major Ebenezer Denny, an Officer in the Revolutionary and Indian Wars*. Philadelphia, PA: J.B. Lippincott, 1859, 44.
9. Moore, Frank, *Diary of the American Revolution, from Newspapers and Original Documents, Vol II*. New York, NY: Charles Scribner, 1860, 508.
10. Dohla, Johann Conrad, translated and edited by Bruce E. Burgoyne, *A Hessian Diary of the American Revolution*. Norman, OK: University of Oklahoma Press, 1993, 177-178.
11. Garden, Alexander, *Anecdotes of the American Revolution, Illustrative of the Talents and Virtues of the Heroes and Patriots*. Charleston, South Carolina: A.E. Miller, 1828, 18.
12. Balch, Thomas, translator, *The French in America during the War of Independence of the United States*. Philadelphia, Pennsylvania: Porter & Coates, 1891, 206.
13. Wright, M.W.E., *Memoirs of the Marshal Count De Rochambeau Relative to the War of Independence of the United States*. Paris: 1838, 73.
14. Crowder, Jack Darrell, *Underage Warriors*. Berwyn Heights, MD: Heritage, 2017, 11-12.
15. Seelye, Elizabeth Eggleston, *The Story of Washington*. New York, NY: D. Appleton, 1893, 306.
16. Ross, Charles, editor, *Correspondence of Charles, First Marquis Cornwallis*. London: John Murray, 1859, 126.
17. Duane, William, Translated from a French Manuscript and Thomas Balch, editor, *The Journal of Claude Blanchard, Commissary of the French Auxiliary Army Sent to the United States during the American Revolution, 1780-1783*. Albany, NY: J. Munsell, 1876, 152.
18. Popp, Stephen and Joseph G. Rosengarten, *The Pennsylvania Magazine of History and Biography, Vol. 26, No. 2*. Pennsylvania: University of Pennsylvania Press, 1902, 248.
19. Dohla, *A Hessian Diary of the American Revolution*, 177.
20. Johnston, Henry P., *The Yorktown Campaign and the Surrender of Cornwallis 1781*. New York, NY: Harper & Brothers, 1881, 156.
21. Custis, George Washington Parke, *Recollections and Private Memoirs of Washington by His Adopted Son, George Washington Parke Custis*. New York, NY: Derby & Jackson, 1860, 249. The horse died at Mount Vernon many years after the Revolution. After Washington stopped riding him, the horse was never ridden again.
22. Thacher, *A Military Journal during the American Revolutionary War, from 1775 to 1783*, 346.
23. Lossing, Benson John, *The Pictorial Field-book of the Revolution, Vol. 1,* New York; N.Y., Harper Brothers, 1850, 524.
24. Custis, George Washington Parke, *Recollections and Private Memoirs of Washington by His Adopted Son, George Washington Parke Custis*. New York, NY: Derby & Jackson, 1860, 248. On April 19, 1775 as the British regulars under General Percy marched out of Boston toward Lexington and Concord, they played "Yankee Doodle Dandy" to taunt the Americans along the way. When the defeated British troops marched back to Boston, they were taunted by Americans playing "Yankee Doodle Dandy." One of the British soldiers was asked how he liked the tune. His reply was, "They made us dance it till we were tired."
25. Balch, *The French in America during the War of Independence of the United States*, 207.
26. Johnston, *The Yorktown Campaign and the Surrender of Cornwallis 1781*. New York, NY: 157.
27. Dohla, *A Hessian Diary of the American Revolution*, 178.
28. Feltman, Lieut. William, *The Journal of Lieut. William Feltman of the First Pennsylvania Regiment 1781-1782*. Philadelphia, PA: Henry Carey Baird, 1853, 22.
29. Riley, *St George Tucker's Journal of the Siege of Yorktown, 1781*, 375-395.
30. Stevens, John Austin, *Yorktown Centennial Handbook*. New York: C.R. Coffin & Rogers, 1881. 25.
31. Dohla, *A Hessian Diary of the American Revolution*, 178.
32. Tustin, Joseph P., editor, *Diary of the American War A Hessian Journal of Captain Johann Ewald*. New Haven, CT, 1979, 342.

33. Stone, Edwin Martin, *Our French Allies Rochambeau and His Army, Lafayette and His Devotion, D'Estaing, DeTernay, Barras, DeGrasse and Their Fleets in the Great War of the American Revolution from 1778-1782.* Providence, RI: Providence Press Co., 1884, 481.
34. *Founder Online,* National Archives.
35. Gallatin, Gaspard de, *Journal of the Siege of York-Town.* Washington D.C.: Government Printing Office, 1931, 27.
36. Riley, *St George Tucker's Journal of the Siege of Yorktown, 1781,* 375-395.
37. Lossing, *Mary and Martha, The Mother and the Wife of George Washington,* 210-211.
38. Ford, Worthington Chauncey, editor, *The Writings of George Washington.* New York, NY: G.P. Putnam's Sons, 1891, 186-187.
39. Tilghman, Tench, *Memoir of Lieut. Col. Tench Tilghman Secretary and Aid to Washington,* Albany, NY: J. Munsell, 1876, 38.
40. *Founders Online,* National Archives.
41. Bugbee, James M., *The Journal of Ebenezer Wild 1776-1781, Who Served as an Corporal, Sergeant, Ensign, and Lieutenant in the War of the Revolution.* Cambridge, MA: John Wilson & Son, 1891, 80.

Chapter 14 Personal Accounts of the Surrender

1. Dohla, Johann Conrad, translated and edited by Bruce E. Burgoyne, *A Hessian Diary of the American Revolution.* Norman, OK: University of Oklahoma Press, 1993, 176-177.
2. Graham, Colonel James J., *Memoir of General Graham with Notices of the Campaigns in Which He Was Engaged from 1779 to 1801.* Edinburgh, Scotland: R. & R. Clark, 1862, 64-65.
3. Laughton, John Knox, editor, *Journal of Rear-Admiral Bartholomew James 1752-1828.* London: Printed for the Navy Records Society, 1896, 126-127.
4. Popp, Stephen and Joseph G. Rosengarten, *The Pennsylvania Magazine of History and Biography, Vol. 26, No. 2.* Pennsylvania: University of Pennsylvania Press, 1902, 249.
5. ____, *Proceedings of the Massachusetts Historical Society 1875-1876.* Boston, MA: Published by the Society, 1876, 43.
6. Martin, Joseph Plumb, *Narrative of Some of the Adventures, Dangers and Sufferings of a Revolutionary Soldier.* Hallowell, Maine: Glazier, Masters & Co., 1830, 173-174.
7. ____, *The Pennsylvania Magazine of History and Biography Vol. XIX.* Philadelphia, PA: Historical Society of Pennsylvania, 1895, 63.
8. Riley, Edward M., *St George Tucker's Journal of the Siege of Yorktown, 1781.* The William and Mary Quarterly Vol. 5 No. 3, July, 1948, 375-395.
9. Crowder, Jack Darrell, *Women Patriots in the American Revolution.* Baltimore, MD: Clearfield, 2018. 17.
10. Johnston, Henry P., *The Yorktown Campaign and the Surrender of Cornwallis 1781.* New York, NY: Harper & Brothers, 1881, 177-178.
11. Lee, Henry, *Memoirs of the War in the Southern Department of the United States.* New York, NY: University Publishing Co. 1869, 512-513.
12. Harper, Lillie De Puy Van Culin, *Colonial Men and Times, containing the Journal of Col. Daniel Trabue.* Philadelphia, PA: Innes & Sons, 1915. 114-116.
13. Denny, Major Ebenezer, *Military Journal of Major Ebenezer Denny, an Officer in the Revolutionary and Indian Wars.* Philadelphia, PA: J.B. Lippincott, 1859, 44-45.
14. *Founders Online,* National Archives.

Chapter 15 The Prisoners Begin to Leave

1. Morse, Jedidiah, *Annals of the American Revolution or a Record of the Cause and Events.* Hartford, CT: 1824, 362.

2. Ross, Charles, editor, *Correspondence of Charles, First Marquis Cornwallis*. London: John Murray, 1859, 127.
3. Ibid, 127.
4. Chadwick, French Ensor, editor, *The Graves Papers and Other Documents Relating to the Naval Operations of the Yorktown Campaign, July to October, 1781*. New York, NY: De Vinne Press, 1916, 151.
5. *Founders Online,* National Archives.
6. Stone, Edwin Martin, *Our French Allies Rochambeau and His Army, Lafayette and His Devotion, D'Estaing, DeTernay, Barras, DeGrasse and Their Fleets in the Great War of the American Revolution from 1778-1782*. Providence, RI: Providence Press Co., 1884, 482.
7. Crowder, Jack Darrell, *African Americans and American Indians in the Revolutionary War*. Jefferson, NC: McFarland, 2019, 14-15.
8. ____, *Letters and Papers Relating Chiefly to the Provincial History of Pennsylvania with some Notices of the Writers*. Philadelphia, PA: Crissy & Markley, 1855, 286.
9. Dohla, Johann Conrad, translated and edited by Bruce E. Burgoyne, Burgoyne, *A Hessian Diary of the American Revolution*. Norman, OK: University of Oklahoma Press, 1993, 182.
10. Tustin, Joseph P., editor, *Diary of the American War A Hessian Journal of Captain Johann Ewald*. New Haven, CT, 1979, 342.
11. Ibid, 342-343.
12. Ibid, 343.
13. ____, *Diary of a French Officer 1781, The Magazine of American History with Notes and Queries, Vol. VII, Oct., No. 4*. New York: A.S. Barnes, 1881, 293.
14. ____, *The Magazine of American History with Notes and Queries Vol. VIII*. New York, NY: A.S. Barnes & Company, 1882, 196. Government records showed that the U.S. owed Steuben $8,500. He was paid $1,700 and the rest was in a Treasury Certificate with interest. Later the Baron had no luck selling it for ten cents on the dollar.
15. Cutter, William, *The Life of General Lafayette*. Cincinnati, OH: H.W. Derby, 1856, 139.
16. Custis, George Washington Parke, *Recollections and Private Memoirs of Washington by His Adopted Son, George Washington Parke Custis*. New York, NY: Derby & Jackson, 1860, 251. Discussion between Colonels Laurens and Tarleton.
17. Ibid, 251.
18. Ibid, 252.
19. Lafayette, Marie Joseph Paul Yves Roch Gilbert De Motier, *Correspondence and Manuscripts of General Lafayette Published by His Hand*. Paris: Saunders, 1837, 444.
20. Martin, Joseph Plumb, *Narrative of Some of the Adventures, Dangers and Sufferings of a Revolutionary Soldier*. Hallowell, Maine: Glazier, Masters & Co., 1830, 176.
21. Balch, Thomas, translator, *The French in America during the War of Independence of the United States*. Philadelphia, Pennsylvania: Porter & Coates, 1891,152.
22. Thompson, Parker C., *From Its European Antecedents to 1791—The United States Army Chaplaincy*. Washington D.C., Department of the Army, 1978, 201.
23. *Founders Online,* National Archives.
24. *Founders Online,* National Archives.
25. Denny, Major Ebenezer, *Military Journal of Major Ebenezer Denny, an Officer in the Revolutionary and Indian Wars*. Philadelphia, PA: J.B. Lippincott, 1859, 45.
26. Dohla, *A Hessian Diary of the American Revolution*. Norman, OK: University of Oklahoma Press, 1993. 182-183.
27. Balch, *The French in America during the War of Independence of the United States,* 152-153.
28. Harper, Lillie De Puy Van Culin, *Colonial Men and Times, Containing the Journal of Col. Daniel Trabue*. Philadelphia, PA: Innes & Sons, 1915, 117. When Daniel got home he found that in the summer and fall he

had sold goods amounting to $1,000. In specie, 163,000 pounds in paper money, one Wagon, one Cart, several watches, and 7 valuable horses. The paper money, of course, depreciated quickly.

29. Egle, William Henry, *Journals and Diaries of the War of the Revolution with Lists of Officers and Soldiers, 1775-1783, Journal of Lieut. William McDowell.* Harrisburg, PA, 1893, 305.
30. ____, *The Historical Magazine and Notes and Queries concerning the Antiquities, History and Biography of America, Vol VII.* New York, NY: John G. Shea, 1864, 301.

Chapter 16 Final Days

1. ____, *The Historical Magazine and Notes and Queries concerning the Antiquities, History and Biography of America, Vol VII.* New York, NY: John G. Shea, 1864, 111.
2. *Founders Online,* National Archives, Oct. 22, 1781
3. Thacher, James M.D., *A Military Journal during the American Revolutionary War, from 1775 to 1783.* Boston, MA: Richardson and Lord, 1827, 349-350.
4. Ibid, 351.
5. Harper, Lillie De Puy Van Culin, *Colonial Men and Times, Containing the Journal of Col. Daniel Trabue.* Philadelphia, PA: Innes & Sons, 1915, 117-118.
6. Sparks, Jared, *The Library of American Biography Vol. III.* New York: Harper & Brothers, 1848. 322.
7. Mellick, Andrew D., Jr., *The Story of an Old Farm or the Life in New Jersey in the 18th Century.* Somerville, NJ: The Unionist-Gazette, 1889, 406.
8. Dohla, Johann Conrad, translated and edited by Bruce E. Burgoyne, *A Hessian Diary of the American Revolution.* Norman, OK: University of Oklahoma Press, 1993, 183.
9. Graham, Colonel James J., *Memoir of General Graham with Notices of the Campaigns in Which He Was Engaged from 1779 to 1801.* Edinburgh, Scotland: R. & R. Clark, 1862, 66-67.
10. ____, *The Pennsylvania Magazine of History and Biography Vol. XXXV.* Philadelphia, PA: Historical Society of Pennsylvania, 1911, 400-401.
11. ____, *Diary of a French Officer 1781, The Magazine of American History with Notes and Queries, Vol. VII, Oct., No. 4.* New York: A.S. Barnes, 1881, 293.
12. ____, *The Historical Magazine and Notes and Queries concerning the Antiquities, History and Biography of America, Vol VII,* 111.
13. Pickering, Octavius, *The Life of Timothy Pickering, Vol. I.* Boston, MA: Little, Brown, and Company, 1867, 309.
14. Pickering, *The Life of Timothy Pickering, Vol. I,* 309.
15. Simcoe, Lieut. Col. J.G., *Simcoe's Military Journal, a History of the Operations of a Partisan Corps, called The Queen's Rangers.* New York, NY: Bartlett & Welford, 1844, 254.
16. Feltman, Lieut. William, *The Journal of Lieut. William Feltman of the First Pennsylvania Regiment 1781-1782.* Philadelphia, PA: Henry Carey Baird, 1853, 22.
17. Dohla, Johann Conrad, *A Hessian Diary of the American Revolution.* Norman, OK: University of Oklahoma Press, 1993, 184.
18. Popp, Stephen and Joseph G. Rosengarten, *The Pennsylvania Magazine of History and Biography, Vol. 26, No. 2.* Pennsylvania: University of Pennsylvania Press, 190, 249.
19. Chadwick, French Ensor, editor, *The Graves Papers and Other Documents Relating to the Naval Operations of the Yorktown Campaign, July to October, 1781.* New York, NY: De Vinne Press, 1916, 141-142.
20. *Founders Online,* National Archives.
21. ____, *The Pennsylvania Magazine of History and Biography Vol. XXXV,* 401.
22. Krafft, Johann Carl Philipp von, *Journal of John Charles Philip von Krafft 1776-1784.* New York, NY: 1888, 152.
23. Leslie, Frank, *Popular Monthly Vol. XII, July to December 1881.* New York, NY: Frank Leslie's Publishing House, 1881, 655.

24. Moore, Frank, *Diary of the American Revolution, from Newspapers and Original Documents, Vol II.* New York, NY: Charles Scribner, 1860, 518.
25. ____, *The Pennsylvania Magazine of History and Biography Vol. XXXV,* 402.
26. Ibid, 402.
27. Biddle, Henry D., editor, *Extracts from the Journal of Elizabeth Drinker.* Philadelphia, PA: J.B. Lippincott, 1889, 137.

Conclusion

1. Martin, Joseph Plumb, *Narrative of Some of the Adventures, Dangers and Sufferings of a Revolutionary Soldier.* Hallowell, Maine: Glazier, Masters & Co., 1830, 175.
2. Green, Samuel Abbott, *My Campaigns in America, a Journal Kept by Count William De Deux-Ponts.* Boston, MA: J.K. Wiggin and Wm. Parsons Lunt, 1868, 153.
3. Ibid, 153.
4. Parole of Charles Cornwallis, Early Cornwallis, 28 October 1781, Special Collections, Library of Virginia, Richmond, Virginia.
5. ____, *The Shot Heard Round the World, From Lexington to Yorktown.* Boston, MA: The John Adams Lee Publishing Company, 1892, 344.
6. Knight, Charles, *The Popular History of England.* New York, NY: I.K. Funk & Co., 1880, 898.
7. Johnston, Henry P., *The Yorktown Campaign and the Surrender of Cornwallis 1781.* New York, NY: Harper & Brothers, 1881, 180.
8. ____, *Campaign of the Allies, The Surrender of Lord Charles Cornwallis, The Magazine of American History with Notes and Queries, Vol. VII, Oct., No. 4.,* New York, NY: A.S. Barnes, 1881, 265.
9. Foster, Sophie Lee, *Revolutionary Reader, Reminiscences and Indian Legends.* Atlanta, Georgia: Byrd Printing Company, 1913, 139.

Bibliography

Acomb, Evelyn M., editor and translator, *The Revolutionary Journal of Baron Ludwig Von Closen 1780-1783*. Chapel Hill, NC: University of North Carolina Press, 1958.

Adolphus, John, *The History of England from the Accession to the Decease of King George the Third, Vol. III*. London: John Lee, 1841.

_____, *The American Revolution Writings from the War of Independence, Letter from James Robertson to Lord Amherst*. New York, New York: Literary Classics of the United States, 2001.

Anderson, Joseph, editor, *The Town and City of Waterbury Connecticut, From the Aboriginal Period to the year Eighteen Hundred and Ninety-five, Vol. I, A Journal of Josiah Atkins*. New Haven, CY: The Price & Lee Company, 1896.

_____, *Annual Report of the American Historical Association for the Year 1896*. Washington D.C.: Government Printing Office, 1897.

_____, *Autobiography of Philip Van Cortlandt Brigadier General of the Continental Army, The Magazine of American History with Notes and Queries, Vol. II*. New York: 1878.

Axelrod, Alan, *The Real History of the American Revolution*. New York, NY: Sterling, 2007.

Balch, Thomas, translator, *The French in America during the War of Independence of the United States*. Philadelphia, Pennsylvania: Porter & Coates, 1891.

Biddle, Henry D., editor, *Extracts from the Journal of Elizabeth Drinker*. Philadelphia, PA: J.B. Lippincott, 1889.

Boudinot, Elias, *Journal or Historical Recollections of American Events during the Revolutionary War*. Philadelphia, PA: Frederick Bourquin, 1894.

Brooks, Noah, *Henry Knox A Soldier of the Revolution*. New York: G.P. Putnam's Sons, 1900.

Broughton-Mainwaring, Major Rowland, *Historical Record of the Royal Welch Fusiliers Late the Twenty-Third Regiment on Royal Welsh Fusiliers*. London: Hatchards, 1889.

Bugbee, James M., *The Journal of Ebenezer Wild 1776-1781, Who Served as an Corporal, Sergeant, Ensign, and Lieutenant in the War of the Revolution*. Cambridge, MA: John Wilson & Son, 1891.

_____, *Campaign of the Allies, The Surrender of Lord Charles Cornwallis, The Magazine of American History with Notes and Queries, Vol. VII, Oct., No. 4.*, New York, NY: A.S. Barnes, 1881.

Carrington, Henry B., *Battles of the American Revolution*. New York, NY: A.S. Barnes, 1876.

Chadwick, French Ensor, editor, *The Graves Papers and Other Documents Relating to the Naval Operations of the Yorktown Campaign, July to October, 1781*. New York, NY: De Vinne Press, 1916.

Chamberlain, Mellen, *Memorial of Captain Charles Cochrane, a British Officer in the Revolutionary War, 1774-1781*. Cambridge, MA: J. Wilson & Son, 1891.

Clinton, Sir Henry, *Narrative of the Campaign in 1781 in North America,* Philadelphia, PA: John Campbell, 1865.

Cornwallis, Earl, *Answer to Sir Henry Clinton's Narrative of the Campaign in 1781 in North America*. Philadelphia, PA: John Campbell, 1866.

Crowder, Jack Darrell, *African Americans and American Indians in the Revolutionary War*. Jefferson, NC: McFarland, 2019.

Crowder, Jack Darrell, *Chaplains of the Revolutionary War*. Jefferson, NC: McFarland, 2017.

Crowder, Jack Darrell, *The First 24 Hours of the American Revolution*. Baltimore, MD: Clearfield, 2018.

Crowder, Jack Darrell, *Underage Warriors.* Berwyn Heights, MD: Heritage, 2017.

Crowder, Jack Darrell, *Women Patriots in the American Revolution.* Baltimore, MD: Clearfield, 2018.

Custis, George Washington Parke, *Recollections and Private Memoirs of Washington by His Adopted Son, George Washington Parke Custis.* New York, NY: Derby & Jackson, 1860.

Cutter, William, *The Life of General Lafayette.* Cincinnati, OH: H.W. Derby, 1856.

Davis, Burke, *The Campaign that Won America.* New York, NY: Harper Collins, 2007.

Dawson, Henry B., *Battles of the United States by Sea and Land. Vol. I.* New York, NY: Johnson, Fry, and Co., 1858.

De Chastellux, Marquis, *Travels in North America in the Years 1780-1782 by the Marquis De Chastellux.* New York, NY: 1828.

Denny, Major Ebenezer, *Military Journal of Major Ebenezer Denny, an Officer in the Revolutionary and Indian Wars.* Philadelphia, PA: J.B. Lippincott, 1859.

_____, *Diary of Captain James Duncan of Colonel Moses Hazen's Regiment in the Yorktown Campaign.* Ancestry.com.

_____, *Diary of Capt. John Davis, of the Pennsylvania Line, The Virginia Magazine of History and Biography, Vol. I, No.1.* July 1893.

_____, *Diary of a French Officer 1781, The Magazine of American History with Notes and Queries, Vol. VII, Oct., No. 4.* New York: A.S. Barnes, 1881.

_____, *Diary of Anna Rawle, The Pennsylvania Magazine of History and Biography, Vol. 35.* Pennsylvania: University of Pennsylvania Press, 1911.

Dohla, Johann Conrad, translated and edited by Bruce E. Burgoyne, *A Hessian Diary of the American Revolution, 1913 Edition.* Norman, OK: University of Oklahoma Press, 1993.

Douglas, Robert B., Translated and edited, *A French Volunteer of the War of Independence.* Paris: Charles Carrington, 1898.

Drake, Francis S., *Life and Correspondence of Henry Knox.* Boston, MA: Samuel G. Drake, 1873.

_____, *Drill Regulations for the siege artillery, United States Army.* Washington D.C.: Government Printing, 1897.

Duane, William, editor, *Extracts from the Diary of Christopher Marshall.* Albany, New York: Joel Munsell, 1877.

Duane, William, Translated from a French Manuscript and Thomas Balch, editor, *The Journal of Claude Blanchard, Commissary of the French Auxiliary Army Sent to the United States during the American Revolution, 1780-1783.* Albany, NY: J. Munsell, 1876.

Egle, William Henry, *Journals and Diaries of the War of the Revolution with Lists of Officers and Soldiers, 1775-1783, Journal of Captain James Duncan.* Harrisburg, PA, 1893.

Egle, William Henry, *Journals and Diaries of the War of the Revolution with Lists of Officers and Soldiers, 1775-1783, Journal of Lieut. William McDowell.* Harrisburg, PA, 1893.

_____, *Extracts from the Journal of Lieutenant John Bell Tilden, Second Pennsylvania Line, 1781-1782, The Pennsylvania Magazine of History and Biography, Vol. XIX.* Philadelphia, PA: Historical Society of Pennsylvania, 1895.

Feltman, Lieut. William, *The Journal of Lieut. William Feltman of the First Pennsylvania Regiment 1781-1782.* Philadelphia, PA: Henry Carey Baird, 1853.

Fleming, Thomas J., *Beat the Last Drum The Siege of Yorktown, 1781.* New York, NY: St. Martin's Press, 1963.

Ford, Henry Jones, *Alexander Hamilton.* New York, NY: Charles Scribner's Sons, 1920.

Ford, Worthington Chauncey, editor, *The Writings of George Washington*. New York, NY: G.P. Putnam's Sons, 1891.

Foster, Sophie Lee, *Revolutionary Reader, Reminiscences and Indian Legends*. Atlanta, Georgia: Byrd Printing Company, 1913.

Garden, Alexander, *Anecdotes of the American Revolution, Illustrative of the Talents and Virtues of the Heroes and Patriots*. Charleston, SC: A.E. Miller, 1822.

Garden, Alexander, *Anecdotes of the American Revolution, Illustrative of the Talents and Virtues of the Heroes and Patriots*. Charleston, SC: A.E. Miller, 1828.

Gallatin, Gaspard de, *Journal of the Siege of York-Town*. Washington D.C.: Government Printing Office, 1931.

Godfrey, Carlos E., *The Commander-in –Chief's Guard*. Washington, D.C.: Stevenson-Smith, 1904.

Graham, Colonel James J., *Memoir of General Graham with Notices of the Campaigns in Which He Was Engaged from 1779 to 1801*. Edinburgh, Scotland: R. & R. Clark, 1862.

Green, Samuel Abbott, *My Campaigns in America, a Journal Kept by Count William De Deux-Ponts*. Boston, MA: J.K. Wiggin and Wm. Parsons Lunt, 1868.

Griswold, Rufus Wilmot, *Washington and The Generals of the American Revolution, Vol. I*. Philadelphia, PA: Carey & Hart, 1848.

Guild, Curtis, *Yorktown, The Lesson That It Teaches*. The American Monthly Magazine, Vol. XXXVII, December 1910, No. 6.

Hamilton, Alexander, *Hamilton's Letters*. Founders Online, National Archives.

Hamilton, John C., *The Works of Alexander Hamilton Comprising His Correspondence and His Political and Official Writings*. New York, NY: John F. Trow, 1850.

Hannay, David, editor, *Letters Written by Sir Samuel Hood in 1781-1783*. Printed for the Navy Records Society, 1895.

_____, *The Historical Magazine and Notes and Queries concerning the Antiquities, History and Biography of America, Vol VII*. New York, NY: John G. Shea, 1864.

Harper, Lillie De Puy Van Culin, *Colonial Men and Times, Containing the Journal of Col. Daniel Trabue*. Philadelphia, PA: Innes & Sons, 1915.

Heath, William, *Heath's Memoirs of the American War*. New York, New York, A. Wessels, 1904.

Humphreys, Frank Landon, *Life and Times of David Humphreys, Soldier—Statesman—Poet*. New York, NY: G.P. Putnam's Sons, 1917.

Irvine, General William, *Extracts from the Papers of General William Irvine, The Pennsylvania Magazine of History and Biography Vol. 5 No. 3*. Pennsylvania: University of Pennsylvania Press, 1881.

Johnson, Joseph, *Traditions and Reminiscences Chiefly of the American Revolution in the South*. Charleston, SC: Walker & James, 1851.

Johnston, Henry P., *The Yorktown Campaign and the Surrender of Cornwallis 1781*. New York, NY: Harper & Brothers, 1881.

Johnson, William J., *George Washington the Christian*. New York: The Abingdon Press, 1919.

_____, *Journal of the Siege of York in Virginia (Engineers), The Magazine of American History with Notes and Queries, Vol. IV, No. 6, June*. New York: A.S. Barnes, 1880.

Judd, Jacob, *The Revolutionary War Memoir and Selected Correspondence of Philip Van Cortlandt*. Tarrytown, NY: Sleepy Hollow Restorations, 1976.

Kapp, Friedrick, *The Life of Frederick William Von Steuben Major General in the Revolutionary Army.* New York, NY: Mason Brothers, 1859.

Ketchum, Richard M., *Victory at Yorktown The Campaign that Won The Revolution.* New York, NY: Henry Holt, 2004.

Knight, Charles, *The Popular History of England.* New York, NY: I.K. Funk & Co., 1880.

Krafft, Johann Carl Philipp von, *Journal of John Charles Philip von Krafft 1776-1784.* New York, NY: 1888.

_____, *Ladies Home Journal, Philadelphia December 1895 Vol. XIII, No. 1.*

Lafayette, Marie Joseph Paul Yves Roch Gilbert De Motier, *Correspondence and Manuscripts of General Lafayette Published by His Hand.* Paris: Saunders, 1837.

Landers, Colonel H.L., *The Virginia Campaign and the Blockade and Siege of Yorktown 1781.* Washington D.C.: Government Printing Office, 1931.

Laughton, John Knox, editor, *Journal of Rear-Admiral Bartholomew James 1752-1828.* London: Printed for the Navy Records Society, 1896.

Laurens, John, *The Diary of Col. John Laurens, The Collector, A Magazine for Autograph and Historical Collectors, Vol XV, No. 10, August.* New York: 1902.

Leake, Isaac Q., *Memoir of the Life and Times of General John Lamb an Officer of the Revolution.* Albany, NY: Joel Munsell, 1850.

Lee, Henry, *Memoirs of the War in the Southern Department of the United States.* New York, NY: University Publishing Co. 1869.

Lee, Henry, *Memoirs of the War in the Southern Department of the United States, Vol. II.* Philadelphia, PA: Bradford and Inskeep, 1812.

Lengel, Edward G., *General George Washington: A Military Life.* New York: Random House, 2005.

Leslie, Frank, *Popular Monthly Vol. XII, July to December 1881.* New York, NY: Frank Leslie's Publishing House, 1881.

_____, *The Letters of Horace Walpole Earl of Oxford, Vol. IV.* Philadelphia, Pennsylvania: Lea and Blanchard, 1842.

Lengel, Edward G., editor, *A Companion to George Washington.* New York: John Wiley, 2012.

_____, *Letters of De Fersen Aid-De Camp to Rochambeau Written to His Father in Sweden, The Magazine of American History with Notes and Queries, Vol. III, part 2.* New York: A.S. Barnes, 1879.

_____, *Letters from the Field, The Magazine of American History with Notes and Queries.* New York: A.S. Barnes, 1880.

_____, *Letters and Papers Releating Chiefly to the Provincial History of Pennsylvania with some Notices of the Writers.* Philadelphia, PA: Crissy & Markley, 1855.

Levasseur, A. *Lafayette in American in 1824 and 182, Vol. 1.* Philadelphia, PA: Carey and Lea, 1829.

Linn, John Blair and William H. Egle, editors, *Pennsylvania in the War of the Revolution Battalions and Line 1175-178, Vol. II.* Harrisburg, PAQ: Lane & Hart, 1880.

Lodge, Henry Cabot, *Alexander Hamilton.* Boston, MA: Houghton, Mifflin and Co., 1893.

Lossing, Benson J., *Hours with the Living Men and Women of the Revolution.* New York, NY: Funk & Wagnalls, 1889.

Lossing, Benson J., *Mary and Martha, The Mother and the Wife of George Washington.* New York, NY: Harper & Brothers, 1886.

Lossing, Benson John, *The Pictorial Field-book of the Revolution, Vol. 1,* New York; NY Harper Brothers, 1850.

Lowell, Edward J., *The Hessians and the other German Auxiliaries of Great Britain in the Revolutionary War.* New York, NY: Harper & Brothers, 1884.

Lynn, John Blair & William H. Egle, editors, *Pennsylvania in the War of the Revolution Battalions and Line 1775-1778, Vol. I.* Harrisburg, PA, 1880.

MacKenzie, Frederick, *The Diary of Frederick MacKenzie, Vol. 1 & 2.* Cambridge, MA: Harvard University Press, 1930.

_____, *The Magazine of American History with Notes and Queries Vol. VIII.* New York, NY: A.S. Barnes & Company, 1882.

Marshall, John, *The Life of George Washington Written for the Use of Schools.* Philadelphia, PA: James Crissy, 1839.

Majorum, Gloria, *Memoir of Lieut. Col. Tench Tilghman, Secretary and Aid to Washington.* Albany, NY: J. Munsell, 1876.

Martin, Joseph Plumb, *Narrative of Some of the Adventures, Dangers and Sufferings of a Revolutionary Soldier.* Hallowell, Maine: Glazier, Masters & Co., 1830.

Mellick, Andrew D., Jr., *The Story of an Old Farm or the Life in New Jersey in the 18th Century.* Somerville, NJ: The Unionist-Gazette, 1889.

Meras, E. Jules, *Memoirs of the Duc De Lauzun.* New York, NY: Sturgis & Walton, 1912.

Miller, John Chester, *The World by the Ears: Thomas Jefferson and Slavery.* New York: Free Press, 1877.

Miller, Ken, *Dangerous Guests: Enemy Captives and Revolutionary Communities during the War for Independence.* New York: Cornell University Press, 2014.

McNeill, J.R., *Malarial Mosquitoes Helped Defeat British in Battle that Ended Revolutionary War.* Washington Post, October 18, 2010.

Middlekauff, Robert, *Washington's Revolution The Making of America's First Leader.* New York, NY: Alfred A. Knopf, 2015.

Moore, Frank, *Diary of the American Revolution, from Newspapers and Original Documents, Vol II.* New York, NY: Charles Scribner, 1860.

Moore, H.N., *Life and Services of Gen. Anthony Wayne.* Philadelphia, PA: John B. Perry, 1845.

Morse, Jedidiah, *Annals of the American Revolution or a Record of the Cause and Events.* Hartford, CT: 1824.

Muhlenberg, Henry A., *The Life of Major-General Peter Muhlenberg of the Revolutionary Army.* Philadelphia, PA: Carey and Hart, 1849.

Nelson, Paul David, *Anthony Wayne, Soldier of the Early Republic.* Bloomington, IN: Indiana University Press, 1985.

_____, *New York Continental Line, Magazine of American History, Vol. VII, December 1881, No. 6.* New York: A,S.

Oberholtzer, Ellis Paxson, *Robert Morris Patriot and Fanancier.* New York, NY, MacMillian, 1903.

_____, *Orderly Book of the Siege of Yorktown from September 26th, 1781, to November 2nd, 1781.* Philadelphia, Pennsylvania, 1865.

Patton, Jacob Harris, *Yorktown.* New York, NY: Fords, Howard, & Hulbert, 1882.

_____, *The Pennsylvania-German Society Vol. XVII.* Allentown, PA: Published by the Society, 1908.

_____, *The Pennsylvania Magazine of History and Biography Vol. V.* Philadelphia, PA: Historical Society of Pennsylvania, 1881.

_____, *The Pennsylvania Magazine of History and Biography Vol. XIX.* Philadelphia, PA: Historical Society of Pennsylvania, 1895.

_____, *The Pennsylvania Magazine of History and Biography Vol. XXXV.* Philadelphia, PA: Historical Society of Pennsylvania, 1911.

Pickering, Octavius, *The Life of Timothy Pickering, Vol. I.* Boston, MA: Little, Brown, and Company, 1867.

Popp, Stephan, *Popp's Journal, 1777-1783.* Philadelphia, PA, 1902.

Popp, Stephen and Joseph G. Rosengarten, *The Pennsylvania Magazine of History and Biography, Vol. 26, No. 2.* Pennsylvania: University of Pennsylvania Press, 1902.

_____, *The Primitive Methodist Magazine for the year 1883.* London: Ralph Fenwick, 1883.

_____, *Proceedings of the Massachusetts Historical Society 1875-1876.* Boston, MA: Published by the Society, 1876.

Rakove, Jack, *Revolutionaries A New History of the Invention of America.* New York, NY: Houghton Mifflin Harcourt, 2010.

Randall, Willard Sterne, *George Washington.* New York, NY: Henry Holt and Co. 1997.

Raphael, Ray, *A People's History of the American Revolution.* New York, NY: Perennial, 2001.

Rhoades, Lillian Ione, *The Story of Philadelphia.* New York: American Book Company, 1900.

Rice, Howard C., editor, *The American Campaigns of Rochambeau's Army: 1780, 1781, 1782, 1783, Vol. 2,* Princeton, NJ: Princeton University Press, 1972.

Richards, Sarah J., and others, *The Town and City of Waterbury, Connecticut, from the Aboriginal Period to the Year Eighteen Hundred and Ninety-five, Vol. I.* New Haven, CT: The Price & Lee Company, 1896.

Riley, Edward M., *St George Tucker's Journal of the Siege of Yorktown, 1781.* The William and Mary Quarterly Vol. 5 No. 3, July, 1948.

Rosengarten, J.G., *The German Allied Troops in the North American War of Independence 1776-1783.* Albany, NY: Joel Munsell's Sons, 1893.

Ross, Charles, editor, *Correspondence of Charles, First Marquis Cornwallis.* London: John Murray, 1859.

Rousselet, Louis, *The Drummer Boy, A Story of the Days of Washington.* London: Sampson Low, Marston, Searle, & Rivington, 1883.

Schwamenfeld, Steven, *The Foundation of British Strength: National Identity and the Common British Soldier.* Ph.D. dissertation, Florida State University, 2007.

Seelye, Elizabeth Eggleston, *The Story of Washington.* New York, NY: D. Appleton, 1893.

Selig, Robert A., *Military History Magazine.* February 2003.

Selig, Robert A., *The William and Mary Quarterly Vol. 50, No. 3 July, 1993.*

Shea, John Gilmary, *The Operations of the French Fleet Under the Count De Grasse in 1781-1782.* New York, 1864.

Shepherd, William, *A History of the American Revolution, Published in London under the Superintendence of the Society for the Useful Knowledge.* Columbus, OH: Isaac N. Whiting, 1834.

_____, *The Shot Heard Round the World, From Lexington to Yorktown.* Boston, MA: The John Adams Lee Publishing Company, 1892.

Simcoe, Lieut. Col. J.G., *Simcoe's Military Journal, a History of the Operations of a Partisan Corps, called The Queen's Rangers.* New York, NY: Bartlett & Welford, 1844.

Smith, Hermon Dunlap, *Revolutionary War Journals of Henry Dearborn 1775-1783*. Chicago: The Caxton Club, 1939.

Sparks, Jared, *The Library of American Biography Vol. III*. New York: Harper & Brothers, 1848.

Sparks, Jared, *The Writings of George Washington being His Correspondence, Addresses, Messages, and other Papers, Official and Private*. Boston, MA: Russell, Odiorne, and Metcalf, 1835.

_____, *Spy Letters of the American Revolution from the Clinton Collection*. University of Michigan on line.

Stedman, C., *The History of the Origin, Progress, and Termination of the American War, Vol. II*. London, J. Murray, 1794.

Stille, Charles J., *Major-General Anthony Wayne and The Pennsylvania Line in the Continental Army*. Philadelphia: PA: J.B. Lippincott, 1893.

Stevens, John Austin, *Yorktown Centennial Handbook*. New York: C.R. Coffin & Rogers, 1881.

Stone, Edwin Martin, *Our French Allies Rochambeau and His Army, Lafayette and His Devotion, D'Estaing, DeTernay, Barras, DeGrasse and Their Fleets in the Great War of the American Revolution from 1778-1782*. Providence, RI: Providence Press Co., 1884.

_____, *The Storm of the Yorktown Redoubts, The Magazine of American History with Notes and Queries*. New York: A.S. Barnes, 1879.

Symonds, Craig L., *A Battlefield Atlas of the American Revolution*. Baltimore, Maryland: The Nautical & Aviation Publishing Co. of America, 1986.

Tarleton, Colonel, *A History of the Campaigns of 1780 and 1781, in the Southern Provinces of North America*, London: T. Cadell, 1787.

Taylor, Alan, *American Revolutions A Continental History, 1750-1804*. New York, NY: W.W. Norton, 2016.

Thacher, James M.D., *A Military Journal during the American Revolutionary War, from 1775 to 1783*. Boston, MA: Richardson and Lord, 1827.

Thompson, Parker C., *From Its European Antecedents to 1791 The United States Army Chaplaincy Vol. 1*. Department of the Army Washington D.C., 1978.

Thorne, John Calvin, *Rev. Israel Evans, Chaplain of the American Army*. Concord, NH, 1902.

Tilghman, Tench, *Memoir of Lieut. Col. Tench Tilghman Secretary and Aid to Washington*, Albany, NY: J. Munsell, 1876.

Tilton, Dr. James, *Economical Observations of Military Hospitals; and the Prevention and Cure of Diseases Incident to an Army*. Wilmington, DE: J. Wilson, 1813.

Toner, J.M., *Washington's Rules of Civility and Decent Behavior in Company and Conservation*. Washington D.C.: W.H. Morrison, 1888.

Tuchman, Barbara W., *The First Salute A View of the American Revolution*. New York, NY: Random House, 2014.

Tustin, Joseph P., editor, *Diary of the American War A Hessian Journal of Captain Johann Ewald*. New Haven, CT, 1979.

Upham, Charles W., *The Life of Timothy Pickering Vol. II*. Boston, MA: Little, Brown, and Co., 1873.

Unknown person, *War Diary, May 26, 1781-July 4, 1782*. Connecticut Society of the Sons of the American Revolution.

Walpole, Horace, *Journal of the Reign of King George the Third from the Year 1771 to 1783*. London: Richard Bentley, 1859.

Washington, George, *Washington's Diary.* Founders Online, National Archives.

Williams, Catherine R., *Biography of Revolutionary Heroes: Contains the Life of Gen. William Barton and also, of Captain Stephen Olney.* Providence, RI: published by the author, 1839.

Wilson, Samuel Farmer, *History of the American Revolution.* Baltimore, MD: M. Hickman, Cushing & Sons, 1836.

Wormeley, Katharine Prescott, translator, *Diary and Correspondence of Count Axel Fersen.* London: William Heinemann, 1902.

Wright, M.W.E., *Memoirs of the Marshal Count De Rochambeau Relative to the War of Independence of the United States.* Paris: 1838.

Wrong, George Martin and Walter Sage, *The Story of Canada.* Toronto: The Ryerson Press, 1931.

Government Records

Bounty Land Warrants. Ancestry.com database.

Census records. Ancestry.com database.

Journals and diaries of the war of the revolution with lists of officers and soldiers, 1775-1783. Ancestry.com database.

Pension List of 1792-1795. Ancestry.com database

U.S. Pension Records. Ancestry.com database.

U.S. Pensioners 1818-1872.

Ancestry.com database.

INDEX

A
abatis, 14,15,110,114,115

Abercrombie, Colonel Robert, 23,131,164

Adams, John, 8

Andromaque, 203

Armstrong, Archibald, 128,160

Arnold, General Benedict, 194

Atkins, John, 102

B
Beal, Shadrach, 53

Bettisworth, Charles, 49

Blanchard, Claude, 50,52,93,98,102,141,162,189,190

Bonetta, 151,153,167,171,190

Boudy, John, 197

Bradford, Captain Samuel, 145

Bradshaw, John, 190

Brady, Thomas, 67

Breeden, Enoch, 49

Broyhill, James,179

Brown, William, 124

Burch, John, 20

Burgoyne, General John, 189,195

Burrnett, William, 190

Butler, Richard, 19,33,39,41,45,50,54,66,79,97,132,148,157,193,196,197

C
Cameron, Lieutenant Allan, 36

cannons, siege, 76,77

Chapman, Erasmus, 36

Charon, 13,87,89,100

Charlton, John, 179

Chesapeake Bay, 17,26,197,198

Clifford, Anna Rawle, 195,198,200,201

Clinton, General Henry, 8,9,12,26,31,39,44,49,87,95,110,128,130,138,150,152,156,183,184,204,

Cobb, Colonel David, 97,121

Cochrane, Major Charles, 86,100

Cook, Henry, 166

Corbin, Margaret Cochran, 206

Cornwallis, General Charles, 8, 10,58,79,85,87,88,100,185,186,196,197,203-205; cave, 105; defense of Yorktown, 9,12-15,23,27,31,32,101; escape, 86,127-130,134,135; letters, 95,130,184; surrender, 138,140-142,150-154,156-160,165,167

Cortlandt, General Philip Van,35,37,82

Craik, Doctor ,168,169

Cromwell, Oliver,207

Cusick, Nicholas, 207

Custis, Jacky, 168,169

D
Davenport, Richard, 84

Davis, John, 41,66

Deane, John, 67

Dearborn, Henry, 132,1454,203

de Barras, Admiral, 156

de Creveoeur, General Francois-Jean, 168

de Bourg, Baron Cromot, 181, 186,196

de Chastellux, General, 74,166

de Chatelus, Chevalier, 128

de Chosy, General, 34,46,49

de Fersen, Axel, 33,91,131,135,156

de Gallatin, Gaspard, 167

de Grasse, Admiral, 8,41,42,140,185,185,198,204

de Lameth, Charles, 32,118

de Noailles, Vicomte, 152,153

235

de Rochambeau, General, 8,20,33,35,39,74,112,123, 124,135,141,151,156,158,159,168,188,190,196

de Rouvroy, Major-General Claude-Anne, 203

de Verger, Jean Baptiste Antoine, 108,119

de Vomenil, Baron, 198,109,118,191

de Lauzun, Duc, 20,23,41,46,48-50,129,151,188

Denny, Ebenezer, 22,55,84,97,121

Deux-Ponts, Count de, 33, 40,92,107,108,112,118, 119,

Dohla, Johann Conrad, 18,27,32,44,53,62,63,80,86, 95,100,107,108,128,139,147,157,158,162,164,173,185,190,195,197

Drinker, Elizabeth, 201

Duncan, Captain James 41,45,50,64,66,96,106,119

Dundas, Lieutenant Colonel,151

Dye, William, 160

E

Elley, Edward, 25,69,83

Evans, Walter, 68

Evens, Chaplain Israel, 188

Ewald, Captain Johann, 44,128,130,165,185

F

fascines, 14

Feltman, Lieutenant William, 21,24,28,35,41,45,52, 53,85,98,101,107,149,164,197

Fisher, James, 70

Flohr, Georg Daniel, 119

Fontaine, Colonel William, 175

Foreman, David, 144,170,198

Forge, Valley, 67

Franklin, Benjamin, 206

French, Joseph,68

French fleet, 17

Fusiliers, Royal Welsh, 31,32

G

Germain, Lord George,204-206

Gillett, Asa, 134

Gildewell, William, 87

Gloucester, 9,12-14,20,24,34,39,41,46,48-51,86,97,109,129,130,135,153,154,166,167,171

Graham, Captain Samuel, 12,17,81,109,173,191,194,195

Graves, Admiral Samuel, 44,198

Greene, General Nathanael, 21,28,204

Groom, Major, 28

Guadeloupe, 32,80

Gunn, Sterling, 83

H

Hamilton, Colonel Alexander,65,103,104,108,113-115,124,125,133,134,150,157,161,168

Hamilton, Elizabeth, 103,104

Hayes, Henry, 153

Hessians, 17,129,165,190,198

Hill. William, 181

Howitzers, 78,82

Hudson, John, 41,64,82,90,131,201,202

Humphreys, Colonel David,154

Hyde, Irvine,194

I

J

James, Bartholomew, 17,26,40,51,53,66,81,87,96,105,108,128,148,173

Jefferson, Thomas,12

Jenkins, Caleb, 118

K

Kercheval, John, 112

King George III,205

Knox, General Henry, 73,74,99,121,155,164

Kymes, Conrad,190

L

Lafayette, General Marquis de, 9,57,64,89,108,112, 115,117,133,148,151,158,164,183-185,205

Lafayette, James Armistead, 205

Lamb, General John, 59,73,131

Laurens, John, 60,91,115,140,151-153,187

Lee, General Charles, 38,87

Lee, General Henry, 93,177

Lincoln, General Benjamin, 121,152,189

Lowry, Thomas, 24

M

Madding, Chapness, 69

Martin, Joseph Plumb, 19,21,53,54,58,64,84,115,134,144,174,187,203

McDowell, Lieutenant William,34,191

McKean, Thomas,1323,169,199,200

McMahan, John, 159

McNeal, Samuel, 113

Moore, George, 75

Moore House,151-153

Moreland, Charles,25

Morgan, General Daniel, 194,195

Mortars, 77,82

Muhlenberg, General Peter, 124,166

Muirhead, Henry, 28

Munson, Doctor Eneas,38,119

N

Neel, William, 180

Nelson, Thomas Jr., 86,89,90

Nelson, William, 86

O

O'Hara, General, 138,158-160,167,184,186,203

Ollis, Boston, 159

Olney, Captain Stephen, 113-117,134

Organ, Corporal, 54

Osborn, Aaron, 70,174,175

Osborn, Sarah, 70,174,175

Overstreet, Henry, 68

P

Painter, George, 159

Pickering, Colonel Thomas, 37,40,98,99,144,196

Popp, Stephen, 26,32,81,86,108,138,147,162,173,197

Prison base, 55

Q

R

Rasor, Christian, 180

Redoubt15,32,

redoubt 9,13,97,101,108,112-115,119,121,124,125,127

redoubt 10,13, 97,101,108,112-115,119,121,124,125,127

Robertson, James,138

Robin, Abbe, 162

Ross, Major Alexander,151-153

Royal, John, 58

S

sappers and miners, 115,116

Saunders, John, 79

Scammell, Colonel Alexander, 36-38, 4,62

Schwerin, Wilhelm Graft von, 64

Seely, Colonel Sylvanus149

Simcoe, Colonel John, 47, 48,135,166,196

Slaves, 14,187,196

Steuben, Baron Von, 39,92,96,97,148,157,196

Strange, John, 117

Strong, Charles, 20

Suddarth, John, 31

Surveillante, 188

Symonds, Captain Thomas, 184

T

Tarleton, Colonel Banastre, 13,23,24,32,46-51,64,80,96,109,127,148,166,167,187,193,194

Thacher, Doctor James, 28,33,37,59,62,78,84,89,105,137,143,149,150,162,

Tilden, John Bell, 37,52,143,174

Tilghman, Colonel Tench, 59,64,170,199,200

Trabue, Colonel Daniel, 57,87,141,177,190,191

Trumbull, Colonel Jonathan, 54, 89,102,140,143,173

Tucker, St. George, 31,28,38,45,46,52,55,58,67,87,99,121,132,143,148,165,167,174

U

V

Vernon, Mount168,169

Ville de Paris, 188

Viomenil, Baron, 23

W

Walpole, Horace, 8

Washington, George, 8,10,18,20,26,35,39,43,66,104,124,185,186,206; arrival at Yorktown, 24,25,32; at New York, 9; capture redoubts, 101,107,108; death of step-son, 168,169exposed to danger, 27,51,84,121; general orders, 34,183,188; letters, 7,32,42,132,155; orderly Book,62; parallels, 54,95,96; speeches, 27,113; surrender, 138,142,145,151,154,158,159,162,163,170

Blanchard, Claude, 50,52,93,98,102,141,162,189,190

Wayne, General Anthony, 50,51,97

Weedon, General George, 20,23,34,41,49

Whitely, Robert, 68,162

Whittemore, Samuel, 206

Wild, Ebenezer, 23,52,67,143,150,171,203

Wilson, Robert, 161

Williamsburg, 18,36,117,166,195

X

Y

Yankee Doodle,154,164

Yorktown (the village), 11-16

Z

www.ingramcontent.com/pod-product-compliance
Lightning Source LLC
Chambersburg PA
CBHW080732300426
44114CB00019B/2563